A College Grammar of English

Longman English and Humanities Series
Series Editor: Lee Jacobus
University of Connecticut, Storrs

A College Grammar of English

Sidney Greenbaum

Longman
New York & London

A College Grammar of English

Longman Inc., 95 Church Street, White Plains, N.Y. 10601

Associated companies:
Longman Group Ltd., London
Longman Cheshire Pty., Melbourne
Longman Paul Pty., Auckland
Copp Clark Pitman, Toronto
Pitman Publishing Inc., New York

For Isaac
with affection

Executive editor: Gordon T. R. Anderson
Production editor: Camilla T. K. Palmer
Text design: Jill Francis Wood
Cover design: Kevin C. Kall
Production supervisor: Kathleen Ryan

Library of Congress Cataloging-in-Publication Data

Greenbaum, Sidney.
    A college grammar of English / by Sidney Greenbaum. — 1st ed.
        p. cm.—(Longman English and humanities series)

    Bibliography: p.
    Includes index.
    ISBN 0–582–28597–6
    1. English language—Grammar—1950– I. Title. II. Series.
PE1112.G68 1989
428.2—dc19
                                             88–14814
                                                CIP

ISBN 0-582-28597-6

93 92 91 90 89 88 9 8 7 6 5 4 3 2 1

Contents

Preface

In writing this book I had in mind the many students who enter college without any knowledge of English grammar. Others may have encountered some grammatical terms but feel insecure in applying them or feel a need for a more systematic knowledge of grammar. The book introduces students to basic grammatical concepts and categories that are common to the competing theoretical schools of linguistics. I have deliberately avoided raising theoretical issues in this introductory book.

I begin with an introductory chapter on the nature of grammar and on varieties of English. Part I provides an outline description of English grammar, beginning in Chapter 2 with an overview of sentence types, which are examined in greater detail in Chapter 6. Part II applies the grammatical information from Part I, giving students guidance on punctuation, on solving problems of usage, on improving their writing style, and on ways to analyze the language of literature. The Appendix on spelling includes spelling rules for inflections, such as the plurals of nouns. The Glossary briefly explains the many terms that are needed for a study of grammar.

The exercises at the ends of sections will help students understand the text and give them practice in applying the grammar. Some of the exercises point to topics that are not included in the book.

I am indebted to Charles F. Meyer (University of Massachusetts—Boston) for the exercises. I am grateful for helpful comments from readers of an earlier version of this book: Alexander J. Butrym (Seton Hall University, New Jersey), Geoffrey Kaye (IBM, United Kingdom), Donald M. Lance (University of Missouri at Columbia), and Claudia Ross (Holy Cross College, Massachusetts).

I am happy to record my thanks to Camilla T. K. Palmer and Ilene McGrath for their careful guidance of the manuscript into print. Thanks are also due to Justin Lauzkron for reading the proofs. Finally, I express my gratitude to Marie Gibney for patiently typing the manuscript in its various drafts.

March 1988   Sidney Greenbaum

ACKNOWLEDGMENTS

Excerpt from "The Waste Land" in *Collected Poems 1909–1962* by T.S. Eliot, copyright 1936 by Harcourt Brace Jovanovich, Inc., copyright © 1963, 1964 by T.S. Eliot, reprinted by permission of Harcourt Brace Jovanovich and Faber and Faber Ltd.

"in Just-" is reprinted from *Tulips & Chimneys* by E.E. Cummings, edited by George James Firmage, by permission of Liveright Publishing Corp. and Grafton Books, a division of the Collins Publishing Group. Copyright 1923, 1925, and renewed 1951, 1953 by E.E. Cummings. Copyright © 1973, 1976 by the Trustees for the E.E. Cummings Trust. Copyright © 1973, 1976 by George James Firmage.

"in" is reprinted from *Xaipe* by E.E. Cummings, edited by George James Firmage. (Liveright, 1979).

Excerpt from "The Mystery of the Charity of Charles Peguy" is reprinted from *Somewhere Is Such a Kingdom: Poems 1952–1971* by Geoffrey Hill, by permission of Andre Deutsch Ltd.

"This Bread I Break" by Dylan Thomas from *Poems of Dylan Thomas*. Copyright © 1967 by the Trustees for the Copyrights of Dylan Thomas. Reprinted by permission of New Directions Publishing and David Higham Associates Ltd.

CHAPTER ONE

Rules and Varieties

1.1 WHAT IS GRAMMAR?

I will be using the word **grammar** in this book to refer to the set of rules that
allow us to combine words in our language into larger units. Another term for
grammar in this sense is **syntax**.

Some combinations of words are possible in English, and others are not.
As a native speaker of English (that is, having acquired English from early childhood), you can judge that Home computers are now much cheaper is a possible
English sentence whereas Home computers now much are cheaper is not, because you know that much is wrongly positioned in the second example. Your
ability to recognize such distinctions is evidence that in some sense you know
the rules of grammar even if you have never studied any grammar. Similarly,
you operate the rules whenever you speak or write (you can put words in the
right order) and whenever you interpret what others say (you know that Susan
likes Tom means something different from Tom likes Susan). But knowing the
rules in evaluative and operational senses does not mean that you can say what
the rules are.

You acquire a working knowledge of your native language simply through
being exposed to the language from early childhood: nobody taught you, for
example, where to position much. You study grammar, however, if you want
to be able to analyze your language. The analytic grammar makes explicit the
knowledge of the rules with which you operate when you use the language.
There is a clear difference between the operational grammar and the analytic
grammar. After all, many languages have never been analyzed and some have
been analyzed only relatively recently. People were speaking and writing English long before the first English grammars appeared at the end of the sixteenth
century.

═══ EXERCISE 1.1 ═══

Informally describe the rules that change the (a) sentences into the (b) sentences.

EXAMPLE
   a.   World War II was a tragedy for everyone involved.
   b.   Was World War II a tragedy for everyone involved?
   Sentence (b) is a question formed by interchanging the first two parts of sentence (a).

1. a.   The students were late for class.
   b.   Were the students late for class?
2. a.   The instructor should have been on time.
   b.   Should the instructor have been on time?
3. a.   The students waited for ten minutes and then left.
   b.   Did the students wait for ten minutes and then leave?
4. a.   A few of the students wrote the Dean a letter of complaint.
   b.   A few of the students wrote a letter of complaint to the Dean.
5. a.   The Dean ignored the students' complaints.
   b.   The students' complaints were ignored by the Dean.
6. a.   The Dean asked the students to leave.
   b.   The students were asked by the Dean to leave.
7. a.   Then the students gave the Dean an ultimatum.
   b.   The students then gave the Dean an ultimatum.
8. a.   However, the Dean refused to listen.
   b.   The Dean, however, refused to listen.

1.2 GRAMMAR AND OTHER ASPECTS OF LANGUAGE

Linguistic communications are channeled mainly through our senses of sound and sight. Grammar is the central component of language. It mediates between the system of sounds or of written symbols, on the one hand, and the system of meaning, on the other. **Phonology** is the usual term for the sound system in the language: the distinctive sound units and the ways in which they may be combined. **Orthography** parallels phonology in that it deals with the writing system in the language: the distinctive written symbols and their possible combinations. Despite some eccentricities in our spelling, the alphabetic letters in English are basically related to the individual sound units. **Semantics** is concerned with the system of meanings in the language: the meanings of words and the combinatory meanings of larger units.

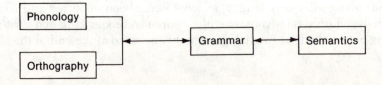

Three other aspects of language description are often distinguished: phonetics, morphology, and pragmatics. **Phonetics** deals with the physical characteristics of the sounds in the language and how the sounds are produced. Sounds and letters combine to form words or parts of words. **Morphology** refers to the set of rules that describe the structure of words. The word computer, for example, consists of two parts: the base compute (used separately as a verb) and the suffix -er (found in other nouns derived from verbs, e.g., blender). **Pragmatics** is concerned with the use of particular utterances within particular situations. For example, Will you join our group? is a question that, depending on the speaker's intention, is a request for information or a request for action.

For descriptive purposes, it is convenient to deal with the components of language separately, but because of the central place of grammar in the language system, it is sometimes necessary to refer to the other components when we discuss the grammar.

1.3 GRAMMARS OF ENGLISH

There are many grammars of English, that is, books describing English grammar. They differ in how much of the grammar they cover and in how they set out the rules. There are also some differences in the categorization and terminology they use. Nevertheless, most categories and terms are widely shared, deriving from a tradition of grammatical description.

The grammatical analysis in this book follows the approach found in *A Comprehensive Grammar of the English Language* by Randolph Quirk, Sidney Greenbaum, Geoffrey Leech, and Jan Svartvik. First published in 1985, that reference work on contemporary English grammar contains nearly 1,800 pages. Future reference works of this scope are likely to be even longer. Despite the immense amount of research on contemporary English in the last few decades, many grammatical phenomena have yet to be discovered and described.

——————— WHICH ENGLISH? ———————

1.4 NATIONAL VARIETIES

English is an international language. It is the native language of about 300 million people, the majority of whom live in the United States and therefore speak American English. There are other national varieties of English, such as those in Canada, the British Isles, the Caribbean, South Africa, Australia, and New Zealand.

English is a second language for a similar number of people who speak another language as their native tongue. For example, the first language for French Canadians is French and for millions of Americans it is Spanish; most of them learn the majority language for practical reasons.

English is also a second language in countries where only a small minority speak English as their native language. It has official functions in administration, law, or higher education, and may be used between speakers who have no other language in common. These countries, which were once under American or British rule, include the Philippines, India, and Nigeria. The English in each of these countries has certain distinctive features, so that it is reasonable to refer to such national varieties as, for example, Indian English or Nigerian English.

Finally, English is studied as the primary foreign language in most other countries in the world. It is the most important language for international communication in commerce and tourism, in economic and military aid, and in scientific and technological literature. It is used throughout the world for air and sea communications as well.

EXERCISE 1.2

Briefly describe how your use of English differs from the use of English in the examples below. Consult a dictionary for meanings of words that you are not familiar with.

1. I shall call you tomorrow. (British English)
2. John spilled coke on his shirt and asked the waitress to bring him a serviette to wipe it up with. (Canadian English)
3. Dat man be botherin' me all de time. (Black English)
4. I might could do the work if I had the time. (Southern American English)
5. Take the lift up to the third floor and go to room 38. (British English)
6. Let's store the food down in the cellar. (Northeastern American English)
7. Our ride hasn't shown up yet even though it's quarter to seven. (Midwestern American English)
8. My friends plan to meet me at the pub at ten. (British English)
9. I really enjoyed my job sacking groceries at a local grocery store. (Southern American English)
10. My father used an electric grass-cutter to trim the grass in the field. (Indian English)

1.5 STANDARD AND NONSTANDARD ENGLISH

In addition to differences between national varieties of English, there are differences within each national variety. Each has a number of dialects, but one dialect is used nationally for official purposes. It is generally called **Standard English.**

Standard English is the dialect that normally appears in print. American standard English in its written form is also called "edited American English," because the final or "edited" draft of a written work is expected by writers and publishers to conform with the standard language. Standard English is taught in schools and is the norm for dictionaries and grammars. You generally hear it in national broadcasts of news and documentary programs on radio or on television.

There is no standard pronunciation of American English, although one type of pronunciation, known as "network English," is normal for news broadcasts. The relative uniformity of standard American English is confined to vocabulary and grammar.

Within standard American English there is some regional variation, minor differences in vocabulary or grammar. For example, some say <u>tap</u> where others say <u>faucet</u>; some make <u>dived</u> the past tense of <u>dive</u> and others use <u>dove</u>; the same time may be variously expressed as <u>five to nine</u>, <u>five till nine</u>, <u>five until nine</u>, or <u>five before nine</u>.

Standard English is one of a number of dialects in American English. It is not intrinsically better than other dialects, although many believe it is, but it has prestige because it is associated with education and with higher-income groups. Also, it has developed a range of styles to suit different kinds of writing. For these reasons this book focuses on standard American English.

Other dialects are often called **nonstandard.** Nonstandard dialects may be restricted to a particular region or to a particular ethnic group. Because of the lower prestige of their dialect, students speaking a nonstandard dialect may be wrongly labeled as unintelligent or slow learners. In recent years there have been attempts to make teachers aware of the dangers of self-fulfilling predictions: expectations by teachers influence the demands they make of students.

The variation we have been considering so far depends on the language of the group with which speakers identify themselves. Many people speak more than one dialect; for example, they may use different dialects at home and at work.

EXERCISE 1.3

Rewrite the sentences below in standard American English.

EXAMPLE

I knowed you wasn't from New York.
I knew you weren't from New York.

1. Them guys should try to be more helpful.
2. I ain't gonna do the work if I don't get paid for it.
3. We didn't do nothin' but listen to records while we were visiting our friends.

4. Youse people should wait in line over there.
5. Our parents is gonna meet us later for dinner.
6. Didn't nobody have enough time to finish the work?
7. Me and him thought it would be a good idea not to go to school today.
8. That book is mines, not yours.
9. They my best friends.
10. The children wanted to play by theirselves.

1.6 VARIATION ACCORDING TO USE

Some variations reflect the uses to which speakers put their language. We can distinguish three major types of variation that depend on the use of the language.

(A) Variation According to Domain

When we turn from one **domain** (type of activity) to another, we necessarily introduce some changes in language. The changes are often merely differences in vocabulary, as when we turn from discussing politics to commenting on the recent football results. Similarly we need different words when we are buying a new car than when we are explaining a mathematical formula. Some domains also tend to have particular grammatical features. For example, recipes for cooking use many imperatives (<u>Mix the ingredients well</u>, rather than <u>You should mix the ingredients well</u>). Certain domains are more clearly recognized than others; some examples are scientific English, literary English, journalistic writing, legal English, and religious English.

===== **EXERCISE 1.4** =====

Identify the domain that each sentence below belongs to. Explain your choices.

EXAMPLE
Lessee shall pay Lessor the sum of $600.00 for rent of said premises.
The sentence contains words such as <u>lessee</u> and <u>lessor</u> that indicate that it belongs to the domain of law.

1. We humbly beseech thee, Lord, that thou remove us our sins.
2. He dribbles down the court, Larry Bird does, and passes off to Robert Parish, who slams the ball through the net for two points.
3. Through the words and deeds of the Canterbury pilgrims, Geof-

frey Chaucer gives us a realistic portrayal of life during the Middle Ages.

4. The activation of the rocket booster engine during reentry is caused by the ignition of gases within the engine.
5. Council Chairman Frank Clark predicted at the Common Council meeting yesterday that the building contract would be awarded soon. Sources close to Clark said that the firm to receive the contract would be named once Mayor Flynn gave his final approval.
6. Stir in three cups of flour. Mix until substance is firm. Then add a cup of vinegar and a cup of chopped onions.

(B) Variation According to Medium

Some variation depends on the **medium,** the channel of communication. The major distinction here is between spoken and written language. Conversation, the most common type of speech, involves immediate interchange between the participants, who convey their reactions either in words or through facial expressions and body movements. The person addressed can indicate lack of understanding, thereby giving the speaker the opportunity to clarify, elaborate, or exemplify. Conversational speech relies on these possibilities, so it can afford to be inexplicit. Writing, on the other hand, generally needs to be fully explicit, since obscurities and misunderstandings cannot be removed immediately. Writers have the time to formulate their language carefully; they can anticipate difficulties and be more concise and elegant than they would be in speech. They also know that their readers will be able to read and reread their writing and will hold them responsible for every word. People therefore feel more committed to what they write, and they tend to be more careful in writing than in speech.

Another major difference between spoken and written language is that speech has many devices such as stress and intonation to convey distinctions that are only partially paralleled in writing. On the other hand, some distinctions conveyed by punctuation—paragraphs and quotation marks, for example—are not paralleled in speech.

EXERCISE 1.5

Explain whether the sentences below were taken from writing or from conversation.

EXAMPLE
Did you like the movie we saw yesterday?

The sentence was taken from conversation because it involves an immediate exchange between speaker and hearer and because many of the references (<u>movie</u>, for instance) are inexplicit.

1. Hey, Fred, why don't you come over here and read the book?
2. One should study diligently if he or she wishes to do well in school.
3. I wouldn't do that if I were you! You'll get hurt.
4. I wonder if it'll rain today, I mean tomorrow.
5. City of Boston employees are going on strike because they desire higher wages and better working conditions.

(C) Variation According to Attitude

Language also varies according to the **attitude** of the speaker or writer toward the listener or reader, toward the topic, and toward the purpose of communication. The contrast ranges from the most formal to the most informal, with much of language being neutral in attitude. Differences in formality are conspicuous in both vocabulary and grammar. <u>Slipshod</u>, <u>comprehend</u>, and <u>animate</u> are more formal than their respective equivalents: <u>sloppy</u>, <u>understand</u>, and <u>put new life into</u>. Similarly, <u>This is the student to whom I gave the message</u> is more formal than <u>This is the student I gave the message to</u>. There is considerable interdependence among the types of variation. On the whole, we expect personal letters to be more informal than business letters. Legal statutes must be in formal writing, whereas coaching of a football team would be conducted through informal speech.

EXERCISE 1.6

For each group of sentences below, describe how the (a), (b), and (c) sentences differ in formality.

EXAMPLE

One should try one's hardest to succeed in school.
The example is quite formal because of the use of the pronoun <u>one</u>, which distances the writer or speaker from the audience being addressed.

1. a. If you weren't such an ignorant clod, you wouldn't get into so many accidents.
   b. If you were a little more careful, you'd be less accident prone.
   c. Individuals who are accident prone must learn to be more careful.
2. a. The guy I sent the package to wasn't home.

   b. The man whom I sent the package to wasn't home.

   c. The person to whom I sent the package was not home.

3. a. You should try a lot harder to get to work on time.

   b. You should try much harder to get to work on time.

   c. One should strive to arrive at work promptly.

4. a. You can rent the apartment for $600 a month.

   b. The apartment rents for $600 a month.

   c. Lessee shall pay the sum of $600 a month for rent of said premises.

1.7 DESCRIPTIVE AND PRESCRIPTIVE RULES

At the beginning of this chapter I said that the rules of grammar state which combinations of words are possible in the language and which are not. My example of an impossible sentence in English was <u>Home computers now much are cheaper</u>. The rule that disallows that sentence is a **descriptive** rule, a rule that describes how people use their language. The validity of this descriptive rule depends on whether it is true that <u>Home computers are now much cheaper</u> is a possible English sentence and <u>Home computers now much are cheaper</u> is an impossible English sentence. The evidence to validate this rule is drawn from the knowledge that native English speakers have of their language as well as from samples of their actual use of the language. Of course the descriptive rule must be accurately formulated to make the valid distinctions.

    Sometimes people speaking the same dialect disagree in their evaluation of particular sentences. For example, some speakers of standard American English find <u>They seem fools</u> acceptable; others find it odd and require instead <u>They seem to be fools</u>; still others insist on <u>They seem foolish</u> or <u>They seem to be foolish</u>.

    A number of differences in the use of standard American English have acquired social importance. Some speakers of the standard dialect consider that certain usages mark their user as uneducated. Rules that specify which usages to adopt or avoid are called **prescriptive** rules. Examples of prescriptive rules are the following:

> Don't use <u>like</u> as a conjunction, as in <u>He speaks like his father does</u>.
> Don't use <u>between you and I</u>.
> You may use <u>It's me</u> in speech.
> Avoid splitting an infinitive.

Speakers of the standard dialect tend to pay greater attention to prescriptive rules when they are on their best behavior, in particular when they are writing in a formal style.

Usages and attitudes vary and may change. Since, unlike some countries, America does not have a Language Academy that issues rulings on disputed usages, individual writers have established themselves as authorities on the language. They base their decisions on their own attitudes or on those of previous authorities. It is therefore not surprising that they sometimes disagree or object to usages that most speakers of the standard dialect find perfectly acceptable.

═══ EXERCISE 1.7 ═══

Briefly explain whether the rules below are descriptive or prescriptive rules.

EXAMPLE

Articles (<u>a</u>, <u>an</u>, and <u>the</u>) precede nouns.
This is a descriptive rule because it describes where articles are placed in English.

1. Never split infinitives.
2. In questions, the verb usually begins the sentence.
3. You should never end a sentence with a preposition.
4. Don't use the pronoun <u>you</u> in writing.
5. Imperative sentences (e.g., <u>Leave at once!</u>) usually lack a subject.
6. Avoid using the word <u>hopefully</u> to mean <u>It is hoped</u>.
7. Adverbs such as <u>however</u> can be moved around in sentences.
8. Sentences should never begin with a conjunction such as <u>and</u> or <u>but</u>.

1.8 WHY STUDY GRAMMAR?

The study of language is a part of general knowledge. We study the complex working of the human body to understand ourselves; there is the same reason for studying the marvelous complexity of human language.

Everybody has attitudes toward the English language and its varieties and has opinions on specific features. These attitudes and opinions affect relationships with other people. If you understand the nature of language, you will realize the grounds for your linguistic prejudices and perhaps moderate them; you will also more clearly assess linguistic issues of public concern, such as support for bilingual education or worries about the state of the language. Studying the English language has a more obvious practical application: it can help you to use the language more effectively.

In the study of language, grammar occupies a central position. However, there is also a practical reason to emphasize the study of grammar. It is easy to learn to use dictionaries by yourself to find the pronunciation, spelling, or meanings of words, but it is difficult to consult grammar books without a considerable knowledge of grammar.

There are several applications of grammatical study: (1) A recognition of grammatical structures is often essential for punctuation; (2) A study of one's native grammar is helpful when one studies the grammar of a foreign language; (3) A knowledge of grammar is a help in the interpretation of literary and nonliterary texts, since the interpretation of a passage sometimes depends crucially on grammatical analysis; (4) A study of the grammatical resources of English is useful in composition: in particular, it can help you to evaluate the choices available to you when you come to revise an earlier written draft.

This book provides a survey of the grammar of standard American English. It also includes applications to disputed usages, punctuation, composition style, and the analysis of literary language. It ends with an Appendix on spelling and a Glossary of terms used in the book.

PART I

The Grammar

CHAPTER TWO

The Sentence

2.1 WHAT IS A SENTENCE?

Grammar deals with the rules for combining words into larger units. The largest unit that is described in grammar is normally the **sentence.** You may therefore think that grammarians should be embarrassed at not being able to offer a simple definition of the term "sentence."

It is sometimes said that a sentence expresses a complete thought. This is a **notional** definition, that is, it defines the term by the notion or idea it conveys. The difficulty with this definition lies in fixing what is meant by a "complete thought." There are notices, for example, that seem to be complete in themselves but are not generally regarded as sentences:

> Exit
> Danger
> 50 m.p.h. limit

On the other hand, there are sentences that clearly consist of more than one thought. Here is one relatively simple example:

> This week marks the 300th anniversary of the publication of Sir Isaac Newton's "Philosophiae Naturalis Principia Mathematica," a fundamental work for the whole of modern science and a key influence on the philosophy of the European Enlightenment.

How many "complete thoughts" are there in this sentence? We should at least recognize that the part after the comma introduces two additional points about Newton's book: (1) that it is a fundamental work for the whole of modern science, and (2) that it was a key influence on the philosophy of the European

Enlightenment. Yet this example would be acknowledged by all as a single sentence, and it is written as a single sentence.

We can try another approach by defining a sentence as a string of words beginning with a capital letter and ending with a period. This is a **formal** definition: it defines a term by the form or shape of what the term refers to. We can at once see that as it stands this definition is inadequate, since (1) many sentences end with a question mark or an exclamation mark, and (2) capital letters are used for names, and periods are used for abbreviations. Even if we amend the definition to take account of these objections, we still find strings of words in newspaper headlines, titles, and notices that everyone would recognize as sentences even though they do not end with a period, a question mark, or an exclamation mark:

> Trees May Be a Source of Pollution
> Dr. Potatohead Talks to Mothers (title of poem)
> Do not enter

The most serious objection, however, is that the definition is directed only toward **orthographic** sentences, that is, sentences that appear in the written language. Spoken sentences, of course, do not have capital letters and periods.

It is in fact far more difficult to determine the limits of sentences in natural conversation, to say where sentences begin and end. That is so partly because people may change direction as they speak and partly because they tend to make heavy use of connectors such as <u>and</u>, <u>but</u>, <u>so</u>, and <u>then</u>. Here is a typical example of a speaker who strings sentences together with <u>and</u>. (The period marks a short pause and the dash a longer pause, and the vertical line marks the end of a rhythmic unit in the intonation.)

> I'd been working away this week| trying to clear up| . the backlog of mail| caused by me being three weeks away| . and I thought I was doing marvelously| . and at about| . six o'clock last night| . I was sorting through . stuff on the desk| and I discovered . a fat pile of stuff| — all carefully opened| and documented by Sally| that I hadn't even seen|.

How many orthographic sentences correspond to A's story? There is no one correct answer. In writing we have a choice: we could punctuate it as one sentence or we could split it into two or more sentences, each of the later sentences beginning with <u>and</u>.

Grammarians are not worried about the difficulties in defining the sentence. Their approach to the question is formal because they are interested in grammatical form. Like many people who are not grammarians, they are generally confident of recognizing sentences, and they specify the possible patterns for the sentences. Combinations of words that conform to those patterns are then **grammatical** sentences.

2.2   IRREGULAR SENTENCES AND NONSENTENCES

Sentences that conform to the major patterns (cf. 3.13) are **regular** sentences, and they are the type that will generally concern us in this book. Sentences that do not conform to the major patterns are **irregular** sentences.

If I ask you to write down the first sentences that come into your mind, you are likely to produce regular sentences. Here are some regular sentences in various major patterns:

> David and Doris have three sons.
> The liquid smelled spicy to Justin.
> Some people give their children a daily dose of vitamins.
> About a million visitors come to our city every summer.

Most irregular sentences are **fragmentary** sentences. These leave out words that we easily supply, usually from the preceding verbal context. Here is a typical example in an exchange between two speakers:

> A: Where did you put the letter?
>
> B: In the top drawer.

We interpret B's reply as I put the letter in the top drawer, and that reconstructed sentence would be regular. Similarly, the headline Hypertension Linked to Erratic Diets corresponds to the regular Hypertension is linked to erratic diets, and the headline Archbishop of Manila to Visit Soviet to the regular The Archbishop of Manila is to visit the Soviet Union. Fragmentary sentences can therefore be viewed as directly derivable in their interpretation from regular sentences.

Finally, we often say or write things that are not grammatical sentences. These nonsentences may simply be mistakes, but they may also be perfectly normal, although they cannot be analyzed grammatically as sentences. Normal nonsentences include such common expressions as Hi!; Yes; No; So long!; Thanks!; Heck! and they include many headlines, headings, titles, labels, and notices:

> A Jazzman's Farewell
> Interest Rates
> A History of the United States
> Pure Lemon Juice
> No Smoking

In the next chapter we will be looking at the patterns of regular sentences, but first there are a few more general things to say about sentences.

===== **EXERCISE 2.1** =====

Below you will find a group of fragmentary sentences. Rewrite them so that they are regular sentences.

EXAMPLE

On my way to work this morning.
I was involved in an accident on my way to work this morning.

1. On the dresser located in the back bedroom.
2. Leader of Contras to visit Washington this week.
3. In the cupboard above the dishwasher.
4. Man taken to hospital after accident.
5. Higher taxes seen as solution to budget crisis.
6. Three miles to next rest stop.
7. If only I'd met you sooner.
8. Need more time to fill out the form?

2.3 SIMPLE AND MULTIPLE SENTENCES

Here are two sentences placed next to each other:

[1]   I'm just a country boy. I'd never been out of the state before.

I can combine the two sentences in [1] merely by putting <u>and</u> between them:

[2]   I'm just a country boy, <u>and</u> I'd never been out of the state before.

I can also combine them by putting a different connecting word in front of the first sentence:

[3]   <u>Since</u> I'm just a country boy, I'd never been out of the state before.

I can make a small change in the first sentence:

[4]   <u>Being</u> just a country boy, I'd never been out of the state before.

A sentence or a sentence-like construction contained within a sentence is called a **clause.** Constructions like <u>Being just a country boy</u> in [4] resemble sentences in that they can be analyzed to a large extent in similar ways (cf. 6.8). The sentences in [2], [3], and [4] therefore all consist of two clauses. (Strictly speaking, the separate sentences in [1] are also clauses, but since they have only one clause each, it is convenient to refer to them just as sentences.)

A sentence that does not contain another clause within it is a **simple** sentence. If it contains one or more clauses, it is a **multiple** sentence.

Here are some more examples of multiple sentences with connecting words:

> You can't insist <u>that</u> your children love each other.
> The building was emptied <u>before</u> the bomb-disposal squad was called.
> <u>When</u> we returned three hours later, no wolves were in sight.
> My father always hoped <u>that</u> I would become a doctor <u>and</u> that must have been <u>why</u> he took me along <u>when</u> he visited his patients.

We will be looking more closely at multiple sentences in Chapter 6. Meanwhile, I will be using simple sentences to illustrate general matters about sentences.

EXERCISE 2.2

Identify whether each sentence below is a simple sentence or a multiple sentence.

EXAMPLE
American automobiles are competing in the marketplace with Japanese automobiles. *(simple sentence)*

1. Many Americans are becoming increasingly concerned about their health.
2. They are eating better and they are exercising more.
3. If individuals want to eat healthfully, they must reduce their intake of saturated fats.
4. Red meat is very high in saturated fat.
5. Consequently, it should be eaten sparingly.
6. Because fish is low in saturated fat, it is a healthy alternative to red meat.
7. People must also exercise regularly if they want to stay healthy.
8. Many individuals have taken up jogging, but others prefer to walk.
9. It is important that all individuals become health-conscious.
10. If they do, they'll live happier and more productive lives.

2.4 SENTENCE TYPES

There are four major types of sentences:

(1) Declaratives (or declarative sentences)

Last year many Californian couples exchanged vows aboard
   hot-air balloons.
Analysts anticipate an improvement in the U.S. merchandise
   trade deficit this year.

(2) Interrogatives (or interrogative sentences)

Do you have your own personal computer?
Where are you spending your vacation this summer?

(3) Imperatives (or imperative sentences)

Open the door for me.
Take a seat.

(4) Exclamatives (or exclamative sentences)

How well you look!
What a large piece you've given me!

These four sentence types differ in their form (cf.6.2–4). They correspond
in general to four major uses:

1. STATEMENTS are used chiefly to convey information.
2. QUESTIONS are used chiefly to request information.
3. DIRECTIVES are used chiefly to request action.
4. EXCLAMATIONS are used chiefly to express strong feeling.

It is usual to refer to interrogatives more simply as questions.
   We will be discussing these sentence types and their uses in a later chapter
(cf. 6.1–5). Declaratives are the basic type and I will therefore generally be using
them for illustrative purposes.

===== **EXERCISE 2.3** =====

Identify whether each sentence below is a statement, question, directive, or exclamation.

EXAMPLE
   If I'm paid tomorrow, I'll go shopping with you. *(statement)*

   1. It will probably be cold tomorrow.
   2. Do you know when you'll be coming over?
   3. Leave immediately!
   4. What a lovely apartment you have!
   5. Stop your arguing.
   6. If I don't get a new job, I think that I'll go crazy.
   7. Will your father be coming with you, or will he be staying behind?
   8. How much weight you've lost!
   9. It's been nice having a short vacation from my job.
   10. Do you have a lot of work to do tonight?

2.5 POSITIVE AND NEGATIVE SENTENCES

Sentences are either **positive** or **negative.** If an **auxiliary** ("helping") verb is present, we can usually change a positive sentence into a negative sentence by inserting <u>not</u> or <u>n't</u> after the auxiliary. In the following examples, the auxiliaries are <u>has</u>, <u>is</u>, and <u>can</u>:

> POSITIVE: Nancy <u>has</u> been working here for over a year.
> NEGATIVE: Nancy <u>has not</u> been working here for over a year.
>
> POSITIVE: Dan <u>is</u> paying for the meal.
> NEGATIVE: Dan <u>isn't</u> paying for the meal.
>
> POSITIVE: I <u>can</u> tell the difference.
> NEGATIVE: I <u>can't</u> tell the difference.

The rules for inserting <u>not</u> and <u>n't</u> are somewhat complicated. I will be referring to them later (cf.3.3f).
   A sentence may be negative because of some other negative word:

> She <u>never</u> had a secretary.
> <u>Nobody</u> talked to us.
> This is <u>no</u> ordinary painting.

Most sentences are positive, and I will therefore generally be using positive sentences for examples.

═══════════════════════ **EXERCISE 2.4** ═══════════════════════

Make the negative sentences below positive and the positive sentences negative.

EXAMPLE
    John isn't coming to the party.
    John is coming to the party.

1. I will not take public transportation to work.
2. Every election, candidates make election promises.
3. Nobody likes to have to pay taxes.
4. The instructor was late for class again.
5. There is nothing you can do about missing work today.
6. The agency accepts late payments.
7. The leader of the Senate was not able to get the bill passed.
8. Many people like classical music.
9. I never talk to strangers.
10. You should drive cautiously during a snowstorm.

2.6 ACTIVE AND PASSIVE SENTENCES

We can often choose whether to make a sentence active or passive (cf. 4.15). The choice involves differences in position of the words and differences in the form of the verb:

    ACTIVE: Charles Dickens wrote many novels.
    PASSIVE: Many novels were written by Charles Dickens.

Charles Dickens and many novels are at opposite ends of the two sentences; in the passive sentence by comes before Charles Dickens, and the active wrote corresponds to the longer were written.
    Here are two further examples of active and passive sentences:

    ACTIVE: The Department identified meat inspection as a
               new area for public health reform.
    PASSIVE: Meat inspection was identified by the Depart-
               ment as a new area for public health reform.

ACTIVE: The researchers had marked this female timber
           rattlesnake six years ago.
PASSIVE: This female timber rattlesnake had been marked
           by the researchers six years ago.

Actives are far more numerous than passives. Their relative frequency varies with the type of language. For example, passives tend to be heavily used in formal scientific writing.

The example sentences in the chapters that follow will generally be active rather than passive.

EXERCISE 2.5

Identify whether each sentence below is active or passive.

EXAMPLE

The workers completed the job. *(active)*

1. The bill was approved by most senators in attendance.
2. The policeman chased the suspect who had held up a local bank.
3. The astronomers calculated the distance between the two galaxies.
4. The class was attended by a group of unruly students.
5. The fossil was estimated by archeologists to be two thousand years old.
6. The President notified Congress that he would veto the bill.
7. The artist painted the picture in only a few hours.
8. The board chairman was quoted inaccurately by a reporter who interviewed him.

EXERCISE 2.6

Make the active sentences below passive and the passive sentences active.

EXAMPLE

The work was completed by the construction firm. (passive)
The construction firm completed the work. (active)

1. The building was destroyed by a very powerful earthquake.
2. Geoffrey Chaucer wrote *The Canterbury Tales* toward the end of his life.
3. Scientists discovered nuclear energy during the 1940s.

4. Senator Kennedy was questioned by the press during a recent news conference.
5. The decline in the dollar will force many tourists to vacation at home this summer.
6. Over a million dollars were withdrawn from the account by anxious investors.
7. The leader of the gang was arrested by two police officers.
8. The artist painted the picture in a very short period of time.

CHAPTER THREE

The Parts of the Simple Sentence

3.1 STRUCTURE, FORM, FUNCTION

Consider this sentence:

> [1]   A heavy snowfall has blocked the mountain passes.

There are various ways of analyzing the sentence. One way is to say that it contains three units:

> A heavy snowfall
> has blocked
> the mountain passes

We cannot simply arrange the units in any way that we like. For example, [1a] is not an English sentence:

> [1a]   The mountain passes has blocked a heavy snowfall.

Sentence [1] has a **structure** in that there are rules that decide the units that can co-occur in the sentence and the order in which they can occur.

    The three units in [1] are **phrases.** Phrases also have a structure. We cannot rearrange the internal order of the three phrases in [1]. These are not English phrases: heavy snowfall a; blocked has; the passes mountain.

    A heavy snowfall and the mountain passes are noun phrases (cf. 4.2) and has blocked is a verb phrase (cf. 4.11). We characterize them as these types of phrases because of their structure: in the noun phrases a noun is the main word, while in the verb phrase a verb is the main word. That kind of characterization describes the structure of each of the three units.

    We can also look at the three units from a different point of view: their

function, or how they are used in a particular sentence. For example, in [1] <u>A heavy snowfall</u> is the **subject** of the sentence and <u>the mountain passes</u> is the **direct object** of the sentence (cf. 3.5–7):

[1]   <u>A heavy snowfall</u> has blocked the <u>mountain passes</u>.

However, in [2] below <u>a heavy snowfall</u> is the direct object and in [3] <u>the mountain passes</u> is the subject:

[2]   They encountered <u>a heavy snowfall</u>.
[3]   <u>The mountain passes</u> are now open.

We therefore see that identical phrases may have different functions in different sentences.

Turning back to [1], we can combine the descriptions by structure and function. <u>A heavy snowfall</u> is a noun phrase functioning as subject, and <u>the mountain passes</u> is a noun phrase functioning as direct object. In this chapter we will be examining only the function of the phrases, not their structure. In the next section we will take a preliminary look at the functions of the parts of a sentence.

=========================== **EXERCISE 3.1** ===========================

Briefly explain what is wrong with the structure of each of the sentences below.

EXAMPLE
   The car crashed the mountain into.
   The preposition <u>into</u> comes after <u>the mountain</u> rather than before it.

1.   The mountain passes has blocked a heavy snowfall.
2.   Police not will let any vehicles travel over roads leading to the passes.
3.   Truckers many have had to take alternate routes.
4.   Stranded tourists staying have been in motels near the passes.
5.   Authorities hope to open the roads a day or two in.
6.   However, feel they that if the blizzard doesn't end soon roads could be closed for up to a week.
7.   Angry trucker an remarked that he was losing over a hundred dollars a day by having to take an alternate route.
8.   Owners of ski resorts, however, are looking forward to business the that the snow will generate.

3.2 SUBJECT, PREDICATE, VERB

It is traditional to divide the sentence into two main constituents: the **subject** and the **predicate.** The predicate consists of the verb and any other elements of the sentence apart from the subject:

subject	predicate
I	learned all this later.
The chef	is a young man with a broad experience of the world.
The fate of the land	parallels the fate of the culture.

The most important constituent of the predicate is the verb. Indeed, it is the most important element in the sentence, since regular sentences may consist of only a verb: imperatives such as Help! and Look! The verb of the sentence may consist of more than one word: could have been imagining. The **main verb** in this verb phrase comes last: imagining. The verbs that come before the main verb are **auxiliary verbs** ("helping verbs"), or simply **auxiliaries:** could have been.

I have been following traditional practice in using the word verb in two senses:

1. Like the subject, the verb is an element of sentence structure. In [1] the verb of the sentence is stroked and in [2] it is has been working:

[1] Marty stroked his beard.
[2] Ellen has been working all day.

2. A verb is a word, just as a noun is a word. In this sense, [2] contains three verbs: the auxiliaries has and been and the main verb working. The three verbs in [2] form a unit, the unit being a verb phrase (cf. 4.11).

=========================== **EXERCISE 3.2** ===========================

Place a slash between the subject and the predicate of the sentences below.

EXAMPLE
The tourists/visited the many historical monuments in Washington, D.C.

1. Most people enjoy listening to good music.
2. People's musical tastes vary considerably.
3. Some people favor classical music over rock music.
4. Others prefer country and western or folk music.

5. People listen to music for various reasons.
6. Some types of music have a calming value for people seeking relief of stress.
7. Loud and obnoxious kinds of rock music allow some people to let off steam.
8. Music with a fast rhythm is good for dancing.
9. Compact disk players have improved the quality of recorded music.
10. One can now hear quality music at home.

========================== EXERCISE 3.3 ==========================

Underline the verb in each sentence.

EXAMPLE
The students were taking the exam.

1. Charlie Chaplin's childhood was spent in the darkest of London slums.
2. His father had been an alcoholic for many years.
3. His mother sewed blouses for a living.
4. Chaplin made many enemies because of his political views.
5. After the Second World War he retired to Switzerland.
6. In 1972 he was given an Academy Award.
7. A few years later Queen Elizabeth II knighted him.
8. Chaplin may have thought a great deal about death.
9. His film adventures were always ending in a fading twilight.
10. He has had an incalculable effect on the art of making motion pictures.

3.3 OPERATOR

In section 3.2 I divided the sentence into two parts: the subject and the predicate. I then pointed to the verb as the most important constituent of the predicate.

We can now identify an element in the verb that has important functions in the sentence: the **operator.** Another way of analyzing the sentence is to say that it consists of three constituents: the subject, the operator, and the rest of the predicate.

As a first approximation, I will say that the operator is the first or only auxiliary in the verb of the sentence. In [1] the verb is <u>could have been imag</u>ining:

> [1]   You <u>could have been imagining</u> it.

The operator is <u>could,</u> the first auxiliary. In [2] the verb is <u>can get</u>:

> [2]   Karen <u>can get</u> to the heart of a problem.

The operator is <u>can,</u> the only auxiliary.

The operator plays an essential role in the formation of certain sentence structures:

1.   We form most types of questions by interchanging the positions of the subject and the operator:

> [1]   You <u>could</u> have been imagining it.
> [1a] <u>Could</u> you have been imagining it?

This is known as **subject–operator inversion.**

2.   We form negative sentences (cf. 2.5) by putting <u>not</u> after the operator. In informal style, <u>not</u> is often contracted to <u>n't,</u> and in writing <u>n't</u> is attached to the operator; some operators have very different positive and negative forms (e.g., <u>will</u> in [3] and <u>won't</u> in [3a]):

> [3]   Barbara and Charles <u>are</u> getting married in April.
>
> [3a] Barbara and Charles $\left. \begin{array}{l} \text{\underline{are not}} \\ \text{\underline{aren't}} \end{array} \right\}$ getting married in April.
>
> [4]   Nancy <u>will</u> be staying with us.
>
> [4a] Nancy $\left\{ \begin{array}{l} \text{\underline{will not}} \\ \text{\underline{won't}} \end{array} \right\}$ be staying with us.

3.   Operators can carry the stress in speech to convey emphasis:

> [5]   A: Finish your homework.
>   B: I HAVE finished it.
> [6]   A: I am afraid to tell my parents.
>   B: You MUST tell them.

4.   Operators are used in various kinds of reduced clauses to substitute for the predicate:

> [7]   A: Are you leaving?
>   B: Yes, I <u>am.</u>
> [8]   Karen and Tom haven't seen the movie, but Jill <u>has.</u>
> [9]   I'll take one if you <u>will.</u>

=========== **EXERCISE 3.4** ===========

Underline the operator in the sentences below.

EXAMPLE

Archeologists <u>have</u> been studying ancient ruins for decades.

1. We are traveling to Providence, Rhode Island, tomorrow.
2. The visitors to the city did not like the information that the convention bureau sent them.
3. Your parents would enjoy receiving an occasional letter from you.
4. The Internal Revenue Service has unfortunately decided to audit my return for 1987.
5. You may be eligible for student aid.
6. We were discussing the novel in English class last week.
7. The principal of the school has spoken to the teachers about the new attendance policy.
8. Employees of the company should take advantage of the health insurance benefits.

=========== **EXERCISE 3.5** ===========

Contract the operator and the negative in each sentence below.

EXAMPLE

I do not like food that is very spicy.
I don't like food that is very spicy.

1. My husband and I do not plan on attending our high school reunion this summer.
2. Most politicians would not favor a reduction in federal election funds.
3. The inventors of a computer with a very large memory capability have not as yet applied for a patent.
4. Convicted felons should not be allowed to leave prison on work furloughs.
5. Economists are not predicting a recession in the near future.
6. Most congressional members do not favor a tax increase.
7. A rise in interest rates would not be healthy for the economy.
8. Inflation has not risen very much in the past few years.

3.4   DUMMY OPERATOR <u>DO, BE</u>

In section 3.3 I identified the operator as the first or only auxiliary. But many sentences have no auxiliary, as in [1]:

[1]   Terry <u>works</u> for a public authority.

Here there is only the main verb <u>works</u>. If we want to form the structures specified in 3.3, we have to introduce the **dummy operator** <u>do</u> with the appropriate endings (<u>do</u>, <u>does</u>, <u>did</u>):

[1a]   <u>Does</u> Terry work for a public authority?
[1b]   Terry <u>doesn't</u> work for a public authority.
[1c]   Terry <u>DOES</u> work for a public authority, and her sister <u>does</u> too.

The auxiliary <u>do</u> in these sentences is a dummy operator because it is introduced to perform the functions of an operator in the absence of "true" operators such as <u>can</u> and <u>will</u>.

There is one operator that is not an auxiliary. The verb <u>be</u> is used as an operator even when it is the main verb, provided it is the only verb.

[2]   It <u>was</u> an awful system.
[2a]   A: <u>Was</u> it an awful system?
        B: It <u>was</u>.

=========================== **EXERCISE 3.6** ===========================

Turn the sentences below into questions, adding the dummy operator <u>do</u> or the operator <u>be</u>. If a sentence contains the verb <u>have</u>, you can form a question two ways: by adding the operator <u>do</u> (most common) or by inverting <u>have</u> and the subject (less common).

EXAMPLES
   Many students try too hard to obtain high grades.
   Do many students try too hard to obtain high grades?

   Insomniacs have a very difficult time sleeping.
   Do insomniacs have a very difficult time sleeping? (most common)
   Have insomniacs a very difficult time sleeping? (less common)

1. Positive role models are very important for young children.
2. They help children learn healthy behavioral patterns.
3. Many children grow up in environments of crime and poverty.
4. In these environments they rarely see normal, healthy behaviors.

5. They have little opportunity to mature into healthy adults.
6. Many schools now realize the need to give their students exposure to adults with positive outlooks.
7. Consequently, they bring successful adult professionals to speak to students.
8. These speakers show students how to succeed.

3.5 SUBJECT AND VERB

Regular sentences consist of a subject and a predicate, and the predicate contains at least a verb (cf. 3.2). Here are some sentences consisting of just the subject and the verb:

subject	verb
A door	opened.
The sun	is setting.
The baby	was crying.
You	must leave.
Many of us	have protested.
They	have been drinking.

Sentences usually contain more than just the subject and the verb. Here are several examples, with the subject (S) and the verb (V) underscored and labeled:

His black boots (S) had (V) pointed toes and fancy stitching.
It (S) rained (V) every day of our vacation.
Every kind of medical equipment (S) was (V) in short supply.

The subject need not come first in the sentence:

Eventually the president (S) intervened (V) in the dispute.
Over the years she (S) had collected (V) numerous prizes for academic achievement.

Sometimes, a word or phrase comes between the subject and the verb:

They (S) often stay (V) with us for their vacations.

Or there is an interruption between parts of the verb:

We (S) can (V) never thank (V) this country enough.

The easiest way to identify the subject in a declarative sentence is to turn this sentence into a **yes-no question** (one expecting the answer <u>yes</u> or <u>no</u>). The operator (op) and the subject change places:

[1] <u>The baby</u> (S) <u>has</u> (op) been crying.
[1a] <u>Has</u> (op) <u>the baby</u> (S) been crying?

[2] <u>Every kind of medical equipment</u> (S) <u>was</u> (op) in short supply.
[2a] <u>Was</u> (op) <u>every kind of medical equipment</u> (S) in short supply?

[3] Eventually <u>the president</u> (S) intervened in the dispute.
[3a] <u>Did</u> (op) <u>the president</u> (S) eventually intervene in the dispute?

It may be necessary to turn other types of sentences into declarative sentences to identify the subject for this test and the next. For example, the subject in [1a] is that part of the sentence that changes place with the operator when the question is turned into a declarative sentence.

Another way of identifying the subject of a declarative sentence is to ask a question introduced by <u>who</u> or <u>what</u> followed by the verb (without subject-operator inversion). The subject is the element that <u>who</u> or <u>what</u> questions:

[4] <u>The World Bank president</u> (S) <u>predicted</u> (V) another world recession in the near future.
[4a] <u>Who</u> (S) <u>predicted</u> (V) another world recession in the near future? <u>The World Bank President.</u>

[5] <u>Tourism</u> (S) <u>ranks</u> (V) foremost as a growth industry.
[5a] <u>What</u> (S) <u>ranks</u> (V) foremost as a growth industry? <u>Tourism.</u>

[6] <u>Barbara</u> (S) <u>is marrying</u> (V) Charles.
[6a] <u>Who</u> (S) <u>is marrying</u> (V) Charles?

We can identify the verb of the sentence because it changes its form or contains auxiliaries to express differences in time (for example, past and present) or attitude (for example, possibility, permission, and obligation). Here are some examples with the verb <u>predict</u>:

predicts	was predicting	might predict
predicted	may predict	could have predicted
is predicting	will predict	should have been predicting

We could use any of these forms of <u>predict</u> as the verb in this sentence:

He <u>predicted</u> (V) another world recession.

EXERCISE 3.7

Turn each sentence into a question. Underline the subject of the sentence in the original statement and in the question. Some of the sentences contain more than one clause.

EXAMPLE

<u>Terrorists</u> kidnapped a former Italian premier and killed his five body-guards.

Did <u>terrorists</u> kidnap a former Italian premier and kill his five bodyguards?

1. A small school bus braked slowly.
2. Fourteen teenagers stepped out.
3. All of them wore dark sweaters.
4. They placed a bouquet of carnations before the memorial to the murdered five bodyguards.
5. Pinned to the cross on the memorial were five photos of the dead.
6. The memorial is all that marks the site of the terrorist kidnapping.
7. A few blocks away, border police checked every tenth car or so.
8. The drivers were asked to show identification while their trunks were searched.
9. Police believe that a team of foreign terrorists may have committed the attack and then turned the former premier over to local terrorists.
10. The cabinet has given the police greater power in interrogation and arrests.

EXERCISE 3.8

Identify and underline the subjects of the questions and exclamations below.

EXAMPLES

Have <u>they</u> been drinking?
(Think of declarative: *<u>They</u> have been drinking.*)
How sensibly <u>she</u> speaks!
(It may help to turn it into a question: *Does <u>she</u> speak sensibly?*)

1. Has the project been completed yet?
2. What a wonderful party it was!
3. How long your hair has gotten!
4. Will the caterers be on time for the wedding reception?

5. Should the school be notified about the flu epidemic?
6. How little humankind has progressed over the centuries!
7. Can the appointment be postponed until next week?
8. What bad weather we've been having!

3.6 SUBJECT

Many grammatical rules refer to the subject. Here are some examples, including several that I mentioned earlier:

1. There are rules for the position of the subject. The subject normally comes before the verb in declaratives, but in questions it comes after the operator.

[1]   They (S) accepted (V) full responsibility.
[1a] Did (op) they (S) accept (V) full responsibility?

The subject comes before the verb even in questions if who or what is the subject:

[1b] Who (S) accepted (V) full responsibility?

2. The subject is normally absent in imperatives:

Help (V) me with the baggage.

3. Most verbs in the present have a distinctive form ending in -s when the subject is singular and refers to something or someone other than the speaker or the person or persons being addressed:

The older child (singular S) feeds (singular V) the younger ones.
The older children (plural V) feed (plural V) the younger ones.
The senator (singular S) has (singular V) a clear moral position on racial equality.
The senators (plural S) have (plural V) a clear moral position on racial equality.

4. Some **pronouns** (words like I, you, she, he, they) have a distinctive form when they function as subject of the sentence:

She (S) knows me well.
I (S) know her well.

5. The subject decides the form of **reflexive pronouns** (those ending in -self, such as <u>herself</u>, <u>ourselves</u>, <u>themselves</u>) that appear later in the sentence:

> <u>I</u> (S) hurt <u>myself</u> badly.
> <u>He</u> (S) hurt <u>himself</u> badly.
> <u>You</u> (S) can look at <u>yourself</u> in the mirror.
> <u>She</u> (S) can look at <u>herself</u> in the mirror.

6. When we turn an active sentence into a passive sentence (cf. 2.6), we change the subjects:

> ACTIVE: <u>The police</u> (S) called <u>the bomb-disposal squad</u>.
> PASSIVE: <u>The bomb-disposal squad</u> (S) was called by <u>the police</u>.

We can also omit the subject of the active sentence when we form the passive sentence, and indeed we generally do so:

> PASSIVE: <u>The bomb-disposal squad</u> was called.

EXERCISE 3.9

Explain how the rules for subjects distinguish the (a) and (b) sentences.

EXAMPLE
   a.   Leave immediately.
   b.   You should leave immediately.
   Sentence (a) is an imperative sentence. It differs from sentence (b) because it lacks a subject (you).

1. a.   We took ourselves out to dinner and a movie last night.
   b.   We took them out to dinner and a movie last night.
2. a.   A good lecturer keeps the audience interested in the topic of discussion.
   b.   Good lecturers keep the audience interested in the topic of discussion.
3. a.   The lab workers analyzed the sample promptly.
   b.   The sample was analyzed promptly by the lab workers.
4. a.   The project is scheduled for completion in early 1990.
   b.   Is the project scheduled for completion in early 1990?
5. a.   He worked well into the evening on the tax audit.
   b.   The office gave him until Thursday to complete the audit.
6. a.   Let me give you a cup of coffee before you leave.
   b.   You should let me give you a cup of coffee before you leave.

3.7 TRANSITIVE VERBS AND DIRECT OBJECT

If a main verb requires a **direct object** to complete the sentence, it is a **transitive** verb. The term "transitive" comes from the notion that a person (represented by the subject of the sentence) performs an action that affects some person or thing: there is a "transition" of the action from the one to the other. Indeed, the direct object (dO) typically refers to a person or thing directly affected by the action described in the sentence:

> Polly snatched my letter (dO).
> Ronald stroked his beard (dO).
> They have eaten all the strawberries (dO).
> I dusted the bookshelves in my bedroom (dO).

One way of identifying the direct object in a declarative sentence is by asking a question introduced by who or what followed by the operator and the subject. The object is the element that who or what questions:

> [1]   Carter has been photographing light bulbs lately.
> [1a] What (dO) has (op) Carter (S) been photographing lately? Light bulbs.
> [2]   Sandra recorded the adverse effects of the changes.
> [2a] What (dO) did (op) Sandra (S) record? The adverse effects of the changes.
> [3]   Don is phoning his mother.
> [3a] Who (dO) is (op) Don (S) phoning? His mother.

Some grammatical rules refer to the direct object.

1. The direct object normally comes after the verb (but cf. section 3.11).

> Carter has been photographing (V) light bulbs (dO) lately.

2. Some pronouns have a distinctive form when they function as direct object (cf. 3.6 (4)):

> She phoned us (dO) earlier this evening.
> We phoned her (dO) earlier this evening.

3. If the subject and direct object refer to the same person or thing, the direct object is generally a reflexive pronoun (cf. 3.6(5)):

> The children hid themselves.

4. When we turn an active sentence into a passive sentence, the direct object of the active sentence becomes the subject of the passive sentence.

> ACTIVE: Radio telescopes have detected <u>cosmic radiation</u> (dO).
>
> PASSIVE: <u>Cosmic radiation</u> (S) has been detected by radio telescopes.

In this section I have discussed one basic sentence structure:

> SVO: Subject + (Transitive) Verb + (Direct) Object

================ **EXERCISE 3.10** ================

Underline the direct objects.

EXAMPLE
   We drove <u>the car</u> yesterday.

1. The doctor canceled all appointments.
2. He drove the car to the airport.
3. He met the two men there.
4. He then drove them back to his house.
5. On the way, he described certain landmarks.
6. The father and his son admired the house.
7. However, they preferred a motel.
8. The boy's father demanded a church wedding.
9. The girl's father opposed the idea.
10. However, they convinced him in the end.

3.8   LINKING VERBS AND SUBJECT COMPLEMENT

If a verb requires a **subject complement** (SC) to complete the sentence, the verb is a **linking verb.** The subject complement (underscored in the examples that follow) typically identifies or characterizes the person or thing denoted by the subject:

[1]   Sandra is <u>my mother's name.</u>
[2]   Your room must be <u>the one next to mine.</u>
[3]   The upstairs tenant seemed <u>a reliable person.</u>

[4]   A university is <u>a community of scholars</u>.
[5]   The receptionist seemed <u>very tired</u>.
[6]   You should be <u>more careful</u>.
[7]   The distinction became <u>quite clear</u>.
[8]   The corridor is <u>too narrow</u>.

The most common linking verb is <u>be</u>. Other common linking verbs (with examples of subject complements in parentheses) include <u>appear</u> (the best plan), <u>become</u> (my neighbor), <u>seem</u> (the wrong person), <u>feel</u> (a fool), <u>get</u> (ready), <u>look</u> (cheerful), <u>sound</u> (foolish). Subject complements are typically noun phrases (cf. 4.2), as in [1]–[4] above, or adjective phrases (cf. 4.21), as in [5]–[8] above.

We have now looked at two basic structures:

(3.7) SVO: Subject + (Transitive) Verb + (Direct) Object
(3.8) SVC: Subject + (Linking) Verb + (Subject) Complement

EXERCISE 3.11

Underline the subject complements.

EXAMPLE
    The woman seems <u>very intelligent</u>.

1.   Outside, the company sign seems modest.
2.   Inside, the atmosphere is one of rush and ferment.
3.   The company is a genetic engineering firm.
4.   It has become a leader of a brand-new industry.
5.   The focus of the project is DNA recombination.
6.   DNA recombination is the transfer of pieces of DNA from one type of organism to another.
7.   The leaders of the company are research scientists.
8.   They are also shareholders of the company.
9.   The company is becoming an independent corporation with research.

3.9 INTRANSITIVE VERBS AND ADVERBIALS

If a main verb does not require another element to complete it, the verb is **intransitive**:

[1]   Vietnam veterans (S) <u>were demonstrating</u> (V).
[2]   I (S) <u>agree</u> (V).
[3]   No <u>cure</u> (S) <u>exists</u> (V).
[4]   <u>They</u> (S) <u>are lying</u> (V).

We have now seen three basic sentence structures:

(3.7) SVO: Subject + (Transitive) Verb + (Direct) Object
(3.8) SVC: Subject + (Linking) Verb + (Subject) Complement
(3.9) SV: Subject + (Intransitive) Verb

The structures are basic because we can always add optional elements to them. These optional elements are **adverbials.** We should be careful to distinguish adverbials from adverbs (cf. 5.13). The adverbial, like the subject, is a sentence element; the adverb, like the noun, is a word.

Adverbials (A) convey a range of information about the situation depicted in the basic structure (cf. 3.14). In [1a] below, the adverbial <u>noisily</u> depicts the manner of the action, and the adverbial <u>outside the White House</u> indicates the place of the action.

[1a]   Vietnamese veterans were demonstrating <u>noisily</u> (A) <u>outside the White House</u> (A).

In [2a] <u>entirely</u> is an intensifier of <u>agree</u>, conveying the intensity of the agreeing:

[2a]   I <u>entirely</u> (A) agree.

In [3a] <u>unfortunately</u> supplies the writer's comment:

[3a]   <u>Unfortunately</u> (A), no cure exists.

<u>Therefore</u> in [4a] points to a logical connection between the two sentences. The evidence stated in the first sentence is the reason for the assertion in the second sentence:

[4a]   A reliable witness has testified that they were in Denver on the day they claimed to be in Houston. They are <u>therefore</u> (A) lying.

The sentences [1a]–[4a] with adverbials have the basic structure SV , which we also see in the parallel sentences [1]–[4] without adverbials. In [5] the basic structure is SVO and in [6] it is SVC:

[5]   <u>For all its weaknesses</u> (A) the Continental Congress had won the war against one of the world's mightiest powers.
[6]   Jade is plentiful <u>in this area</u> (A).

In [5] the adverbial has concessive force ("despite all its weaknesses") and in [6] it indicates place.

As [1a] indicates, a sentence may have more than one adverbial.

===================== **EXERCISE 3.12** =====================

Underline the adverbials in the sentences below. Some sentences may contain more than one adverbial.

EXAMPLE
<u>A few days ago</u> a new mayor was elected <u>in New York</u>.

1. The new mayor quietly celebrated New Year's Eve in Manhattan with a few close friends.
2. The next day the mayor was formally inaugurated on the steps of the city hall.
3. The city still faces major economic difficulties.
4. Without federal aid, New York will soon be bankrupt.
5. The imposition of new taxes is unpopular everywhere.
6. Nevertheless, new taxes and cuts in spending must be introduced quickly.
7. New York State may provide increased aid in the near future.
8. The federal administration will probably give some long-term loans.
9. However, the administration wants a balanced city budget first.
10. The mayor will probably make some unpopular decisions this year.

===================== **EXERCISE 3.13** =====================

Insert the adverbials in parentheses into the sentences that precede them.

EXAMPLE
Influenza will attack hundreds of thousands of Americans. (this year)
This year influenza will attack hundreds of thousands of Americans.

1. A few people have died from influenza. (over the past two weeks)
2. It is not an epidemic. (yet)
3. No drugs can lower the initial fever. (effectively)
4. People with the flu should rest. (in bed)

5. They should drink fruit juice. (additionally)
6. Scientists identified a virus as the cause of influenza. (forty years ago)
7. They have discovered several flu viruses. (since then)
8. Experts have distinguished more than one strain of flu viruses. (unfortunately)
9. Doctors gave many people vaccinations against Type A virus. (last year)
10. A vaccine for one strain never gives full protection for other strains. (however)

3.10 ADVERBIAL COMPLEMENT

I explained in section 3.9 that adverbials are optional elements in sentence structure. However, some elements that convey the same information as adverbials are obligatory because the main verb is not complete without them. Such obligatory elements are **adverbial complements** (AC).

Contrast [1] with [1a]:

[1] Vietnamese veterans were demonstrating <u>outside the White House</u> (A).

[1a] Vietnamese veterans were <u>outside the White House</u> (AC).

In [1] the sentence is complete without the adverbial, but in [1a] the sentence is not complete without the adverbial complement.

Typically, adverbial complements refer to space—location or direction:

The city lies <u>225 miles north of Guatemala City</u> (AC).
The nearest inhabitants are <u>a five-day mule trip away</u> (AC).
George is getting <u>into his wife's car</u> (AC).
This road goes <u>to Madison</u> (AC).

Adverbials may convey other meanings:

Their work is <u>in the early stages</u> (AC).
The show will last <u>for three hours</u> (AC).
The children were <u>with their mother</u> (AC).
These letters are <u>for Cindy</u> (AC).

We can now add a fourth basic sentence structure to our set:

(3.7) SVO: Subject + (Transitive) Verb + (Direct) Object
(3.8) SVC: Subject + (Linking) Verb + (Subject) Complement

(3.9) SV: Subject + (Intransitive) Verb
(3.10) SVA: Subject + Verb + Adverbial (Complement)

I have not named the set of verbs that requires an adverbial complement because there is no traditional name for it. The most common verb in the SVA structure is <u>be</u>.

═══════════════════ **EXERCISE 3.14** ═══════════════════

State whether the underlined adverbial in each sentence is obligatory or optional.

EXAMPLES

The lawyer <u>vigorously</u> defended her client. *(optional)*
The dog is <u>in the backyard</u>. *(obligatory)*

1. The Museum of Fine Arts is located <u>in Boston</u>.
2. It is on Huntington Ave, <u>near Northeastern University</u>.
3. Paintings in the museum are displayed <u>tastefully and elegantly</u>.
4. <u>Unfortunately</u>, there are times when the museum is very crowded.
5. <u>At these times</u> it is hard to get a close look at the paintings.
6. There are <u>simply</u> too many people in your way looking at paintings.
7. On Friday evenings, fewer people are <u>in the museum</u>.
8. This is, <u>therefore</u>, a good time to visit the museum.

3.11 DIRECT AND INDIRECT OBJECT

We have seen that a transitive verb requires a direct object to complete the sentence (cf. 3.7). Some transitive verbs can have two objects: an **indirect object** followed by a direct object. The indirect object (iO) refers to a person indirectly affected by the action described in the sentence. The person generally receives something or benefits from something.

[1] Ruth gave <u>my son</u> (iO) <u>a birthday present</u> (dO).
[2] I can show <u>you</u> (iO) <u>my diploma</u> (dO).
[3] My friends will save <u>her</u> (iO) <u>a seat</u> (dO).
[4] You may ask <u>the speaker</u> (iO) <u>another question</u> (dO).
[5] The store is allowing <u>senior citizens</u> (iO) <u>a 20 percent discount</u> (dO).

The indirect object is usually equivalent to a phrase introduced by to or for, but that phrase normally comes after the direct object. Sentences [1a]–[4a] parallel [1]–[4]:

[1a] Ruth gave a birthday present to my son.
[2a] I can show my diploma to you.
[3a] My friends will save a seat for her.
[4a] You may ask another question of the speaker.

The structures in [1]–[4] and those in [1a]–[4a] differ somewhat in their use, since there is a general tendency for the more important information to come at the end (cf. 9.2). For example, if the son has already been mentioned, but not the birthday present, we would expect [1] to be used rather than [1a], though in speech we can indicate the focus of information by giving it prominence in our intonation.

We can question the indirect object in a way similar to the questioning of the direct object:

[1b] Whom (iO) did Ruth give a birthday present?

The grammatical rules that refer to the direct object (cf. 3.7) also refer to the indirect object:

1. The indirect object comes after the verb:
    Ruth gave my son (iO) a birthday present (dO).
    Notice that the indirect object comes before the direct object.
2. Some pronouns have a distinctive form when they function as indirect objects:
    I paid her (iO) the full amount.
    She paid me (iO) the full amount.
3. If the subject and indirect object refer to the same person, the indirect object is generally a reflexive pronoun (cf. 3.6(5)):
    The president of the company paid herself (iO) a huge salary.
4. When we turn an active sentence into a passive sentence, the indirect object of the active sentence can become the subject of the passive sentence:
    The principal granted Tony (iO) an interview.
    Tony (S) was granted an interview.
    The direct object can also become the subject, but in that case the indirect object (if retained) is generally represented by a phrase introduced by to or for:
    An interview was granted to Tony.

We can now add a fifth basic sentence structure:

(3.7) SVO: Subject + (Transitive) Verb + (Direct) Object
(3.8) SVC: Subject + (Linking) Verb + (Subject) Complement
(3.9) SV: Subject + (Intransitive) Verb
(3.10) SVA: Subject + Verb + Adverbial (Complement)
(3.11) SVOO: Subject + (Transitive) Verb + (Indirect) Object + (Direct) Object

═══════════════════ **EXERCISE 3.15** ═══════════════════

Indicate whether the underlined words are direct objects (dO) or indirect objects (iO).

EXAMPLE

I gave <u>my father</u> *(iO)* <u>a new watch</u> *(dO)* for his birthday.

1. I saw <u>a group of soldiers</u> (   ).
2. The soldiers erected <u>two large tents</u> (   ).
3. They did not make <u>much noise</u> (   ).
4. A lieutenant showed <u>me</u> (   ) <u>a small chess set</u> (   ).
5. He himself had made <u>it</u> (   ).
6. I showed <u>him</u> (   ) <u>my portable radio</u> (   ).
7. I had bought <u>it</u> (   ) last week.
8. He told <u>me</u> (   ) <u>his name</u> (   ).

═══════════════════ **EXERCISE 3.16** ═══════════════════

Certain verbs allow the indirect object in a sentence to be optionally deleted. Indicate whether the indirect objects in the sentences below are optional or obligatory.

EXAMPLE

The man gives <u>his good friends</u> low interest loans. *(optional)*

1. I'll show <u>you</u> my work records after dinner.
2. My sister saved <u>me</u> some milk and cookies.
3. The film was way too long and gave <u>me</u> a throbbing headache.

4. The worker suspected of stealing told <u>his employers</u> a number of lies.
5. The unpaid bills caused <u>the landlord</u> a lot of grief and misery.
6. John is cooking <u>his family</u> dinner tonight.
7. The experience taught <u>the boy</u> a very valuable lesson.
8. The man paid <u>his mother</u> the back rent that he owed.

EXERCISE 3.17

Below are a group of verbs that take direct and indirect objects. Use the verbs as the basis of sentences containing direct and indirect objects.

EXAMPLE
  Give
  The woman gave her husband an expensive gift.

1. Pay
2. Allow
3. Ask
4. Play
5. Show
6. Tell
7. Pour
8. Make
9. Grant
10. Bake

3.12 DIRECT OBJECT AND COMPLEMENT

In 3.11 we saw examples of transitive verbs that require two elements: indirect object and direct object. In this section I will introduce the two remaining structures, each of which consists of a subject, a transitive verb, a direct object, and a complement. In both structures the complement is related to the direct object.

In the first structure, the direct object is followed by an **object complement** (OC):

[1] His jokes made <u>the audience</u> (dO) <u>uneasy</u> (OC).
[2] I declared <u>the meeting</u> (dO) <u>open</u> (OC).
[3] The heat has turned <u>the milk</u> (dO) <u>sour</u> (OC).
[4] They elected <u>her</u> (dO) <u>their leader</u> (OC).

This SVOC structure parallels the SVC structure (cf. 3.8), but in the first structure the complement is related to the direct object and in the second it is related to the subject. Compare [1]–[4] with [1a]–[4a]:

[1a] The audience (S) is uneasy (SC).
[2a] The meeting (S) is open (SC).
[3a] The milk (S) is sour (SC).
[4a] She (S) is their leader (SC).

Finally, the direct object may be followed by an adverbial complement (Ac) required by the main verb (cf. 3.10):

[5] You should put (V) the chicken (dO) in the microwave (AC).
[6] I keep (V) my car (dO) outside the house (AC).
[7] He stuck (V) his hands (dO) in his pockets (AC).

Just as the SVOC structure parallels the SVC structure, so this SVOA structure parallels the SVA structure.

[5a] The chicken (S) is in the microwave (AC).
[6a] My car (S) is outside the house (AC).
[7a] His hands (S) are in his pockets (AC).

We have now looked at four basic structures with transitive verbs and direct objects:

(3.7) SVO: Subject + (Transitive) Verb + (Direct) Object
(3.11) SVOO: Subject + (Transitive) Verb + (Indirect) Object + (Direct) Object
(3.12) SVOC: Subject + (Transitive) Verb + (Direct) Object + (Object) Complement
(3.12) SVOA: Subject + (Transitive) Verb + Direct (Object) + Adverbial (Complement)

═══════════════════ **EXERCISE 3.18** ═══════════════════

At the end of each sentence, indicate whether the underlined constructions are object complements (OC) or adverbial complements (AC).

EXAMPLE
  I placed the sweater in the dresser drawer. *(AC)*

  1. We elected Mary Jones president of the senior class.
  2. Ed drove his car into the garage.

3. The therapist made her client <u>comfortable</u>.
4. The doctors kept the patient <u>alive</u>.
5. The president placed the blame <u>on his close associates</u>.
6. The professor certified the exam <u>valid</u>.
7. I invested all of my savings <u>in the stock market</u>.
8. The minister pronounced the couple <u>husband and wife</u>.
9. The child placed his toys <u>in his playbox</u>.
10. The heater kept the car <u>very warm</u>.

EXERCISE 3.19

Below are a group of verbs that take direct objects and either object complements or adverbial complements. Make up sentences containing the verbs and either an object complement or an adverbial complement.

EXAMPLE
Make
I made my parents very happy.

1. Turn
2. Elect
3. Set
4. Declare
5. Keep
6. Presume
7. Put
8. Rate
9. Place
10. Drive

3.13 THE BASIC SENTENCE STRUCTURES

I will now summarize what has been described so far in this chapter. The following elements function in the basic sentence structures:

subject	S
verb	V
object	O—direct object dO
	O—indirect object iO

complement   C—subject component SC
                            C—object complement OC
                            A—adverbial complement AC

These elements enter into the seven basic sentence structures:

SV: Subject + Intransitive Verb (cf. 3.9)
        <u>Someone</u> (S) <u>is talking</u> (V).

SVA: Subject + Verb + Adverbial Complement (cf. 3.10)
        <u>My parents</u> (S) <u>are living</u> (V) <u>in Chicago</u> (AC).

SVC: Subject + Linking Verb + Subject Complement
        (cf. 3.8)
        <u>I</u> (S) <u>feel</u> (V) <u>tired</u> (SC).

SVO: Subject + Transitive Verb + Direct Object (cf. 3.7)
        <u>We</u> (S) <u>have finished</u> (V) <u>our work</u> (dO).

SVOO: Subject + Transitive Verb + Indirect Object + Direct Object   (cf. 3.11)
        <u>She</u> (S) <u>has given</u> (V) <u>me</u> (iO) <u>the letter</u> (dO).

SVOA: Subject + Transitive Verb + Direct Object + Adverbial   Complement (cf. 3.12)
        <u>You</u> (S) <u>can put</u> (V) <u>your coat</u> (dO) <u>in my bedroom</u> (AC).

SVOC: Subject + Transitive Verb + Direct Object + Object Complement (cf. 3.12)
        <u>You</u> (S) <u>have made</u> (V) <u>me</u> (dO) <u>very happy</u> (OC).

The structures depend on the choice of the main verbs, regardless of the auxiliaries. The same verb (sometimes in somewhat different senses) may enter into different structures. Here are some examples:

SV: I have <u>eaten</u>.
SVO: I have <u>eaten</u> lunch.

SV: It <u>smells</u>.
SVC: It <u>smells</u> sweet.

SVC: He <u>felt</u> a fool.
SVO: He <u>felt</u> the material.

SVO: I <u>made</u> some sandwiches.
SVOO: I <u>made</u> them some sandwiches.

SVO: I have <u>named</u> my representative.
SVOC: I have <u>named</u> her my representative.

SV: The children are <u>growing</u>.
SVO: The children are <u>growing</u> carrots.
SVC: The children are <u>growing</u> hungry.

SVO: She <u>caught</u> me.
SVOO: She <u>caught</u> me a fish.
SVOA: She <u>caught</u> me off my guard.

EXERCISE 3.20

Identify the underlined element by writing down the appropriate abbreviation at the end of the sentence: S (subject), V (verb), dO (direct object), iO (indirect object), SC (subject complement), OC (object complement), A (adverbial), or AC (adverbial complement).

EXAMPLE
   <u>The centennial of Einstein's birth</u> was last year. *(S)*

1.   Some scientists consider Einstein <u>the greatest scientist of all time</u>.
2.   He revealed <u>new concepts of space and time</u>.
3.   Astronomers and physicists <u>rely</u> heavily on his theory of general relativity.
4.   <u>Several of Einstein's important scientific papers</u> appeared in 1905.
5.   Scientists give <u>him</u> the credit for some of the most important scientific theories of this century.
6.   They have also made possible <u>many technological developments</u>.
7.   Einstein received the Nobel Prize in 1922 <u>for his photoelectric theory</u>.
8.   His theory of relativity <u>was</u> not <u>accepted</u> by all scientists at that time.
9.   In his final years Einstein publicly denounced <u>McCarthyism</u>.
10. He considered his political views <u>of great importance</u>.
11. <u>In his last public act,</u> he joined other scholars in pleading for a ban on all warfare.
12. Throughout his life he spoke out <u>courageously</u> against social injustice.

====== **EXERCISE 3.21** ======

Identify each sentence element by writing the appropriate abbreviation in the parentheses after it: S (subject), V (verb), dO (direct object), iO (indirect object), SC (subject complement), OC (object complement), A (adverbial), or AC (adverbial complement). If the verb is split, put V for the auxiliary.

EXAMPLES
   The film industry *(S)* calls *(V)* theater owners *(dO)* exhibitors *(OC)*.
   Movies *(S)* are *(V)* not *(A)* always *(A)* seen *(V)* by exhibitors *(A)*.

1. Several expensive movies (   ) have (   ) recently (   ) failed (   ) badly (   ).
2. The distributor (   ) sends (   ) exhibitors (   ) a brochure about the movie (   ).
3. The brochure (   ) merely (   ) tells (   ) them (   ) the plot and the stars (   ).
4. With that information (   ) the exhibitors (   ) make (   ) a bid for the movie (   ).
5. They (   ) promise (   ) the distributor (   ) a percentage of box office revenues (   ).
6. They (   ) also (   ) guarantee (   ) the distributor (   ) a fixed sum (   ).
7. The industry (   ) calls (   ) that type of booking (   ) blind bidding (   ).
8. Last year (   ) most of the major pictures (   ) were (   ) blinds bids (   ).
9. The National Association of Theater Owners (   ) opposes (   ) blind bidding (   ).
10. The association (   ) is introducing (   ) bills against blind bidding (   ) in most state legislatures (   ).
11. The distributors (   ) are lobbying (   ) against those bills (   ).
12. Would (   ) you (   ) buy (   ) a product (   ) on trust (   )?

===================== **EXERCISE 3.22** =====================

Make up sentences that conform to the structures given below. The abbreviations correspond to the following structures: S (subject), V (verb), dO (direct object), iO (indirect object), SC (subject complement), OC (object complement), A (adverbial), AC (adverbial complement).

EXAMPLE

    S V DO *Nobody wants any more coffee.*

1. S V
2. S V A
3. S V SC
4. S V dO
5. S V iO dO
6. S V dO AC
7. S V dO OC

===================== **EXERCISE 3.23** =====================

These sentences are ambiguous. For each possible meaning, state the structure (set of sentence elements) and give a paraphrase.

EXAMPLE

    They are baking potatoes.
    S + V + SC (They are potatoes for baking.)
    S + V + DO (They are cooking potatoes in the oven.)

1. I left him a wreck.
2. You will make a good model.
3. They are finding me an honest worker.
4. They have elected the deputy mayor.
5. They are flying planes.

3.14   THE MEANINGS OF THE SENTENCE ELEMENTS

The sentence elements are grammatical, not semantic, categories. However, they are associated with certain meanings. In this section I will illustrate some typical meanings.

Subject

(1) agentive

In sentences with a transitive or intransitive verb, the subject typically has an agentive role: the person that performs the action:

> <u>Martha</u> has switched on the television.
> <u>Caroline</u> is calling.

(2) identified

The identified role is typical of structures with a linking verb:

> <u>Jeremy</u> was my best friend.
> <u>Doris</u> is my sister-in-law.

(3) characterized

The characterized role is also typical of structures with a linking verb:

> <u>This brand of coffee</u> tastes better.
> <u>Paul</u> is an excellent student.

(4) affected

With intransitive verbs the subject frequently has the affected role: the person or thing directly affected by the action, but not intentionally performing the action:

> <u>They</u> are drowning.
> <u>The water</u> has boiled.

(5) it

Sometimes there is no participant. The subject function is then taken by <u>it</u>, which is there merely to fill the place of the subject:

> <u>It</u>'s raining.   <u>It</u>'s already eleven o'clock.
> <u>It</u>'s too hot.   <u>It</u>'s a long way to Miami.

Verb

The major distinction in meaning is between verbs that are **stative** and verbs that are **dynamic.**

Stative verbs introduce a **quality** attributed to the subject or a **state of affairs:**

I <u>am</u> an American.
Their children <u>are</u> noisy.
She <u>has</u> two brothers.
I <u>heard</u> your alarm this morning.

Dynamic verbs introduce **events.** They refer to something that happens:

Her books <u>sell</u> well.
We <u>talked</u> about you last night.
Your ball has <u>broken</u> my window.
I <u>listened</u> to her respectfully.

Dynamic verbs, but not stative verbs, occur quite normally with the <u>ing</u> form
(cf. 4.12, 4.14):

Her books are <u>selling</u> well.
We were <u>talking</u> about you last night.
They have been <u>playing</u> in the yard.
She is <u>looking</u> at us.

When stative verbs are used with the -<u>ing</u> form, they have been transformed
into dynamic verbs:

Their children are <u>being</u> noisy. ("behaving noisily")
I am <u>having</u> a party next Sunday evening.

Direct Object

(1) *affected*

This is the typical role of the direct object. See **subject** (4) above.

I threw <u>the note</u> on the floor.
She shook <u>her head</u>.

(2) *resultant*

The direct object may refer to something that comes into existence as a result
of the action:

He's written <u>a paper on his hobbies</u>.
I'm knitting <u>a sweater</u> for myself.

(3) *eventive*

When it has the eventive role, the direct object typically (a) is a noun that is
derived from a verb, (b) carries the main part of the meaning that is normally

carried by the verb, and (c) is preceded by a verb of general meaning, such as <u>do</u>, <u>have</u>, or <u>make</u>:

> They were having <u>a quarrel</u>. [Cf: *They were quarreling.*]
> I have made <u>my choice</u>. [Cf: *I have chosen.*]

Indirect Object

The indirect object typically has a **recipient** role: the person that is indirectly involved in the action, generally the person receiving something or intended to receive something:

> They paid <u>me</u> the full amount.
> He bought <u>Sandra</u> a bunch of flowers.

Subject and Object Complement

The complement typically has the role of **attribute.** It attributes an identification or characterization to the subject (if it is a subject complement) or the direct object (if it is an object complement):

> Susan is <u>my attorney.</u>
> Ronald became <u>a paid agitator.</u>   } OC

> I have made David <u>my assistant.</u>
> The sun has turned our curtains <u>yellow.</u> } SC

Adverbial

Adverbials have a wide range of meanings, some of which apply to adverbial complements (cf. 3.10, 3.12). Here are some typical examples:

(1) space

> My school is <u>on the west side</u>. [*position in space*]
> She has gone <u>to the bank</u>. [*direction*]

(2) time

> They're staying with us <u>for a few weeks</u>. [*duration*]
> We come here <u>quite often</u>. [*frequency*]
> James Madison was born <u>in 1751</u>. [*position in time*]

(3) manner

> The students cheered <u>wildly</u>.
> I examined the statement <u>carefully</u>.

(4) degree

> I like them <u>very much</u>.
> We know her <u>well</u>.

(5) cause

> My brother is sick <u>with the flu</u>.
> They voted for her <u>out of a sense of loyalty</u>.

(6) comment on truth-value [degree of certainty or doubt]

> They <u>certainly</u> can't finish on time.
> <u>Perhaps</u> he's out.

(7) evaluation of what the sentence refers to

> <u>Luckily</u>, they were not hurt.
> He <u>unexpectedly</u> fell asleep.

(8) providing a connection between units

> I was not friendly with them; <u>however</u>, I did not want them
>   to be treated unfairly.
> We arrived too late, and <u>as a result</u> we missed her.

======= EXERCISE 3.24 =======

Identify the meanings that the underlined sentence elements in each sentence
convey.

EXAMPLES
<u>John</u> has written his semester paper. *(agentive)*
A school of fish <u>drifted</u> past our boat. *(event)*
The Rio Grande splits New Mexico <u>vertically</u>. *(manner)*

1. <u>The instructor</u> taught the class the parts of speech.
2. Grammar <u>is</u> my favorite subject.
3. The superintendent <u>spoke</u> to a group of new workers.
4. <u>The man</u> is my father.
5. George baked <u>a cake</u> on his day off last week.
6. <u>The patient</u> died during the operation.

7. The paper was written by the commission in response to a bill that the legislature passed.
8. The car dealer gave me $1,000 for my used car.
9. I had many choices in the matter.
10. I worked for the firm during spring break.
11. Mary cooked dinner for her husband's clients.
12. The paper was written very clearly in language that everyone could understand.
13. The young child seems very immature.
14. The building is located on the south side of the city.
15. It is very cold outside today.
16. The results of the election will probably be known by this evening.

EXERCISE 3.25

Make up sentences containing the meanings given below.

EXAMPLE

Agentive Subject + Dynamic Verb + Affected Object + Degree Adverbial
I kicked the football very hard.

1. Identified Subject + Stative Verb + Attribute Subject Complement
2. Affected Subject + Dynamic Verb
3. Agentive Subject + Dynamic Verb + Recipient Indirect Object + Affected Direct Object
4. Affected Subject + Dynamic Verb + Time Adverbial
5. Agentive Subject + Dynamic Verb + Time Adverbial + Space Adverbial
6. Agentive Subject + Dynamic Verb + Affected Object + Attribute Object Complement
7. Characterized Subject + Stative Verb + Attribute Subject Complement
8. It-Subject + Stative Verb + Time Adverbial
9. Agentive Subject + Dynamic Verb + Manner Adverbial
10. Affected Subject + Stative Verb + Attribute Subject Complement + Cause Adverbial

CHAPTER FOUR

The Structures of Phrases

4.1. KINDS OF PHRASES

When we looked earlier (3.1) at the parts of the simple sentence, we noticed that they can be viewed in terms of either their structure or their function. In Chapter 3 we were concerned mainly with their function in the sentence, and there we distinguished functional elements such as subject and direct object. In this chapter we are concerned mainly with the internal structure of the elements. For the simple sentence, this means the structures of the various phrases that can function in the sentence as subject, verb, and so on.

There are five types of phrases:

noun phrase	a peaceful <u>result</u>
	(main word: noun <u>result</u>)
verb phrase	must have been <u>dreaming</u>
	(main word: verb <u>dreaming</u>)
adjective phrase	very <u>pleasant</u>
	(main word: adjective <u>pleasant</u>)
adverb phrase	very <u>carefully</u>
	(main word: adverb <u>carefully</u>)
prepositional phrase	<u>in</u> the shade
	(introductory word: preposition <u>in</u>)

The first four phrases are named after their main word. The prepositional phrase is different in that the preposition is the introductory word rather than the main word.

In grammar, the technical term <u>phrase</u> is used even if there is only one word—the main word alone; for example, both <u>very pleasant</u> and <u>pleasant</u> are adjective phrases. This may seem strange at first, since in everyday use the word <u>phrase</u> applies to a group of at least two words. There is a good reason for the wider use of the term in grammar. Many rules that apply to an adjective phrase apply also to an adjective. Instead of specifying each time "adjective phrase or adjective," it is simpler to specify "adjective phrase" and thereby include adjectives. For example, the same rules apply to the positions of <u>very pleasant</u> and <u>pleasant</u> in these sentences:

It was a $\left\{ \begin{array}{l} \underline{\text{very pleasant}} \\ \underline{\text{pleasant}} \end{array} \right\}$ occasion.

The party was $\left\{ \begin{array}{l} \underline{\text{pleasant.}} \\ \underline{\text{very pleasant.}} \end{array} \right.$

In the sections that follow we will be looking at the structures of the five types of phrases, but I will make several general points now. First, a phrase may contain another phrase within it. Or, to put it another way, one phrase may be **embedded** within another phrase:

[1] We had <u>some very pleasant times</u> in Florida.
[2] They were standing <u>in the shade of a large oak tree.</u>

In [1] the noun phrase <u>some very pleasant times</u> has the adjective phrase <u>very pleasant</u> embedded between <u>some</u> and <u>times</u>. In [2] the prepositional phrase consists of the preposition <u>in</u> and the noun phrase <u>the shade of a large oak tree;</u> in the noun phrase another prepositional phrase (<u>of a large oak tree</u>) is embedded as a modifier of <u>shade</u> and that phrase contains the noun phrase <u>a large oak tree.</u> A clause (cf. 2.3) may also be embedded in a phrase:

[3] <u>The school that I attend</u> is quite small.

In [3] the relative clause <u>that I attend</u> (cf. 4.5) is embedded in the noun phrase <u>the school that I attend.</u>

A second point is that phrases are defined by their structure, but they are also characterized by their potential functions. For example, a noun phrase may function (among other possibilities) as a subject, direct object, or indirect object.

Third, there is an inevitable circularity in talking about phrases and words: a noun is a word that can be the main word in a noun phrase, and a noun phrase is a phrase whose main word is a noun.

We will be examining classes of words more closely in the next chapter, but the classes must enter into the discussions of phrases in this chapter. The examples should be a sufficient indication of the types of words that are involved.

THE NOUN PHRASE

4.2 THE STRUCTURE OF THE NOUN PHRASE

The main word in a noun phrase is a noun or a pronoun. There are a number of subclasses of nouns and pronouns, but I will postpone discussion of subclasses until we come to look at word classes (cf. 5.4, 5.15).

The structure of the typical noun phrase may be represented schematically in the following way, where the parentheses indicate elements of the structure that may be absent:

(determiners)　(premodifiers)　noun　(postmodifiers)

Determiners (cf. 5.24–28) introduce noun phrases. **Modifiers** are units that are dependent on the main word and can be omitted. Modifiers that come before the noun are **premodifiers,** and those that come after the noun are **postmodifiers.** Here are examples of possible structures of noun phrases:

noun	books
determiner + noun	those books
premodifier + noun	history books
determiner + premodifier + noun	some long books
noun + postmodifier	books about Canada
determiner + noun + postmodifier	some books on astronomy
premodifier + noun + postmodifier	popular books on psychology
determiner + premodifier + noun + postmodifier	some popular books on astronomy

All these examples can fit into the blank in this sentence:

I occasionally read. . . . .

══════ EXERCISE 4.1 ══════

Underline the noun phrases in each sentence below. Some sentences may have more than one noun phrase or a noun phrase embedded in another noun phrase.

EXAMPLE
   The small children played in the yard.

1. Every spring, students go on spring break.
2. Most students travel to Florida.
3. There they and their friends bathe in the sun for a week.
4. In the evenings, students drive their cars along the beaches.
5. Excessive drinking by students is a problem.
6. Police arrest many students during their vacations.
7. Local merchants make much money off students.
8. In fact, without students their profits would decline considerably.
9. Many local residents do not look forward to the rowdiness of spring break.
10. However, spring break is a long tradition and will not end in the near future.

4.3 DETERMINERS

There are three classes of determiners, defined by their potential sequence in a noun phrase (cf. 5.24–28):

1. **predeterminers,** e.g. all, both, half
2. **central determiners,** e.g. a(n), the, those
3. **postdeterminers,** e.g. other, two, first

Here are two examples with determiners from each class:

all those other problems
both our two daughters

A noun phrase usually has only one or two determiners present.

4.4 MODIFIERS

The noun phrase may have more than one premodifier or postmodifier:

a long hot summer
acute, life-threatening crises
a nasty gash in his chin which needed medical attention

There are two postmodifiers in the last example because each separately modifies gash: a nasty gash in his chin; a nasty gash which needed medical attention. The modifier may itself be modified or may require some kind of completion:

a comfortably cool room
the reduction of violence to children
those eyewitnesses willing to testify about what they had seen

=========================== **EXERCISE 4.2** ===========================

Indicate whether each underlined noun phrase contains a premodifier, a post-modifier, or both.

EXAMPLES
> <u>Violence on television</u> is increasing. (*postmodifier*)
> <u>Young children</u> should not watch violent shows. (*premodifier*)

1. <u>Television violence</u> is increasing, according to some experts.
2. They cite as evidence of this trend <u>television shows like "Miami Vice."</u>
3. On this show, <u>numerous people</u> are often killed quite violently.
4. <u>The effects of violence on children</u> has been studied by experts for a number of years now.
5. They have concluded that excessive violence has <u>a very negative effect</u> on children.
6. <u>Younger children who watch violent shows</u> often behave more violently toward their parents and friends.
7. On the other hand, <u>children who do not watch violent shows</u> do not act as violently toward others.
8. <u>Identical tests</u> were performed on older viewers.
9. Again it was found that <u>those in the study who watched violent shows</u> were more likely to commit violent crimes than those who did not.
10. However, researchers cautioned that their findings were tentative and needed <u>further study on different populations</u>.

4.5   RELATIVE CLAUSES

One common type of postmodifier is the **relative clause:**

> He had <u>a nasty gash which needed medical attention</u>.

The relative clause is embedded in the noun phrase. As an independent sentence it might be:

> [1]   The gash needed medical attention.

We might think of the embedding as a process that takes place in stages. The first stage puts the sentence close to the noun it will be modifying:

> [1a]   He had a nasty <u>gash</u>. <u>The gash</u> needed medical attention.

You will notice that the two sentences share nouns (gash) that refer to the same thing. The next stage changes the noun phrase into a **relative pronoun** (5.22)—here which:

[1b] He had a nasty gash <u>which</u> needed medical attention.

The relative pronoun <u>which</u> functions as subject in the relative clause just as <u>The gash</u> functions as subject in [1a].

Here is another example:

[2] The woman is a premedical student. The woman was sitting next to you.

[2a] The woman (The woman was sitting next to you) is a premedical student.

[2b] The woman <u>who</u> was sitting next to you is a premedical student.

In both [1b] and [2b] the relative pronoun can be replaced by relative <u>that</u>:

[1c] He had a nasty gash <u>that</u> needed medical attention.

[2c] The woman <u>that</u> was sitting next to you is a premedical student.

For the choice of relative pronouns, see 5.22.

=========================== **EXERCISE 4.3** ===========================

Combine the (a) and (b) sentences in each group below, making one of the sentences a relative clause.

EXAMPLE

(a) A man was hospitalized yesterday.

(b) The man was seriously injured in an auto accident.

A man who was seriously injured in an auto accident was hospitalized yesterday.

1. **a.** Many cacti retract their heads into the soil during dry hot spells.
   b. These cacti are small and single-stemmed.
2. **a.** Industries have been replacing oil-guzzling driers and kilns with devices.
   b. These devices burn scrap wood.

3. a. They checked the earlier measurements.
  b. The measurements were performed by federally funded laboratories.
4. a. The town fighters battled an inferno.
  b. The inferno was fueled by toxic chemicals at an illegal stockpile.
5. a. The regulations list over five hundred industrial processes and materials as hazardous.
  b. The regulations took effect last fall.
6. a. The drugs inevitably damage a patient's healthy cells as well.
  b. The drugs are used in chemotherapy.
7. a. Human infants pass through a critical period.
  b. This period lasts a few years.
8. a. Scientists discovered a new compound during a recent experiment.
  b. The experiment took place at a lab in Southern California.

4.6 APPOSITIVE CLAUSES

Another type of clause that is often embedded in a noun phrase is the **appositive clause.** It is introduced by the conjunction <u>that</u>:

> the assumption <u>that he will return home</u>
> the fact <u>that she rejected his offer of marriage</u>
> the knowledge <u>that she rejected his offer of marriage</u>
> the reason <u>that I am here today</u>

The conjunction <u>that</u> in appositive clauses differs from the relative <u>that</u> (cf. 4.5) because the conjunction does not have a function within its clause. The appositive clause can be a sentence without <u>that</u>:

> [1]   You know the reason <u>that I am here today</u>.
> [1a] I am here today.

The relative clause cannot be a sentence without the relative <u>that</u>:

> [2]   He had a nasty gash <u>that needed medical attention</u>.

We can convert the noun phrase containing the appositive clause into a sentence by inserting a form of the verb <u>be</u> before the clause:

> [3]   the assumption <u>that he will return</u>
> [3a] The assumption <u>is</u> that he will return.

===================== **EXERCISE 4.4** =====================

Determine whether each underlined clause is a relative clause or an appositive clause. To help you make the appropriate choice, apply the tests for these kinds of constructions.

EXAMPLE

I rejected the idea that I should stay late.
The clause is an appositive clause because it can stand alone as a sentence (I should stay late) and because we can construct a sentence containing a form of the verb be that links the clause to the noun before it (The idea is that I should stay late).

1. We contacted the agency that books acts for comedy nightclubs.
2. The book contradicted my belief that a nuclear war is inevitable.
3. One cannot dispute the fact that a college education helps an individual get a good job.
4. The speeding car hit the bus that was picking up children for school.
5. The manager lacked the knowledge that would enable him to advance in the business.
6. Many individuals are frightened by the knowledge that cancer in the United States is on the increase.
7. The man was hired by a company that offered him a large increase in pay.
8. We like the idea that we control our fate here on earth.

4.7 APPOSITIVES

The relation of **apposition** is also common between two noun phrases:

> Paul Peterson, a rock and alpine climber, was the first to volunteer.

As with the appositional clause, we can show that a rock and alpine climber is appositive to (or in apposition to) Paul Peterson by converting the two phrases into a sentence:

> Paul Peterson is a rock and alpine climber.

Here are some other examples of noun phrases in apposition:

> vitamin B_{12}, a complex cobalt-containing molecule,
> the witness, a burly man with a heavy stubble,

the first phase of the project—<u>an underground building
topped by an above-ground glass pyramid</u>—
the rattlesnake, <u>a venomous animal capable of causing death
in human beings,</u>

Appositives are often signaled by expressions such as <u>namely</u> and <u>that is to say</u>:

You can read the story in the first book of the Bible, <u>namely</u>
Genesis.

==================== **EXERCISE 4.5** ====================

Underline the appositives in the sentences below. Some sentences may contain
more than one appositive.

EXAMPLE
My English instructor, <u>a woman with a Harvard Ph.D.,</u> is quite good.

1. The accelerator hurled ions of carbon and neon at a foil target of
   bismuth, a metal related to lead.
2. They removed genes from the cells of one strain of mice, genes
   which make them resistant to a toxic drug.
3. Berkeley scientists have finally realized the medieval alchemist's
   dream: transmuting a base metal into gold.
4. Wood can fill 5 percent of our energy needs, leaving 95 percent
   that must come from other sources—solar, wind, coal, nuclear, bio-
   mass.
5. In 1969 two University of Nevada psychologists, Beatrice and R.
   Allen Gardner, claimed to have taught Washoe, a chimpanzee, to
   communicate in a human language.
6. Most cells contain many mitochondria, semi-independent structures that supply the cell with readily usable energy.
7. Scientists have discovered two sets of hydrothermal vents (ocean
   hot springs).

4.8 COORDINATION

As with other types of phrases, we can coordinate (link) noun phrases with <u>and</u>
or <u>or</u>:

all the senators <u>and</u> some of their aides
law schools <u>or</u> medical schools
my sister, her husband, <u>and</u> their three children

We can also coordinate parts of a noun phrase. Coordinated modifiers may apply as a unit:

> underline{wholesome and tasty} food [*food that is both wholesome and tasty*]
>
> a underline{calm and reassuring} gesture [*a gesture that is both calm and reassuring*]
>
> an appetizer of underline{blackberries and raspberries} [*an appetizer that consists of both blackberries and raspberries*]

Or they may apply separately:

> electric and magnetic fields [*electric fields and magnetic fields*]
>
> large or small classes [*large classes or small classes*]
>
> houses along the coast and on the lower hills [*houses along the coast and houses on the lower hills*]
>
> the chemical and the biological analysis of plants [*the chemical analysis of plants and the biological analysis of plants*]

A determiner may serve two or more nouns or modified nouns:

> his wife and two sons [*his wife and his two sons*]
>
> some friends and close acquaintances [*some friends and some close acquaintances*]
>
> the reactions of the students and teachers [*the reactions of the students and the reactions of the teachers*]

It is sometimes possible to interpret coordination of parts of phrases in more than one way:

frustrated and desperate men

1. frustrated men and desperate men
2. men who are both frustrated and desperate

old men and women

1. old men and old women
2. women and old men

their cats and other pets

1. their cats and their other pets
2. other pets and their cats

═══ EXERCISE 4.6 ═══

The coordinated noun phrases below are ambiguous. Rewrite the phrases, capturing the different meanings that the phrases expresss.

EXAMPLE
    my friends and good neighbors
    (a) *good neighbors and my friends*
    (b) *my friends and my good neighbors*

1. lying and unscrupulous thieves
2. aged cheese and wine
3. his books and assorted notes
4. my favorite foods and beverages
5. very old and wonderful memories
6. our properties and other businesses

4.9 COMPLEXITY

Noun phrases can display considerable structural complexity, because it is easy to embed in them clauses, appositional structures, and linked noun phrases. Here are some examples taken from newspapers:

The latest certified horror story involved <u>a Delta Air Lines jumbo jet that drifted 60 miles (about 100 kilometers) off course over the North Atlantic and came within 100 feet (30 meters) of colliding with a Continental Airlines jet on Wednesday</u>. (*The International Herald Tribune*, July 3, 1987, p. 4, taken from *The Washington Post*)

Last month, for instance, the Bangkok exchange opened <u>a second board through which overseas buyers can trade among themselves in stocks in which the limit of foreign ownership has been reached</u>. (Patrick L. Smith in *The International Herald Tribune*, July 15, 1987, p. 13)

Working hard on the incline, the solitary Clere passed <u>two cattle farms, a field with grazing sheep, another full of newly baled hay, a garage, several private houses, a snack restaurant, a spartan hotel and a bakery with a sign announcing a bowling competition in nearby Flammerecourt that offered a pig and a lamb among its prizes</u>. (Samuel Abt in *The International Herald Tribune*, July 8, 1987, p. 19)

4.10 FUNCTIONS

Following is a brief list, with illustrations, of the possible functions of noun phrases:

1. subject

The people in the bus escaped through the emergency exit.

2. direct object

They are testing some new equipment.

3. indirect object

The bank gave her a loan.

4. subject complement

The performance was a test of their physical endurance.

5. object complement

Many Democrats consider her a future presidential candidate.

6. complement of a preposition

The study of Latin appeals to some Spanish-speaking students.

7. premodifier of a noun or noun phrase

Milk production is down this year.
I have not yet paid my state income tax.
He suffers from lower back problems.

8. adverbial

The semester finishes next week.
You will not succeed that way.

=========================== **EXERCISE 4.7** ============================

Underline each noun phrase and state its function by writing above it S (subject), dO (direct object), iO (indirect object), SC (subject complement), OC (object complement), cP (complement of a preposition), pM (premodifier of a noun or noun phrase), or A (adverbial).

EXAMPLE

S   *dO*   *cP*

Some <u>people</u> oppose <u>competitiveness</u> in <u>games</u>.

1. Games are usually competitive activities.
2. Most sports programs develop skills through competition.
3. In competitive games someone loses every time.
4. The games give the losers a feeling of inferiority.
5. The losers feel rejected.
6. They consider the games a test of their capabilities.
7. Noncompetitive games are becoming increasingly popular.
8. In noncompetitive games, scorekeeping can be eliminated.
9. Nobody wins and nobody loses.
10. Do you object to competitive games?

_____ **THE VERB PHRASE** _____

4.11   THE STRUCTURE OF THE VERB PHRASE

The typical structure of the verb phrase consists of a main verb preceded optionally by a maximum of four auxiliary verbs. The four belong to different subclasses of auxiliaries.

(aux 1)	(aux 2)	(aux 3)	(aux 4)	main verb

It is very unusual for all four auxiliaries to appear in one verb phrase, but if two or more auxiliaries co-occur they must appear in the sequence indicated in the diagram, e.g., 1 + 3, 1 + 2 + 4, 2 + 3. For the four subclasses, see 4.17 below.

4.12 MAIN VERBS

Regular main verbs have four forms that are constructed in this way:

1. **base form** The base form is what we find in dictionary entries: <u>laugh</u>, <u>mention</u>, <u>play</u>.
2. **-s form** The -s form adds to the base form an ending in -s: <u>laughs</u>, <u>mentions</u>, <u>plays</u>.
3. **-ing participle** The -ing participle adds to the base form an ending in -ing: <u>laughing</u>, <u>mentioning</u>, <u>playing</u>.
4. **-ed form** (past or -ed participle) The -ed form adds to the base form an ending in -ed: <u>laughed</u>, <u>mentioned</u>, <u>played</u>.

The addition of the endings involves some rules of pronunciation and spelling that depend on how the base form ends. For example, the -ed ending is pronounced as a separate syllable in <u>loaded</u> but not in <u>laughed</u>; the final consonant of the base form is doubled in the spelling of <u>plotted</u> but not in the spelling of <u>revolted</u>. Similarly, the -s ending is pronounced as a separate syllable and spelled -es in <u>passes</u>. For the spelling rules, see A.4. in the Appendix.

The -ed form represents two distinct functions that are differentiated in some irregular verbs:

(a) past
(b) -ed participle

Contrast the one form for <u>laugh</u> in the following sets of sentences with the two forms for <u>give</u> and <u>speak</u>:

past	She <u>laughed</u> at us.
	She <u>gave</u> us a smile.
	She <u>spoke</u> to us.

-ed participle	She has <u>laughed</u> at us.
	She has <u>given</u> us a smile.
	She has <u>spoken</u> to us.

Irregular main verbs have either fewer or more forms than main verbs. For example, <u>put</u> has only three forms: <u>put</u>, <u>puts</u>, <u>putting</u>. Put serves as both the base form and the -ed form in the functions of the past and of the -ed participle:

base form	They always <u>put</u> the cat out at night.
-ed form: past	They <u>put</u> the cat out last night.
-ed form: -ed participle	They have <u>put</u> the cat out.

The irregular verb <u>be</u> has the most forms, eight in all:

base form   <u>be</u>
present   <u>am</u>, <u>is</u>, <u>are</u>
past   <u>was</u>, <u>were</u>
-ing participle   <u>being</u>
-ed participle   <u>been</u>

For the differences in the present forms and in the past forms of <u>be</u>, see 4.13.

================================ **EXERCISE 4.8** ================================

Identify whether the underlined verb in each sentence is the base form, present form, past form, -ing participle form, or -ed participle form. Then write out all forms of the verb.

EXAMPLE
   The father is <u>taking</u> his children to the zoo.
   -ing participle form of verb
   take, takes, took, taking, taken

1.   In the past, sports has <u>been</u> available mainly to males.
2.   Adults <u>viewed</u> sports as unsuitable or even harmful to girls.
3.   Several court cases may have <u>helped</u> the crusade for women's sports.
4.   Federal law <u>forbids</u> sex discrimination in any educational institution that <u>receives</u> federal funds.
5.   Federal funds are <u>denied</u> to an institution that has been <u>practicing</u> sex discrimination.
6.   The administration has <u>had</u> some limited success at the elementary and secondary levels.
7.   On the intercollegiate level, the administration would <u>prefer</u> encouragement to intervention.
8.   Society's attitude to women athletes must <u>shift</u>.
9.   Women athletes should be <u>given</u> the same opportunities as men athletes.

4.13 TENSE, PERSON, AND NUMBER

The first or only verb in the verb phrase is marked for **tense, person,** and **number.**

Tense is a grammatical category referring to the time of the situation; the tense is indicated by the form of the verb. There are two tense forms: **present** and **past.** There are three persons: **first person** (the person or persons speaking or writing), **second person** (the person or persons addressed), and **third person** (others). There are two numbers: **singular** and **plural.**

For all verbs except <u>be</u>, there are two forms for the present: the -<u>s</u> form and the base form. The -<u>s</u> form is used for the third person singular, that is, with <u>he</u>, <u>she</u>, <u>it</u>, and singular noun phrases as subject:

> He <u>plays</u> football every day.
> The road <u>seems</u> narrower.

The base form is used for all other subjects: <u>I</u>, <u>you</u>, <u>we</u>, <u>they</u>, and plural noun phrases:

> I <u>play</u> football every day.
> The roads <u>seem</u> narrower.

<u>Be</u> has three forms for the present tense:

> <u>am</u>   first person singular
> <u>is</u>   third person singular
> <u>are</u> others

For all verbs except <u>be</u>, there is only one past form:

> He (<u>or</u> They) <u>played</u> football yesterday.
> The road (<u>or</u> roads) <u>seemed</u> narrower.

<u>Be</u> has two forms for the past:

> <u>was</u>   first and third person singular
> <u>were</u> others

The two tenses are related to distinctions in time, but they do not correspond precisely to the difference between present and past in the real world. The present tense generally refers to a time that includes the time of speaking but usually extends backward and forward in time:

> Three and five <u>make</u> eight.
> We <u>live</u> in Boston.
> I <u>work</u> in the steel industry.
> They <u>are</u> my neighbors.

Sometimes the present refers to an event that is simultaneous with the time of speaking:

> Here <u>comes</u> the President.
> I <u>nominate</u> Robert.

=============================== **EXERCISE 4.9** ===============================

Specify the tense (present or past), person (first, second, or third), and number (singular or plural) of the underlined verbs in the sentences below.

EXAMPLE
    We <u>like</u> visiting our relatives.
    Tense: present
    Person: first
    Number: plural

1. The price of oil <u>has</u> dropped considerably in the past few years.
2. Prices <u>dropped</u> a few years ago because there was an oil glut.
3. Prices <u>continue</u> to drop because oil-producing nations are refining too much crude oil.
4. OPEC <u>wants</u> prices to rise.
5. However, its members <u>disagree</u> about how to raise prices.
6. "I <u>am</u> in favor of higher prices," an OPEC member was recently quoted as saying.
7. "However, we <u>are</u> not in favor of lowering our production, because of the many debts we have."
8. Unless OPEC nations <u>lower</u> their production quotas, prices will remain low.
9. Some OPEC nations <u>cut</u> production last year.
10. However, because other OPEC nations did not go along with their cuts in production, prices <u>remain</u> low.

4.14 ASPECT

Aspect is a grammatical category referring to the way that the time of the situation is viewed by the speaker or writer; the aspect is indicated by a combination of auxiliary and verb form. Verbs have two aspects: the **perfect** aspect and the **progressive** aspect.

The perfect of a verb combines a form of the auxiliary <u>have</u> with the -ed participle of that verb. The auxiliary has two present tense forms (<u>has</u>, <u>have</u>) and one past form (<u>had</u>). For example, the present perfect of <u>close</u> is <u>has closed</u> or <u>have closed</u> and the past perfect is <u>had closed</u>:

I <u>have closed</u> the store for the day.
The store <u>has closed</u> for the day.
The police <u>had closed</u> the store months ago.

The **present perfect** refers to a situation set in some indefinite period that leads to the present. The situation may be a state of affairs that extends to the present:

> They have been unhappy for a long time.
> I have lived here since last summer.
> We have always liked them.

Or it may be an event or set of events that is viewed as possibly recurring:

> We have discussed your problems.
> I have phoned him every day since he fell sick.
> He has read only newspapers until now.

The **past perfect** refers to a situation earlier than another situation set in the past:

> We had heard a lot about her before we ever met her.

Both the present perfect and the past perfect are often replaced by the past.
Some -ed participle forms may be used as adjectives:

> She was annoyed with them.
> I am worried about you.
> My teachers are pleased with my progress.

The -ed words are adjectives if one or more of these possibilities apply: (1) if they can be modified by very (for example, very annoyed); (2) if they can occur with a linking verb other than be (for example, became annoyed); (3) if they can be linked with another adjective (for example, angry and disappointed).

The progressive combines a form of the auxiliary be with the -ing participle. The **present progressive** and the **past progressive** are illustrated below:

> You are neglecting your work.
> I am resting just now.
> The children were fighting all morning.
> We were waiting for you in the lobby.

The progressive indicates that the situation is in progress. It may therefore also imply that it lasts for only a limited period and that it is not ended.

============ **EXERCISE 4.10** ============

Identify each underlined verb as present perfect, past perfect, present progressive, or past progressive.

EXAMPLE

The family <u>was taking</u> a vacation when their house was robbed. (*past progressive*)

1. The principal <u>has spoken</u> to the truant student many times in the past.
2. We <u>had spoken</u> to the travel agency before we went on a trip to the Far East.
3. The police <u>have taken</u> strong measures to control drug trafficking in the neighborhood.
4. We <u>were taking</u> the exam when the fire alarm sounded.
5. The mayor <u>is planning</u> to hold a news conference to announce that she is running for reelection.
6. The hospital <u>had issued</u> strong warnings to the striking nurses before it decided to dismiss them.
7. The students <u>have made</u> elaborate plans for their graduation party.
8. The sponsors of the benefit <u>are giving</u> away free tickets to the first ten callers.
9. The players <u>are relaxing</u> after a very strenuous game.
10. We <u>had decided</u> not to buy the house even before they accepted our offer of purchase.

4.15 VOICE

Verbs have two voices: **active** and **passive.** The active is the voice that is used most commonly. The active and passive have different verb phrases in that the passive has an additional auxiliary: a form of the auxiliary <u>be</u> followed by an -ed participle. Here are examples of corresponding active and passive verb phrases:

ACTIVE	PASSIVE
loves	is loved
sold	was sold
is fighting	is being fought
has reconstructed	has been reconstructed
will proclaim	will be proclaimed
may have asserted	may have been asserted
should be purifying	should be being purified

The passive is a way of phrasing the sentence so that the subject does not refer to the person or thing responsible (directly or indirectly) for the action. The passive therefore differs from the corresponding active not only in the forms of the verb phrases but also in the positions of certain noun phrases. The direct or indirect object of the active sentence becomes the subject of the corresponding passive sentence, and the subject (if retained) appears after the verb in a <u>by</u>-phrase:

ACTIVE: The FBI (S) is investigating the crime (dO).
PASSIVE: The crime (S) is being investigated by the FBI.

ACTIVE: Three bullets (S) penetrated his heart (dO).
PASSIVE: His heart (S) was penetrated by three bullets.

ACTIVE: The jungle (S) has reclaimed the site (dO).
PASSIVE: The site (S) has been reclaimed by the jungle.

ACTIVE: The President (S) has given congressional leaders (iO) an outline of his budget proposals.
PASSIVE: Congressional leaders (S) have been given an outline of his budget proposals by the President.

Generally the passive sentence does not contain the <u>by</u>-phrase:

Snakes were being skinned outside our restaurant.
Most of the buildings were destroyed.
The decision has already been taken.

The most common reason for using the passive is to avoid referring to the person performing the action. That may be because the identity of the person is not known or because it is felt to be unnecessary to identify the person (perhaps because irrelevant or obvious) or it is felt to be tactless to do so:

He was immediately admitted to the hospital.
The Federalist papers are still considered the most lucid explanation of the Constitution.
The refrigerator door has not been properly closed.

EXERCISE 4.11

Identify whether the sentences below are active or passive.

EXAMPLE
The man was taken to the police station for questioning. (*passive*)

1. Corn is grown in Iowa.
2. Durable goods are manufactured in Chicago.

3. Many people regard the Midwest as the heartland of America.
4. They think that the Midwest has many redeeming qualities lacking in other regions of the country.
5. California is known as the land of fads and fashion.
6. New York is regarded as a city of high prices and high crime rates.
7. In the Midwest, in contrast, people live simple lives.
8. Many don't wear expensive clothes or drive fancy cars.
9. Instead, they value a simpler lifestyle.

EXERCISE 4.12

Identify whether the underlined words are passive participles or adjectives.

EXAMPLE
The woman felt <u>cheated</u> by the high prices. (*adjective*)

1. The driver was <u>stopped</u> by the police.
2. The child seemed <u>upset</u> by all of the loud noises the planes were making.
3. The toy is <u>manufactured</u> by a company that specializes in educational products for children.
4. The ancient tomb was <u>discovered</u> by a group of tourists digging for fossils.
5. I was <u>enraged</u> by the number of cars that were speeding down my block during the festival.
6. The product was <u>made</u> by a group of amateur inventors.
7. The student was <u>interested</u> in English literature.
8. The young child was <u>reprimanded</u> by his parents.

4.16 EXPRESSING FUTURE TIME

In 4.13 I stated that verbs have only two tenses: present and past. How then do we refer to future time?

There are only two tenses in the sense that these are the two distinctions that we make through the forms of the verbs. However, there are various ways of expressing future time. One way is through the simple present tense:

My sister <u>chairs</u> the meeting tomorrow.

The most common way is by combining <u>will</u> (or the contraction '<u>ll</u>) with the base form:

> He <u>will be</u> here soon.
> I'<u>ll talk</u> to you next time.

Two other common ways are the use of <u>be going to</u> and the present progressive:

> I'<u>m going to see</u> them later.
> We'<u>re playing</u> your team next week.

=============== **EXERCISE 4.13** ===============

Identify whether the future tense in the sentences below is expressed through a present tense verb, a full or contracted form of <u>will</u>, the expression <u>be going to</u>, or a present progressive verb.

EXAMPLES
The student plans to enroll in graduate school. (*present tense verb*)
Edith is going to nominate you. (*present progressive verb*)

1. I'll call you later after dinner.
2. The professor is going to give a lecture on Dickens tomorrow.
3. Politicians will say anything to get elected.
4. John starts his new job in a little over a week.
5. Stephanie is attending college in the fall.
6. Business law is going to be a popular field of study in the future.
7. They'll contact you if they're interested in hiring you.
8. The accountant intends to audit the company's books next week.

4.17 THE SEQUENCE OF AUXILIARIES

In 4.11 I referred to the four types of auxiliaries. Here again is the diagram representing the sequence:

(aux 1)	(aux 2)	(aux 3)	(aux 4)	main verb

If we choose to use auxiliaries, they must appear in the following sequence:

1. modal (or modal auxiliary), such as <u>can</u>, <u>may</u>, <u>will</u> (cf. 5.29)

2.   perfect auxiliary <u>have</u>
3.   progressive auxiliary <u>be</u>
4.   passive auxiliary <u>be</u>

These four uses of the auxiliaries specify the form of the verb that follows:

1.   modal, followed by base form: <u>may</u> phone
2.   perfect <u>have</u>, followed by -<u>ed</u> participle: <u>have</u> phon<u>ed</u>
3.   progressive <u>be</u>, followed by -<u>ing</u> participle: <u>was</u> phon<u>ing</u>
4.   passive <u>be</u>, followed by -<u>ed</u> participle: <u>was</u> phon<u>ed</u>

Gaps in the sequence are of course normal:

(1) + (3): will be phoning (modal progressive)
(2) + (4): has been phoned (perfect passive)
(2) + (3): has been phoning (perfect progressive)
(1) + (4): can be phoned (modal passive)

The sequence does not take account of the dummy operator <u>do</u> (3.4), which is introduced when there would otherwise not be an auxiliary in the verb phrase. In this function, <u>do</u> is therefore the only auxiliary present. It is followed by the base form:

I <u>did</u> phone.
<u>Did</u> you phone?
I <u>did</u> not phone.
Martha phoned, and I <u>did</u> too.

There are also **phrasal auxiliaries,** which are intermediate between auxiliaries and main verbs. Here are some examples:

Sandra <u>is going to</u> apply for the job.
I <u>had better</u> eat now.
My parents <u>are about to</u> leave.
We <u>have got to</u> speak to her.
He may <u>be able to</u> help us.
Jennifer <u>is supposed to</u> phone us today.

Only the first word in a phrasal auxiliary is a true auxiliary, since only that word functions as an operator, for example in forming questions (cf. 3.3):

<u>Is</u> Sandra <u>going to</u> apply for the job?
<u>Is</u> Jennifer <u>supposed to</u> phone us today?

The phrasal auxiliaries may come together to make a long string of verbs:

We <u>seem to be going to have to keep on</u> paying the full fee.
They <u>are likely to be about to manage to start</u> working on our project.

EXERCISE 4.14

Identify whether each underlined auxiliary verb is a modal, perfect <u>have</u>, progressive <u>be</u>, or passive <u>be</u>.

EXAMPLE

I <u>am</u> leaving very soon. (*progressive <u>be</u>*)

1. The employment agency <u>should</u> be contacting you soon about the job.
2. The city <u>was</u> contacted about the break in the water main.
3. Linguists <u>have</u> studied the structure of language for centuries.
4. I <u>can</u> be reached in case of an emergency at my office number.
5. Committee members <u>are</u> planning a meeting for early next fall.
6. The economy of Massachusetts <u>has</u> improved considerably since the recession years of the 1970s.
7. The remains <u>were</u> discovered accidentally by a group of paleontologists.
8. The couple <u>are</u> greeting guests at their daughter's wedding.

EXERCISE 4.15

Construct sentences containing the combinations of auxiliaries specified below.

EXAMPLE
modal + perfect <u>have</u>
I must have lost my glasses at the party.

1. modal + progressive <u>be</u>
2. dummy operator <u>do</u>
3. phrasal auxiliary
4. modal + passive <u>be</u>

5. perfect <u>have</u> + progressive <u>be</u>
6. perfect <u>have</u> + passive <u>be</u>
7. modal + perfect <u>have</u>
8. modal + perfect <u>have</u> + passive <u>be</u>

4.18   FINITE AND NONFINITE VERB PHRASES

Verb phrases are either **finite** or **nonfinite.** A finite verb is a verb that carries a contrast in tense between present and past and that may be marked for person and number. In a finite verb phrase the first or only verb is finite, and the other verbs (if any) are nonfinite. In a nonfinite verb phrase all the verbs are nonfinite. <u>Play</u> and <u>played</u> are finite verbs in these sentences:

[1] We <u>play</u> football every day.
[2] We <u>played</u> in a football match last week.

<u>Play</u> is in the present tense in [1] and <u>played</u> is in the past tense in [2]. In [3] <u>plays</u> is the third person singular form of the present:

[3] She <u>plays</u> hockey.

On the other hand, in [4] <u>will</u> is the finite verb (the past of <u>will</u> is <u>would</u>), whereas <u>play</u> is nonfinite:

[4] We <u>will play</u> some football later today.

Similarly, in [5] <u>have</u> is the finite verb and <u>played</u> is nonfinite:

[5] We <u>have played</u> football every day this week.

All the verb phrases in [1]–[5] are finite verb phrases because they begin with a finite verb.
   The following are the nonfinite verb forms:

1. the infinitive, often introduced by <u>to</u>: <u>(to) phone</u>
2. the <u>-ing</u> participle: <u>phoning</u>
3. the <u>-ed</u> participle: <u>phoned</u>

If one of these forms is the first or only verb in the verb phrase, the phrase is a nonfinite verb phrase:

He was afraid <u>to predict</u> the next day's weather.
<u>Having stayed</u> in their apartment, I can remember how frequently they quarreled.

Technicians were then rare, <u>found</u> only in the laboratories of the most senior professors.

The **infinitive** has the base form. It is the infinitive that is used after modals and after the dummy operator <u>do</u>:

I may <u>see</u> you later.
I may <u>be</u> there later.
I did <u>tell</u> them.

Nonfinite verb phrases normally do not occur as the verb phrase of an independent sentence. Contrast:

[6]   His job was <u>to predict</u> the next day's weather.
[7]   He <u>predicted</u> the next day's weather.

The verb of the sentence in [6] is <u>was</u>, not the infinitive <u>to predict</u> (cf. <u>To predict the next day's weather was his job</u>).

EXERCISE 4.16

Specify whether the underlined verbs are finite or nonfinite.

EXAMPLES
The games <u>will</u> be played tomorrow unless it rains. (*finite*)
The conductor is <u>stopping</u> the train to let off the injured passenger. (*nonfinite*)

1.   Computers have <u>revolutionized</u> the twentieth century.
2.   Without them, modern society <u>would</u> not have progressed as far as it has.
3.   Computers can <u>be</u> found just about everywhere.
4.   Most industries now <u>rely</u> heavily on computers to transact business.
5.   Physicians use computers to <u>look</u> up information about drugs they are prescribing.
6.   Utilities have computers that keep track of the amounts of gas or electricity their customers <u>use</u>.
7.   This saves on their <u>having</u> to send out people to read meters.
8.   This practice <u>is</u> time-consuming and costly.
9.   Computers can also be <u>found</u> in people's homes.
10.   Children <u>do</u> their homework on computers.
11.   Adults use computers as a means of <u>keeping</u> track of bills and savings.

4.19 MOOD

Mood refers to distinctions in the form of the verb that express the attitude of
the speaker to what is said. Finite verb phrases have three moods:

1. indicative
2. imperative
3. subjunctive

The **indicative** is the usual mood in declarative, interrogative, and exclamative sentences:

> Roger <u>has known</u> me for a long time.
> How well <u>does</u> Rosalind <u>play</u>?
> What a heavy coat you <u>are wearing</u>!

The **imperative** has the base form. It is used chiefly as a directive to request
action:

> <u>Stop</u> them!

There are two forms of the **subjunctive:** the present subjunctive and the
past subjunctive.
The **present subjunctive** has the base form. It is used in:
1. <u>that</u>-clauses after the expression of such notions as demand or request:

> [1]   We demand that he <u>take</u> the witness stand.
> [2]   I accept your wish that my secretary <u>omit</u> this discussion
>   from the minutes.
> [3]   The boss insisted that I <u>be</u> on time.
> [4]   I move that the meeting <u>be</u> adjourned.

In verbs other than <u>be</u>, the present subjunctive has a distinctive form only in
the third person singular: the base form, which contrasts with the indicative
form ending in -<u>s</u>. In other singular persons and in plurals, the base form is the
same as the indicative present tense form. Contrast [1] with [1a]:

> [1a]   We demand that they <u>take</u> the witness stand.

For all persons, the negative sentence need not have an operator (cf. 3.3f):

> [1b]   We demand that $\left\{ \begin{array}{l} he \\ they \end{array} \right\}$ <u>not take</u> the witness stand.
>
> [4a]   I move that the meeting <u>not be</u> adjourned.

2. certain set expressions:

> Long live the Republic!
> Be that as it may, . . .

The **past subjunctive** were is used chiefly to convey that the speaker is not sure that the situation will happen or is happening:

[5]   If he were to be appointed, I would leave.
[6]   If they were in the city, they would contact us.
[7]   I wish you were here.
[8]   I wish I were somewhere hotter than here.

Were is also the past indicative form, so the subjunctive and indicative are identical except where was is required as a past indicative—in the first and third persons singular (I was, he was). Were therefore is a distinctive form as subjunctive only in [5] and [8]. In fact, except in formal style, indicative was is commonly used in place of the past subjunctive in the first and third persons singular:

[5a]   If he was to be appointed, I would leave.
[8a]   I wish I was somewhere hotter than here.

═══════════════════ **EXERCISE 4.17** ═══════════════════

Specify whether the underlined verb in each sentence is indicative, imperative, present subjunctive, or past subjunctive.

EXAMPLE
   If I were you, I would keep quiet. (*past subjunctive*)

1.   With much commotion a bus rattles by just as the milk truck arrives from the highlands.
2.   Supposing she were here now, what would you do?
3.   It is essential that she return immediately.
4.   After that there were no more disturbances.
5.   I had nothing to do with it, so help me God.
6.   Heaven forbid that we should interfere between husband and wife.
7.   I asked that references be sent to the manager.
8.   If we hear from her, I'll call you.
9.   If it's not raining, take the dog for a walk.

10. They say if you <u>stay</u> here long enough to wear out a pair of shoes, you'll stay permanently.
11. It is essential that you <u>be</u> at the meeting.
12. If you happen to meet them, <u>be</u> more helpful than you were last time.
13. They <u>place</u> radio collars on several sedated baboons to help track the troop.
14. No U.S. warships <u>were</u> in the vicinity at the time.

================================

=========== EXERCISE 4.18 ===========

Each sentence contains an expression of requesting or recommending followed by a subordinate clause. Fill the blank in each subordinate clause with an appropriate verb in the present subjunctive (the base form of the verb).

EXAMPLE
   We accepted the suggestion that the grade *be* based on a series of short tests.

1. I demand that he _____ at once.
2. She is insistent that they _____ dismissed.
3. It is essential that she _____ every day.
4. We suggested that your brother _____ our home this evening.
5. I move that the motion _____ accepted.
6. They rejected our recommendation that student fees_____ lowered.
7. They proposed that David _____ on our behalf.
8. I suggest that she _____ the offer.

================================

4.20 MULTI-WORD VERBS

Multi-word verbs are combinations of a verb and one or more other words. They are called multi-word verbs because in certain respects they behave as a single verb.

   The most frequent types of multi-word verbs consist of a verb followed by one or more **particles** (words that do not change their form) such as <u>at</u>, <u>away</u>, <u>by</u>, and <u>for</u>. The three major types of these combinations are:

   phrasal verbs, e.g. <u>give in</u>, <u>blow up</u>

prepositional verbs, e.g. <u>look after</u>, <u>approve of</u>
phrasal-prepositional verbs, e.g. <u>look down on</u>, <u>catch up on</u>

There are sometimes one-word verbs that are similar in meaning to the multi-word verbs. The one-word verbs are more formal:

phrasal verb:	give in	surrender
prepositional verb:	look after	tend
phrasal-prepositional verb:	put up with	tolerate

Phrasal verbs and **prepositional verbs** are a combination of a verb and one particle, whereas **phrasal-prepositional verbs** have two particles. A prepositional verb requires an object to complete the sentence:

[1]   Peter is <u>looking after</u> his elderly parents.

A transitive phrasal verb also requires an object:

[2]   All the students have <u>handed in</u> their essays.

An intransitive phrasal verb does not require an object:

[3]   I <u>give up</u>.

We can distinguish transitive phrasal verbs from prepositional verbs by testing whether the particle can come before the object as well as after the object. The particle of a phrasal verb can take either position because it is an adverb and, like most adverbs, it is not confined to one position:

[2a]   All the students have <u>handed in</u> their essays.
[2b]   All the students have <u>handed</u> their essays <u>in</u>.

If the object is a personal pronoun, however, the particle in a phrasal verb normally must come after the object:

[2c]   All the students have <u>handed</u> them <u>in</u>.

On the other hand, the particle of a prepositional verb is a preposition and must always come before the object, as in [1] above and in [1a]:

[1a]   Peter is <u>looking after</u> them.

Further examples of intransitive phrasal verbs are in [4]–[6] and transitive phrasal verbs in [7]–[9]:

[4]   The discussions <u>went on</u> for a long time.

[5]   They <u>gave up</u> without a struggle.

[6]   The excitement has <u>died down</u>.

[7]   I can't <u>make out</u> their <u>handwriting</u>.

[7a] I can't <u>make</u> their <u>handwriting</u> <u>out</u>.

[8]   We should <u>put off the decision</u> until the next meeting.

[8a] We should <u>put the decision off</u> until the next meeting.

[9]   Cornelia has finally <u>brought out</u> her <u>new book</u>.

[9a] Cornelia has finally <u>brought</u> her <u>new book</u> <u>out</u>.

There are three types of prepositional verbs. The first type is followed by
a **prepositional object,** which differs from direct and indirect objects in that a
preposition introduces it:

[10] My aunt is <u>looking after</u> my <u>brothers</u>.

[11] The principal <u>called for</u> <u>references</u>.

[12] Heavy smoking <u>leads to</u> <u>cancer</u>.

Like other objects, prepositional objects can be questioned by <u>who</u> or <u>what</u>:

[10a] <u>Who</u> is your aunt looking after?
      <u>My brothers</u>.

[12a] <u>What</u> does smoking lead to?
      <u>Cancer</u>.

They can often be made the subject of a corresponding passive sentence:

[11a] <u>References</u> were called for.

The second type of prepositional verb has two objects: a direct object and
a prepositional object. The direct object comes before the particle, and the prepositional object follows the particle:

[13] He <u>blamed</u> the accident <u>on</u> the weather.

[14] You may <u>order</u> a drink <u>for</u> me.

[15] I have <u>explained</u> the procedure <u>to</u> the children.

[16] They were <u>making</u> fun <u>of</u> you.

[17] I have just <u>caught</u> sight <u>of</u> them.

In some cases the direct object is part of an idiomatic unit, as in <u>make fun of</u>
[16] and <u>catch sight of</u> [17].

The third type of prepositional verb also has two objects, but the first is an
indirect object:

They <u>told</u> us <u>about</u> your success.

She <u>forgave</u> me <u>for</u> my rude remark.
I <u>congratulated</u> her <u>on</u> her promotion.

The preposition in all three types of prepositional verbs ordinarily cannot be moved from its position after the verb. If the style is formal, however, in certain structures such as questions and relative clauses it may move with the object to the front. For example, the prepositional object in [13] is normally questioned like this:

[13a]   What did he blame the weather <u>on</u>?

But we could also place <u>on</u> in front, in formal style:

[13b]   <u>On</u> what did he blame the weather?

Finally, there are two types of phrasal-prepositional verbs, which have two particles (an adverb followed by a preposition). The first type has just the prepositional object:

I have been <u>catching up on</u> my reading.
They <u>look down on</u> their neighbors.

The second type has a direct object and a prepositional object:

I have <u>put</u> his problem <u>down to</u> inexperience.
We <u>put</u> him <u>up for</u> election.

═══════════════════ **EXERCISE 4.19** ═══════════════════

Specify whether the verbs in each sentence are phrasal verbs, prepositional verbs, or phrasal-prepositional verbs. Apply the tests for each type of verb to help you make the appropriate choice.

EXAMPLE
John <u>looked up</u> Mary's number. (*phrasal verb*)

1. The instructor will not <u>put up with</u> your tardiness much longer.
2. The owner <u>opened up</u> the store before his employees arrived.
3. Students must <u>concentrate on</u> their studies if they wish to do well in school.
4. Mary <u>came down with</u> the flu last week.
5. The lawyer <u>drew up</u> the contract for her client.
6. The boy is <u>looking after</u> his younger brother and sister.
7. The children <u>turned in</u> their assignments late.

8. Many teenagers <u>look up to</u> rock stars such as Bruce Springsteen and Michael Jackson.
9. The janitor <u>threw</u> the garbage <u>out</u>.
10. I don't <u>approve of</u> your behavior in this matter.

═══════ EXERCISE 4.20 ═══════

Specify whether the prepositional verbs in the sentences below contain a prepositional object, a direct object and a prepositional object, or an indirect object and a prepositional object.

EXAMPLE

My sister <u>told</u> us <u>about</u> the movie. (*indirect and prepositional object*)

1. The young boy always <u>listens to</u> his mother and father.
2. The students <u>took</u> advantage <u>of</u> the substitute teacher.
3. We <u>looked at</u> the paintings for a very long time.
4. The waiter <u>thanked</u> us <u>for</u> the generous tip we gave him.
5. The principal <u>congratulated</u> us <u>on</u> our graduating from high school.
6. The thief <u>robbed</u> the couple <u>of</u> their watches and money.
7. Many truck drivers cannot <u>cope with</u> the rigors of driving long distances.
8. The scientists could not <u>account for</u> the sudden change in atmospheric conditions.
9. The charity <u>received</u> many donations <u>from</u> state employees.
10. The mother <u>forgave</u> her son <u>for</u> his rude behavior.

─────── THE ADJECTIVE PHRASE ───────

4.21 THE STRUCTURE OF THE ADJECTIVE PHRASE

The main word in an adjective phrase is an adjective. The structure of the typical adjective phrase may be represented in the following way; the parentheses indicate elements of the structure that may be absent:

(premodifier)　　adjective　　(postmodifier)　　(complement)

Modifiers qualify in some respect what is denoted by the adjective, and they are optional. The premodifier comes before the adjective and the postmodifier comes after it. The only postmodifiers of adjectives are the adverbs <u>enough</u> and <u>indeed</u>: <u>good enough</u>; <u>excellent indeed</u>.

Complements complete what is implied in the meaning of the adjective. For example, if we say <u>Tom is afraid</u>, we intend this to mean that Tom is filled with fear in some respect. The complement specifies in what respect:

[1]　　Tom is <u>afraid</u>
$$\begin{cases} \text{of } \underline{\text{spiders}}. \\ \text{for } \underline{\text{his job}}. \\ \text{to say } \underline{\text{anything}}. \\ \text{that } \underline{\text{no one will believe him}}. \end{cases}$$

A few adjectives (at least in certain senses) must have an adjective complement:

[2]　　Mary is <u>fond of us</u>.
[3]　　I am <u>aware that he is abroad</u>.
[4]　　The contract is <u>subject to approval by my committee</u>.

Some adjectives that take complements resemble verbs in their meaning:

[1a]　　Tom <u>fears</u> that no one will believe him.
[2a]　　Mary <u>likes</u> us.
[3a]　　I <u>know</u> that he is abroad.
[4a]　　The contract <u>requires</u> approval by my committee.

Here are some examples of possible structures of adjective phrases:

adjective	<u>happy</u>
premodifier + adjective	<u>very happy</u>
adjective + postmodifier	<u>happy enough</u>
premodifier + adjec- 　　tive + postmodifier	<u>extremely happy indeed</u>
adjective + complement	<u>happy to see you</u>
premodifier + adjective 　　+　complement	<u>very happy that you could join us</u>.

===================== **EXERCISE 4.21** =====================

Underline each adjective phrase.

EXAMPLE
  <u>Fragrant homemade</u> bread is becoming <u>common</u> in many <u>American</u> homes.

  1. In a recent sample, 30 percent of the subscribers to a woman's
     magazine said that they baked bread.
  2. The first bread was patted by hand.
  3. The early Egyptians added yeast and made conical, triangular, or
     spiral loaves as well as large, flat, open-centered disks.
  4. Bakers later devised tools to produce more highly refined flour.
  5. White bread was mixed with milk, oil, and salt.
  6. People used to eat black bread because they were too poor to make
     it white.
  7. Bread lovers now buy black bread by choice.

===================== **EXERCISE 4.22** =====================

Provide complements for each adjective.

EXAMPLE
  The woman is aware.
  The woman is aware that she has to work today.

  1. John is able.
  2. Those living in urban areas are always suspicious.
  3. I am always happy.
  4. It is sometimes possible.
  5. The weightlifter is strong enough.
  6. The computer is suitable.
  7. John was doubtful.
  8. The employee was very loyal.

4.22 FUNCTIONS

The following are the main possible functions of adjective phrases:

(1) premodifier in a noun phrase

Our former enemies and allies are now our economic competitors.

(2) subject complement

The photographs were quite professional.

(3) object complement

My parents made me aware of my filial responsibilities.

(4) postmodifier in a noun phrase

I saw something bizarre on my way to school yesterday.

Indefinite pronouns, such as somebody, require the adjective phrase to follow them:

> I bought something quite expensive today.
> You should choose somebody older.

There are also some set expressions (mostly legal or official designations) where the adjective follows the noun:

> heir apparent   attorney general
> court martial   notary public

Here are a few further examples of adjective phrases as postmodifiers:

> the earliest time possible
> in years past
> the officials present
> the people involved

Central adjectives are adjectives that can fulfill all four possible functions. There are also some adjectives that can be only premodifiers and others that cannot be premodifiers at all (cf. 5.11).

Adjectives can be partially converted into nouns and then, like nouns, can function as heads of noun phrases. Typically, such phrases refer to well-established classes of persons, such as <u>the handicapped</u>, <u>the poor</u>, <u>the sick</u>, <u>the unemployed</u>, <u>the young</u>. Nationality adjectives are commonly used in this way too: <u>the British</u>, <u>the English</u>, <u>the French</u>, <u>the Irish</u>. These noun phrases are plural, even though the adjectives do not have a plural ending:

> <u>The sick require</u> immediate attention.
> <u>The British are</u> coming.

Some adjectives, particularly superlatives (cf. 5.12), function as heads of noun phrases that are abstract. These noun phrases are singular:

> <u>The latest is</u> that our team is winning.
> <u>The best is</u> yet to come.

Here are a few common examples of such phrases in set expressions:

> from <u>the sublime</u> to <u>the ridiculous</u>
> out of <u>the ordinary</u>
> We have much in <u>common</u>.
> I'm leaving for <u>good</u>.
> I'll tell you in <u>private</u>.
> The situation is going from <u>bad</u> to <u>worse</u>.

EXERCISE 4.23

Underline each adjective phrase and state its function by writing above it Pre (premodifier in a noun phrase), SC (subject complement), OC (object complement), or Post (postmodifier in a noun phrase).

EXAMPLE

Pre Pre   *SC*
The <u>heroic old</u> pro lies in his bed. He is <u>sick</u>.

1. He has a rare viral infection.
2. The infection has left him with congestive failure.
3. The drugs he takes make him nauseous and gassy.
4. His body looks no different than it looked before.
5. His shoulders are wide and full, his chest is deep and broad, and his arms are flat-muscled and whip-hanging.
6. His doctor arranges preliminary tests for heart surgery.
7. The surgeon tells him in his slow, subdued voice that he has a very strong heart.

8. His general health is good, but open heart surgery is always some-
    what risky.
9. The energetic suffer most from compulsory inactivity.

_____ THE ADVERB PHRASE _____

4.23 THE STRUCTURE OF THE ADVERB PHRASE

The main word in an adverb phrase is an adverb. The structure of the typical
adverb phrase is similar to that of the typical adjective phrase except for the
class of the main word:

| (premodifier) | adverb | (postmodifier) | (complement) |

As with adjective phrases, the only postmodifiers are <u>enough</u> and <u>indeed</u>:
<u>quickly enough</u>; <u>very severely indeed</u>.
    Here are some examples of possible structures of adverb phrases:

adverb	<u>frankly</u>
premodifier + adverb	<u>very frankly</u>
adverb + postmodifier	<u>frankly enough</u>
premodifier + adverb + postmodifier	<u>very frankly indeed</u>
adverb + complement	<u>surprisingly for her</u>

    There is a more restricted range of adverb complements than of adjective
complements.

================ EXERCISE 4.24 ================

Underline each adverb phrase.

EXAMPLE
    The voters wrote <u>very forcefully</u> to their state representatives.

1. Disposing of nuclear waste is a problem that has recently gained
    much attention.
2. Authorities are having difficulties finding locations where nuclear
    waste can be disposed of safely.

3. There is always the danger of the waste leaking very gradually from the containers in which it is stored.
4. Because of this danger, many people have protested quite vehemently against the dumping of any waste in their communities.
5. In the past, authorities have not responded quickly enough to problems at nuclear waste sites.
6. As a result, people react somewhat suspiciously to claims that nuclear waste sites are safe.
7. The problem of nuclear waste has caused many new nuclear power plants to remain closed indefinitely.
8. Authorities fear that this situation will very soon result in a power shortage.

4.24 FUNCTIONS

Adverbs have two main types of functions, but particular adverbs may have only one of these:

1. modifier of an adjective or an adverb in phrase structure
2. adverbial in sentence structure

Here are examples of adverbs as modifiers:

(1) modifier of an adjective

The description was <u>remarkably</u> <u>accurate</u>.

(2) modifier of an adverb

The new drug was hailed, <u>somewhat</u> <u>prematurely</u>, as the penicillin of the 1990s.

Semantically, most of the modifiers are **intensifiers** (cf. 5.12). They express the degree to which the meaning of the adjective or adverb applies on an assumed scale. The most common modifier is <u>very</u>.

Adverbs are commonly used as adverbials in sentence structure:

<u>Fortunately</u>, American automobile manufacturers are <u>now</u> concentrating on improvements in economy and safety.
<u>Certainly</u> we should be grateful for the ways in which he <u>inadvertently</u> challenged our beliefs, <u>deeply</u> and <u>seriously</u>.

Some adverbials seem to be closely linked to the verb or perhaps the predicate, as in She spoke vigorously or She spoke her mind vigorously, but it is difficult to be precise about the scope of such adverbials. For the range of meanings of adverbials, see 3.14.

Many adverbs can function both as modifiers and as adverbials. The intensifier entirely is a modifier of an adjective in [1] and an adverbial in [2]:

[1]   Michael's amendment is entirely acceptable.

[2]   I entirely agree with you.

=============== **EXERCISE 4.25** ===============

Underline each adverb phrase and state its function by writing above it A (adverbial), M Adj (modifier of adjective), or M Adv (modifier of adverb).

EXAMPLE

A   M Adj

The Navy's military and financial future seems bleak, but it now enjoys quite good morale.

1.   The Navy still has some problems with drugs, alcoholism, and a high desertion rate.
2.   However, it has recovered from the very troubled early 1970s.
3.   No serious racial clashes have occurred recently.
4.   The previous Chief of Naval Operations pleased young sailors greatly by removing unnecessary restrictions on their lives.
5.   He permitted civilian-style haircuts, eliminated the requirements for frequent changes of uniforms, and also allowed longer periods of leave.
6.   The hefty pay raises mean that sailors can now more easily afford apartments.
7.   The most extreme change is that the service has finally put women in uniform.

_____ **THE PREPOSITIONAL PHRASE** _____

4.25   THE STRUCTURE OF THE PREPOSITIONAL PHRASE

The prepositional phrase is a structure with two parts:

preposition   complement

The **prepositional complement** is typically a noun phrase, but it may also be a nominal relative clause (cf. 6.9) or an -ing clause (cf. 6.8). Both the nominal relative clause and the -ing clause have a range of functions similar to that of a noun phrase:

(1) complement as noun phrase

through the window

(2) complement as nominal relative clause

from what I heard ("from that which I heard")

(3) complement as -ing clause

after speaking to you

As its name suggests ("preceding position"), the preposition normally comes before the prepositional complement. There are several exceptions, however, where the complement is moved and the preposition is left stranded by itself. The stranding is obligatory when the complement is transformed into the subject of the sentence:

> Your case will soon be attended to.
> This ball is for you to play with.
> The picture is worth looking at.

In questions and relative clauses the prepositional complement may be a pronoun or adverb that is fronted. In that case, the preposition is normally stranded:

[1] Who are you waiting for?
[2] Where are you coming from?
[3] I am the person (that) you are waiting for? [In relative clauses the pronoun may be omitted.]

In formal style the preposition is fronted with its complement:

[1a] For whom are you waiting?
[2a] From where are you coming?
[3a] I am the person for whom you are waiting.

EXERCISE 4.26

Underline each prepositional phrase and circle each preposition. If a prepositional phrase is within another prepositional phrase, underline it twice.

EXAMPLES

It may come as a surprise (to) you that massage is mentioned (in) ancient Hindu Chinese writings.

It is a natural therapy (for) aches and pains (in) the muscles.

1. The Swedish technique of massage emphasizes improving circulation by manipulation.
2. Its value is recognized by many doctors.
3. Some doctors refer to massage as manipulative medicine.
4. Nonprofessionals can learn to give a massage, but they should be careful about applying massage to severe muscle spasms.
5. The general rule is that what feels good to you will feel good to others.
6. A warm room, a comfortable table, and a bottle of oil are the main requirements.
7. The amount of pressure you can apply depends on the pain threshold of the person.
8. You can become addicted to massages.

EXERCISE 4.27

Rewrite the sentences below, moving prepositions to alternative positions in which they can occur.

EXAMPLE

That's the house which I was born in.
That's the house in which I was born.

1. The president of the corporation is the person whom you should send your application to.
2. Relativity is a theory on which many modern theories in physics are based.
3. Whom are you writing to?
4. This article is one which economics scholars often make reference to.
5. For whom does John plan to do the work?

6. Both of the workers are people whom I have a lot of trust in.
7. Where are you driving your car from?
8. The women are authors whose books we have obtained much valuable information from.

4.26 FUNCTIONS

Prepositional phrases have three main functions:

1. postmodifier of a noun in phrase structure
2. complement of an adjective in phrase structure
3. adverbial in sentence structure

(1) postmodifier of a noun

I took several courses in history.
The utility company is subsidizing the installation of energy-saving devices.

(2) complement of an adjective

We were not aware of his drinking problem.
I was happy with my grades last semester.

(3) adverbial

In my opinion, people behave differently on pedestrian malls.
In actual fact, the economy was showing signs of improvement by 1985.

Two or more prepositional phrases may appear independently side by side. Here is a sentence with three prepositional phrases, each a separate adverbial:

He was reelected in Illinois (A) in 1980 (A) by a large majority (A).

One prepositional phrase may also be embedded within another, as in this prepositional phrase that postmodifies the noun variations:

There were variations in the degree of bitterness of taste.

The embedding can be shown in this way:

prepositional phrase	in the degree of bitterness of taste
noun phrase	the degree of bitterness of taste
prepositional phrase	of bitterness of taste
noun phrase	bitterness of taste
prepositional phrase	of taste

EXERCISE 4.28

Underline each prepositional phrase and state its function by writing above it pN (postmodifier of a noun), cA (complement of an adjective), or A (adverbial).

EXAMPLE

> *pN*   *A*
> The leader of the gang was in a lot of trouble.

1. Politicians in the United States must raise large sums of money if they want to get elected.
2. The days are gone when a candidate could win with little campaign money.
3. Candidates are keenly aware of the need to have lots of money.
4. They will need the money to hire staffs and run ads on television.
5. In recent campaigns, television ads have become quite negative.
6. They frequently distort the records of opposing candidates.
7. In addition, they often look like extravagant Hollywood productions.
8. The ads are making many Americans cynical of politicians.
9. To them, a politician is simply a huckster, a person who will say anything to get in office after the election.
10. Many people hope that political races of the future will be run in a more dignified and honest manner.

EXERCISE 4.29

Indicate whether the underlined prepositional phrases are independent or embedded.

EXAMPLE

> Many years of strife have not solved the problems in Northern Ireland. (*embedded*)

1. The panelist angrily stormed off the stage during the middle of the session <u>on world peace</u>.
2. Driving on the Southeast Expressway can be a nightmare on a Friday afternoon <u>during the summer</u>.
3. Schools of education have been the subject of much criticism <u>in recent years</u>.
4. The representative of the group <u>of protesters</u> was arrested during the demonstration for welfare rights.
5. At the beginning <u>of the month</u>, the company decided to lay off about 500 workers.
6. During spring break <u>in 1982</u>, teachers held a rally demanding that they receive higher pay and better benefits.
7. After the strike <u>against the mining company</u>, the workers went back to work.
8. Bob Stanley walked three runners during the middle innings of a recent game <u>with the Milwaukee Brewers</u>.

=== EXERCISE 4.30: Summary ===

Identify the underlined phrase in each sentence. Write NP (noun phrase), Adj P (adjective phrase), VP (verb phrase), Adv P (adverb phrase), or PP (prepositional phrase) at the end of the sentence.

EXAMPLES

The liberal arts were once <u>the whole college curriculum</u>. (*NP*)
The purpose of higher education was <u>very clear</u>. (*Adj P*)
It enriched the minds of an elite class <u>of students</u>. (*PP*)

1. <u>The students</u> used to read the classics of science, philosophy, and art.
2. A college education gave them a <u>broad, coherent, and intellectually rigorous</u> program of studies.
3. Higher education <u>has</u> subsequently <u>been transformed</u>.
4. College students can generally choose <u>their own program</u>.
5. The old requirements <u>have</u> almost <u>disappeared</u>.
6. Some students specialize <u>too much</u>.
7. Others take a wide range <u>of unrelated courses</u>.
8. A recent report <u>on the college curriculum</u> considers the current general education in colleges a complete failure.
9. Many liberal arts colleges <u>have closed</u> in the last few years.
10. <u>Most undergraduates</u> now take professional programs.
11. Many students have a <u>very poor</u> general knowledge.

12. Some universities <u>are</u> now <u>planning</u> a reformed undergraduate curriculum.
13. They are requiring <u>interdisciplinary programs</u>.
14. Many employers <u>do</u> not <u>want</u> liberal arts graduates.
15. But Americans have to make <u>several career changes</u>.
16. And <u>liberal arts graduates</u> find career changes easier.

EXERCISE 4.31: Summary

Construct sentences containing the phrases given below.

EXAMPLE
  noun phrase + verb phrase + noun phrase + prepositional phrase
  Most people like coffee in the morning.

1. prepositional phrase + noun phrase + verb phrase + adverb phrase
2. verb phrase + noun phrase + adverb phrase
3. adverb phrase + noun phrase + prepositional phrase + verb phrase + adjective phrase
4. noun phrase + verb phrase + noun phrase + prepositional phrase + prepositional phrase
5. prepositional phrase + noun phrase + verb phrase + noun phrase
6. noun phrase + verb phrase
7. adverb phrase + prepositional phrase + noun phrase + verb phrase + adjective phrase + adverb phrase
8. noun phrase + prepositional phrase + verb phrase + noun phrase + prepositional phrase

CHAPTER FIVE

Word Classes

5.1 OPEN AND CLOSED CLASSES

When we looked at phrases in Chapter 4, we often referred to classes of words such as noun and adjective. Word classes are traditionally called **parts of speech.** There is not a fixed number of word classes. We can set up as many classes and subclasses as we need for our analysis. The more detailed our analysis, the more classes and subclasses we need.

Word classes can be divided into **open classes** and **closed classes.** Open classes are readily open to new words; closed classes are limited classes that rarely admit new words. For example, it is easy to create new nouns, but not new pronouns.

Listed below, with examples, are the classes that we will be examining in this chapter. They will be further divided into subclasses:

open classes

noun	Paul, paper, speech, play
adjective	young, cheerful, dark, round
main verb	talk, become, like, play
adverb	carefully, firmly, confidentially

closed classes

pronoun	she, somebody, one, who, that
determiner	a, the, that, each, some
auxiliary (verb)	can, may, will, have, be, do
conjunction	and, that, in order that, if, though
preposition	of, at, to, in spite of

There are also some more minor classes, such as the numerals (one, twenty-three, first) and the interjections (oh, ah, oops). And there are some words that do not fit anywhere and should be treated individually, such as the negative not and the infinitive marker to (as in to say).

The conjunction in order that and the preposition in spite of are complex words even though each is written as three separate words.

5.2   WORD CLASSES AND WORD USES

In 5.1 some examples are listed in more than one class. For instance, play is both a noun and a verb; that is a pronoun, a determiner, and a conjunction. Many more examples could have been given of multiple membership of word classes. We can identify the class of some words by their form, as we will see in later sections of this chapter, but very often we can tell the class of a word only from its use in a context. Reply is a noun in:

[1]   I expect a reply before the end of the month.

It is a verb in:

[2]   You should reply before the end of the month.

It is particularly easy to convert nouns to verbs and to convert verbs to nouns.

Reply in [1] and [2] represents two different words that share the same form. They are two different **lexical items,** though related in meaning; they will be entered separately in dictionaries (lexicons).

If lexical items happen to share the same form and are not related in meaning at all, they are **homonyms;** examples are peer ("person belonging to the same group in age and status") and peer ("look searchingly"), or peep ("make a feeble shrill sound") and peep ("look cautiously"). We can make further distinctions if we wish to emphasize identity in pronunciation or identity in spelling. If homonyms share the same sound but differ in spelling, they are **homophones;** examples are weigh and way or none and nun. On the other hand, if they share the same spelling but differ in pronunciation, they are **homographs;** examples are row ("line of objects") and row ("quarrel").

The examples of word classes in 5.1 are listed as lexical items. A lexical item may have more than one grammatical form. The noun play has the singular play and the plural plays; the verb play has the base form play and the past played. It is common usage to use word for the lexical item and the grammatical form, so we can say that the past of the word see is saw and we can also say that the word saw is spelled with a final w. Sometimes there is **neutralization** in form: rather than having the distinctions found in most words, some words have only one neutral form. For example, the verb cut represents at least three grammatical words:

present tense   I always <u>cut</u> my steak with this kind of knife.
past tense   I <u>cut</u> my finger earlier today.
past participle   I have <u>cut</u> my finger.

The context should make it clear how I am using the word <u>cut</u>.

We recognize the class of a word by its use in context. Some words have **suffixes** (endings added to words to form new words) that help to signal the class they belong to. These suffixes are not necessarily sufficient. For example, -<u>ly</u> is a typical suffix for adverbs (<u>slowly</u>, <u>proudly</u>), but we also find this suffix in adjectives: <u>cowardly</u>, <u>kindly</u>. And we can sometimes convert words from one class to another even though they have suffixes that are typical of their original class: <u>an engineer</u>, <u>to engineer</u>; <u>a politic behavior</u>, <u>to politic</u>; <u>a hopeful candidate</u>, <u>a hopeful</u>.

NOUNS

5.3 NOUN SUFFIXES

A noun is a word that can be the only or main word in a noun phrase (cf. 4.2). We cannot identify all nouns merely by their form, but certain suffixes can be added to verbs or adjectives to make nouns. Here are a few typical noun suffixes with words that exemplify them:

-<u>tion</u> (and variants)	<u>education</u>, <u>relation</u>, <u>invasion</u>, <u>revision</u>
-<u>er</u>, -<u>or</u>	<u>camper</u>, <u>speaker</u>; <u>actor</u>, <u>supervisor</u>
-<u>ing</u>	<u>building</u>, <u>writing</u>
-<u>ity</u>	<u>mentality</u>, <u>normality</u>, <u>reality</u>, <u>sanity</u>
-<u>ness</u>	<u>happiness</u>, <u>compactness</u>

Some suffixes were part of the words when they were borrowed into English: <u>doctor</u>, <u>eternity</u>, <u>courage</u>.

EXERCISE 5.1

Convert the following words into nouns by adding noun suffixes. Some words may be able to take more than one suffix.

EXAMPLE
    talk (*talker*)

1. sew
2. heavy

  3. able
  4. conceive
  5. build
  6. speak
  7. durable
  8. construct
  9. write
 10. sad

=============== **EXERCISE 5.2** ===============

For each word below, circle the suffix that indicates the word is a noun.

EXAMPLE
  mean(ness)

  1. actuality
  2. kindness
  3. dismissal
  4. exploration
  5. walking
  6. reviewer
  7. banality
  8. kindness
  9. computer
 10. configuration

5.4 NOUN CLASSES

Nouns may be **common** or **proper.** Proper nouns are the names of specific people, places, or occasions, and they usually begin with a capital letter: Shakespeare, Chicago, January, Christmas. Names may consist of more than one word: The Hague, New York Times, Kennedy Airport, Captain Andrews, Mount Everest. Proper nouns are sometimes converted into common nouns: the Thompsons I know; the proper noun Thompson cannot ordinarily be made plural, but here the Thompsons means "the family with the name Thompson."

Common nouns are nouns that are not names, such as capital in:

The capital of the Netherlands is The Hague.

Nouns can be further subclassified in two ways:

1. type of referent: concrete and abstract
2. grammatical form: count and noncount

Concrete nouns refer to people, places, or things: <u>girl</u>, <u>kitchen</u>, <u>car</u>. **Abstract** nouns refer to qualities, states, or actions: <u>humor</u>, <u>belief</u>, <u>action</u>. Some nouns may be either concrete or abstract, depending on their meaning:

> **concrete** Thomas can kick a <u>football</u> 50 yards.
> **abstract** Jeremy often plays <u>football</u> on Saturdays.

There is a tendency for abstract nouns to be noncount.

Count nouns refer to entities that are viewed as countable. Count nouns therefore have both a singular and a plural and they can be accompanied by determiners that refer to distinctions in number:

$$\left.\begin{array}{l} \underline{a} \\ \text{one} \\ \underline{\text{every}} \end{array}\right\} \text{student} \qquad \left.\begin{array}{l} \underline{\text{ten}} \\ \underline{\text{many}} \\ \underline{\text{those}} \end{array}\right\} \text{students}$$

Noncount nouns refer to entities that are viewed as a mass that cannot be counted; for example, <u>bread</u>, <u>furniture</u>, <u>music</u>. They are treated as singular and can be accompanied only by determiners that do not refer to distinctions in number:

$$\left.\begin{array}{l} \underline{\text{much}} \\ \underline{\text{your}} \\ \underline{\text{that}} \end{array}\right\} \text{information}$$

Determiners such as <u>the</u> and <u>your</u> can go with both count and noncount nouns. Others can go only with singular count nouns (<u>a</u>) or only with plural count nouns (<u>those</u>).

Some nouns may be either count or noncount, depending on their meaning:

> There is not enough <u>light</u> in here.
> We need another couple of <u>lights</u>.
> Sandra does not have much <u>difficulty</u> with science.
> Benjamin is having great <u>difficulties</u> with arithmetic.

Nouns that are ordinarily noncount can be converted into count nouns with two types of special use:

1. When the count noun refers to different kinds:
   The store has a large selection of <u>cheeses</u>.

2. When the count noun refers to units that are obvious in the situation:
I'll have two <u>coffees</u>, please. ("two cups of coffee")

─────────────────── **EXERCISE 5.3** ───────────────────

Specify whether the underlined nouns as used in the sentences below are common or proper, concrete or abstract, and count or noncount.

EXAMPLE

The <u>strikers</u> are picketing a company that hires nonunion workers. (*common, concrete, count*)

1. Labor unions are on the decline in <u>America</u>.
2. Since the recession of the 1970s, many <u>companies</u> have been unwilling to pay the high wages and benefits that unions wanted.
3. In addition, much <u>work</u> in this country has been transferred to foreign countries.
4. In these countries, the <u>cost</u> of labor is quite low.
5. <u>Workers</u> will manufacture goods for a mere fraction of the salary that a U.S. worker commands.
6. Many economists and politicians also claim that the work produced by U.S. companies has declined in <u>quality</u> over the years.
7. During the 1970s, the <u>Japanese</u> took over the U.S. car market.
8. They manufactured cars that <u>Americans</u> felt were of higher quality than American cars.
9. In recent years, however, American companies have made a strong <u>commitment</u> to upgrade the quality of American goods.
10. Businessmen such as <u>Iacocca</u> have made persistent efforts to compete with foreign manufacturers.

─────────────────── **EXERCISE 5.4** ───────────────────

Make up sentences containing nouns having the characteristics given below and underline the noun that you characterize. There may be more than one noun in the sentence you make up.

EXAMPLE

proper, concrete, noncount
<u>Milwaukee</u> is located in Wisconsin.

1. common, abstract, noncount
2. common, concrete, count
3. common, concrete, noncount
4. common, abstract, count
5. proper, concrete, noncount
6. proper, concrete, count

5.5 NUMBER

Count nouns make a distinction between singular and plural. The regular plural ends in -s. This inflection (grammatical suffix), however, is pronounced in one of three ways, depending on the sound immediately before it. Contrast these three sets:

1. buses, bushes, churches, pages, diseases, garages
2. sums, machines, days, toes
3. tanks, patients, shocks, notes

The plural inflection is pronounced as a separate syllable—spelled -es—when it follows any of the sounds that appear in the singulars of the words listed in (1); in the case of diseases and garages, a final -e is already present in the singular, so only an -s needs to be added in the plural. When -s is added to form the plurals toes in (2) and notes in (3), the -es is not pronounced as a separate syllable, since it does not follow one of the sounds before the inflections in (1). There are also some other exceptions to the usual -s spelling. See also A.4 in the Appendix.

There are a few irregular plurals that reflect older English forms:

man	men	mouse	mice
woman	women	louse	lice

foot	feet	brother	brethren (in special senses)
goose	geese	child	children
tooth	teeth	ox oxen (also oxes)	

There are a large number of classes of other irregular plurals, many of them having foreign plurals (e.g., stimulus, stimuli; curriculum, curricula; crisis, crises).

EXERCISE 5.5

Supply the plural form for the irregular singular nouns listed below.

EXAMPLE

    foot (*feet*)

    1. criterion
    2. deer
    3. datum
    4. analysis
    5. child
    6. phenomenon
    7. life
    8. basis
    9. woman
  10. alumnus

5.6 GENDER

Relatively few nouns are distinguished in **gender,** but there are some male nouns and female nouns; for example:

father	mother	widower	widow
boy	girl	bridegroom	bride
host	hostess	bull	cow
hero	heroine	lion	lioness

    Important distinctions in gender, however, apply to the third person singular pronouns he, she, and it (cf. 5.16). When one of these gender-distinctive pronouns refers to a noun, the sex of the specific person or animal is made manifest:

        The student was absent today because she attended an inter-
           view for a job.

5.7 CASE

Nouns make a distinction in **case,** a distinction that is based on the grammatical function of the noun. Nouns have two cases: the **common case** and the **genitive case.** The common case is the one that is used ordinarily. The genitive case generally indicates that the noun is dependent on the noun that follows it; this case often corresponds to a structure with <u>of</u>:

> Jane's reactions   the reactions <u>of Jane</u>

For regular nouns the genitive is indicated in writing by an apostrophe plus <u>s</u> (<u>student's</u>) in the singular and by an apostrophe following the plural <u>-s</u> inflection in the plural (<u>students'</u>):

	singular	**plural**
common case	the <u>student</u>	the <u>students</u>
genitive case	the <u>student's</u> suggestions	the <u>students'</u> suggestions

In speech, three of these forms are pronounced identically.

Irregular nouns, however, distinguish all four forms in speech as well as in writing:

	singular	**plural**
common case	the <u>child</u>	the <u>children</u>
genitive case	the <u>child's</u> suggestions	the <u>children's</u> suggestions

The same genitive inflection (<u>'s</u>) is attached to both the singular and the plural. On the rules for placing the apostrophe after words ending in <u>-s</u>, see 7.13.

When the genitive is dependent on a following noun, the genitive or genitive phrase usually has a **determinative** function; that is, it functions like words that belong to the class of determiners (cf. 5.24–28). Compare:

> the <u>student's</u> suggestions (determinative genitive)
> <u>their</u> suggestions (possessive determiner, cf. 5.17)

Sometimes the genitive is an **independent genitive;** that is, it is not dependent on a following noun. The noun may be omitted because it can be understood from the context:

> Your ideas are more acceptable than <u>Sandra's</u>. (Sandra's
>   ideas)
> David's comments are like <u>Peter's</u>.

But the independent genitive is also used to refer to places:

> The party's at <u>Alan's</u> tonight.
> I'm shopping at <u>Macy's</u>.

Finally, the independent genitive may combine with the <u>of</u>-structure:

> a friend <u>of Martha's</u>
> a suggestion <u>of Norman's</u>

The independent genitive in the <u>of</u>-structure differs from the normal genitive in its meaning: <u>Martha's friend</u> means "the friend that Martha has," (the speaker assumes that the hearer knows the identity of the friend) whereas <u>a friend of Martha's</u> means "one of the friends that Martha has."

=========== **EXERCISE 5.6** ===========

Specify whether the underlined genitive nouns are determinative or independent.

EXAMPLE
<u>John's</u> job is very time-consuming. (*determinative*)

1. My house is much smaller than <u>Sue's</u>.
2. The committee plans to discuss the <u>regents'</u> plans at its next meeting.
3. I'm another friend of <u>Bill's</u>.
4. Tuition costs in the Commonwealth of Massachusetts will cause the average <u>student's</u> tuition to rise significantly in the next five years.
5. The <u>senator's</u> desire to see peace in the region was expressed at the rally held last Tuesday.
6. The professor introduced a motion at the meeting that was slightly different from her <u>colleague's</u>.
7. The reason for the <u>man's</u> dismissal was kept secret from the rest of the workers.
8. The <u>dog's</u> sleeping area was contaminated with fleas.

_____ **MAIN VERBS** _____

5.8 VERB SUFFIXES

A main verb (or, more simply, a verb) is a word that can be the main word in a verb phrase and is often the only verb (cf. 4.11). Certain suffixes are added to nouns or adjectives to make main verbs. Here are a few common verb suffixes with words that exemplify them:

-ate, -iate	chlorinate, originate, differentiate
-en	darken, hasten, sadden
-ify, -fy	codify, falsify, simplify
-ize	apologize, publicize, rationalize

Like nouns, many verbs have no suffixes: write, walk, reveal, understand. Many of the suffixes that characterize verbs served that function in Latin or French, and so we have words in English that were already suffixed when they were borrowed from these languages: signify, realize.

=========================== **EXERCISE 5.7** ===========================

For each word below, circle the suffix that indicates the word is a verb.

EXAMPLE
   chlorinate

   1. harden
   2. prioritize
   3. magnify
   4. reiterate
   5. conceptualize
   6. loosen
   7. complicate
   8. dignify
   9. legalize
   10. signify

=========================== **EXERCISE 5.8** ===========================

Convert the following words into verbs by adding verb suffixes. Some words may take more than one suffix.

EXAMPLE
   light (*lighten*)

   1. final
   2. real
   3. hyphen
   4. ripe
   5. orchestra

6. material
7. burglar
8. wide
9. tight
10. random

5.9 REGULAR AND IRREGULAR VERBS

I earlier (4.12) distinguished five forms of verbs:

1. base form: laugh, speak
2. -s form: laughs, speaks
3. -ing participle: laughing, speaking
4. past form: laughed, spoke
5. -ed participle: laughed, spoken

There is no distinction between the past and the -ed participle in regular verbs and in many irregular verbs (e.g., sent). In other irregular verbs (e.g., put), three forms are identical: the base, past, and -ed participle. On the other hand, the verb be has eight forms (cf. 4.12).

There are over 250 irregular verbs. If we leave aside the highly irregular verb be, we can group the irregular verbs into seven classes:

1. The past and -ed participle are identical, but the endings are irregular:

bend bent bent   have had had
build built built   make made made

2. The past and -ed participle are different, the base and past vowel are identical, and the -ed participle ends irregularly in -n:

saw sawed sawn   show showed shown
sew sewed sewn   swell swelled swollen

Some of these verbs also have variants that are regular: saw, sawed, sawed.

3. The past and -ed participle are identical, but the endings are irregular and there is a change in the vowel:

keep kept kept   lose lost lost   hear heard heard
buy bought bought   tell told told   say said said

Some of these verbs also have regular variants: kneel, kneeled, kneeled, as well as kneel, knelt, knelt.

4. The past and -ed participle are different, and there is a change of vowel. The participle of most of these verbs also ends irregularly in -n:

speak spoke spoken   blow blew blown
wear wore worn   see saw seen

5. The base, past, and -ed participle are identical. There is no suffix in the past or participle:

cut cut cut   put put put
hurt hurt hurt   split split split

Some also have regular variants: wet, wetted, wetted, as well as wet, wet, wet.

6. The past and -ed participle are identical. There is no suffix and there is a vowel change:

feed fed fed   find found found
win won won   fight fought fought

A few also have regular variants: light, lighted, lighted, as well as light, lit, lit.

7. The past and -ed participle are different. There is no suffix and there is a vowel change:

begin began begun   run ran run
come came come   sing sang sung

Note that the past of go is highly irregular: go, went, gone.

EXERCISE 5.9

Conjugate each verb and identify the class of irregular verbs into which it fits.

EXAMPLE
    drink (*drink, drank, drunk—class 7*)

1. set
2. drive
3. say
4. draw
5. see
6. strive
7. drink
8. send
9. mow
10. swim

ADJECTIVES

5.10 ADJECTIVE SUFFIXES

An adjective is a word that can be the only or main word in an adjective phrase (cf. 4.21). A large number of suffixes are added to nouns and verbs to make adjectives. Here are the most common suffixes and words that exemplify them:

-able, -ible	disposable, suitable, fashionable, audible
-al, -ial	normal, cynical, racial, editorial
-ed	wooded, boarded, aged, crooked
-ful	hopeful, playful, careful, forgetful
-ic	romantic, atmospheric, heroic, atomic
-ical	historical, political, paradoxical, economical
-ish	amateurish, darkish, foolish, childish
-ive, -ative	defective, communicative, attractive, affirmative
-less	tactless, hopeless, harmless, restless
-ous, -eous, -ious	famous, virtuous, erroneous, spacious
-y	tasty, handy, wealthy, really

The suffix -ed is often used to make adjectives from noun phrases: blue-eyed, good-natured, open-minded, open-ended.

Like nouns and verbs, many adjectives have no suffixes: sad, young, happy. Some suffixes were part of the words when they were borrowed into English: sensitive, virtuous.

EXERCISE 5.10

For each word below, circle the suffix that indicates the word is an adjective.

EXAMPLE
    fadd(ish)

1. careless
2. delightful
3. ragged
4. sandy
5. specific
6. boisterous
7. healthy

8. cultural
9. creative
10. erroneous
11. suicidal
12. rustic
13. snobbish

EXERCISE 5.11

Convert the following words into adjectives by adding adjective suffixes. Some words may take more than one suffix.

EXAMPLE
    logic (*logical*)

1. style
2. cycle
3. home
4. like
5. wish
6. cone
7. allergy
8. monster
9. rest
10. point
11. hair
12. style
13. use

5.11 ADJECTIVE CLASSES

We can divide adjectives into three classes according to their function. Used alone or with a modifier or a complement, an adjective can be one or more of the following:

1. premodifier of a noun
2. subject complement
3. object complement

Adjectives are **attributive** (attributing a quality to what is denoted by a noun) when they are being used as premodifiers. They are **predicative** (part of the predicate) when they are being used as complements.

Central adjectives can be used in all three functions:

1. It was a comfortable ride.   **attributive**
2. The ride was comfortable.
3. I made the bed comfortable.   **predicative**

Other examples of central adjectives: clever, brave, calm, hungry, noisy.
Some adjectives are attributive only:

That is utter nonsense.
You are the very person I was looking for.

Other examples: chief, main, sheer. Many words are restricted in this way only in particular meanings. Old is only attributive in:

She is an old friend of mine. (a friend for many years)

It is a central adjective in:

She is an old woman.
She is old.
I consider her old.

Some adjectives are predicative only, with or without complements (cf. 4.21):

He is afraid of dogs.
I am glad that you are here.

Other predicative adjectives must be followed by complements: aware (of + noun phrase), loath (to + infinitive), subject (to + infinitive). Some words have this restriction only with particular meanings. Happy is only predicative in:

We are happy to see you.

It is a central adjective in:

He has a happy disposition.
His disposition is happy.
We made him happy.

EXERCISE 5.12

Indicate whether each adjective below is central or whether it is only attributive or only predicative. To help you reach a decision, make up sentences containing the adjectives.

EXAMPLE
> lovable
> *central*
> *Bella is a lovable dog. (attributive)*
> *Bella is lovable. (predicative)*
> *The children found Bella lovable. (predicative)*

1. ancient
2. extreme
3. tired
4. tantamount
5. poor
6. entire
7. fond
8. rigid
9. main
10. dangerous

EXERCISE 5.13

The adjectives below are central. Make up three sentences for each: one where it is used as a premodifier, one as a subject complement, and one as an object complement.

EXAMPLE
> foolish
> *The foolish student handed in his paper late. (premodifier)*
> *The student was foolish. (subject complement)*
> *The instructor considered the student foolish. (object complement)*

1. useful
2. brave
3. timid
4. difficult
5. industrious
6. nervous

7. new
8. necessary
9. unusual
10. strange

5.12 GRADABILITY AND COMPARISON

Adjectives are typically **gradable:** we can arrange them on a scale. Thus we can say that something is a bit hot, somewhat hot, quite hot, very hot, or extremely hot. We can also compare things and say that something is hotter than something else or that it is the hottest of a number of things.

We use **intensifiers** to indicate the point on the scale. The most common intensifier of adjectives is the adverb very. Other examples of intensifiers are:

> fairly pleasant entirely happy
> pretty difficult incredibly dull
> rather dark too long

There are three degrees of comparison:

1. higher

[1a] Ann is politer than Michael. (**comparative**)
[1b] Ann is the politest child in the family. (**superlative**)

We have a three-term contrast: **absolute,** polite; **comparative,** politer–more polite; **superlative,** politest–most polite.

2. same

[2a] Ann is as happy as Michael.

3. lower

[3a] Ann is less friendly than Michael.
[3b] Ann is the least friendly child in the family.

The superlatives in [1b] and [3b] are required when the comparison involves more than two units or sets of units.

Higher degrees of comparison are expressed either through the inflections -er and -est or through the premodifiers more and most:

	absolute	comparative	superlative
inflection	polite	politer	politest
premodifier	polite	more polite	most polite

There are a few common adjectives that have irregular inflections:

good
well   (healthy) } better best

bad   worse worst

far   { farther farthest
          { further furthest

Words of one syllable generally take inflections: older, oldest; purer, purest. Many words of two syllables can take either form: politer, politest or more polite, most polite; noisier, noisiest or more noisy, most noisy. Words that are longer than two syllables take the premodifiers: more impolite, most impolite.

EXERCISE 5.14

Use each adjective below as the basis of a sentence expressing the degree of comparison given in parentheses.

EXAMPLE
   beautiful (comparative)
   Sue is more beautiful than Mary.

   1.   tall (absolute)
   2.   handsome (superlative)
   3.   risky (comparative)
   4.   good (superlative)
   5.   rugged (absolute)
   6.   bad (comparative)
   7.   temperate (superlative)
   8.   kind (comparative)
   9.   healthy (absolute)
   10. receptive (comparative)

═══════════════════ **EXERCISE 5.15** ═══════════════════

Add a different intensifier to each adjective below.

EXAMPLE
    happy (*extremely happy*)

    1. ugly
    2. small
    3. cute
    4. unhappy
    5. modest
    6. outgoing
    7. pleasant
    8. light
    9. friendly
    10. hostile

─────────────── **ADVERBS** ───────────────

5.13 ADVERB SUFFIXES

An adverb is a word that can be the only or main word in an adverb phrase (cf. 4.23). The suffix -ly is commonly added to adjectives to make adverbs:

        calmly, frankly, lightly, madly, tearfully

If the adjective ends in -ic, the suffix is usually -ically:

        economically, geographically, heroically, romantically

The exception is publicly.
    The suffix -wise is added to nouns to make adverbs:

        clockwise, lengthwise, moneywise, weatherwise

    Like the other word classes, many adverbs have no suffixes. These include, in particular, most time adverbs (now, afterwards), space adverbs (here, outside), and "linking adverbs" (therefore, however).

EXERCISE 5.16

For each word below, circle the suffix that indicates the word is an adverb.

EXAMPLE
sporadic(ally)

1. suddenly
2. edgewise
3. logistically
4. candidly
5. crosswise
6. personally
7. domestically
8. cowardly
9. education-wise
10. clumsily

5.14 GRADABILITY AND COMPARISON

Like adjectives, adverbs are typically gradable and can therefore be modified by intensifiers and take comparison (cf. 5.12): quite calmly, very calmly, less calmly, most calmly. Most adverbs that take comparison require the premodifiers more and most. Those adverbs that have the same form as adjectives have the inflections (e.g., late, later, latest). The following adverbs have irregular inflections; the first three are identical with those for adjectives:

well	better	best
badly	worse	worst
far	farther	farthest
	further	furthest
little	less	least
much	more	most

EXERCISE 5.17

Write out the comparative and superlative forms of each adverb.

EXAMPLES
badly: *worse, worst*; horribly: *more horribly, most horribly*

1. happily
2. soon
3. wisely
4. lazily
5. superficially
6. hard
7. talented
8. cruelly
9. much
10. terribly

PRONOUNS

5.15 PRONOUN CLASSES

Pronouns are essentially special types of nouns and are the main word in a noun phrase or (more usually) the only word in a noun phrase. They fall into a number of classes, here listed with examples:

1.	**personal pronouns**	I, you
2.	**possessive pronouns**	mine, yours
3.	**reflexive pronouns**	myself, yourself
4.	**demonstrative pronouns**	this, these; that, those
5.	**reciprocal pronouns**	each other; one another
6.	**interrogative pronouns**	who, what
7.	**relative pronouns**	who, that
8.	**indefinite pronouns**	some, none

The first three classes are related in that they make distinctions in **person** (first, second, third), **gender** (masculine, feminine, and nonpersonal), and **number** (singular and plural). Most of them also share at least some resemblance in their sound and in their appearance (you, yours, yourself).

Pronouns generally substitute for a noun phrase:

> I went around the hospital with Dr. Thomas. He was highly intelligent, austere, and warm all at the same time. He could perceive almost instantaneously whether a problem was a serious one or not.

The two instances of He refer back to an **antecedent** (something that came before), in this instance Dr. Thomas. The pronouns are used to avoid repeating the noun phrase <u>Dr. Thomas</u>. <u>One</u>, however, replaces the noun head <u>problem</u> (and therefore is literally a pronoun rather than a substitute for a noun phrase). Here is another example of pronoun substitution:

> A big-city mayor ran for reelection. During the campaign <u>he</u> promised to remove rent controls.

In this case the pronoun <u>he</u> replaces a noun phrase that is not identical with the antecedent noun phrase <u>A big-city mayor</u>. If we did not substitute <u>he</u>, we would have to write <u>the big-city mayor</u> or (more economically) <u>the mayor</u>.

The pronoun occasionally comes before its antecedent:

> When <u>she</u> moved into <u>her</u> own apartment, Cindy seemed much more relaxed.

If we assume that <u>she</u> and <u>Cindy</u> refer to the same person, the pronoun <u>she</u> refers to <u>Cindy</u> and so does the determiner <u>her</u> (cf. 5.17).

Pronouns can also refer directly to something that is present in the situation:

> Look at <u>that</u>!
> I'll pick <u>it</u> up.

EXERCISE 5.18

Circle the antecedents of the underlined pronouns and determiners.

EXAMPLE

(The man) tried <u>his</u> hardest to overcome his fear of flying.

1. Scientists have discovered that pets have a therapeutic effect on <u>their</u> owners.
2. A dog, for instance, can improve the health of the people <u>it</u> comes in contact with.
3. In a recent study, the blood pressure of subjects was measured while <u>they</u> were petting their pets.
4. In general, an individual's blood pressure decreased while <u>he</u> was in the act of petting his pet.
5. Since many of the elderly have experienced the loss of a spouse, it is particularly important that <u>they</u> be allowed to have a pet.
6. This is a problem, since the elderly often live in housing complexes whose landlords will not allow <u>their</u> tenants to own pets.

7. Recently, however, a local landlord allowed <u>her</u> tenants to own pets on an experimental basis.

8. This landlord found that when <u>they</u> were allowed to have pets, the elderly proved to be very responsible pet owners.

5.16 PERSONAL PRONOUNS

All the personal pronouns have distinctions in person (first, second, third). Most also have distinctions in number (singular, plural) and in case (subjective, objective, genitive). For the genitive case of the personal pronouns, see the possessive determiners (5.17).

		subjective case	objective case
first person			
singular		<u>I</u>	<u>me</u>
plural		<u>we</u>	<u>us</u>
second person			
singular/plural		<u>you</u>	<u>you</u>
third person			
singular	masculine	<u>he</u>	<u>him</u>
	feminine	<u>she</u>	<u>her</u>
	nonpersonal	<u>it</u>	<u>it</u>
plural		<u>they</u>	<u>them</u>

Some regions have a separate plural for the second person; for example, <u>you all</u>, <u>you guys</u>, <u>youse</u>.

The subjective case applies when the pronouns are the subject of a finite clause:

> <u>I</u> know that <u>she</u> lives in Manhattan and that <u>he</u> lives in Brooklyn.

In all other instances except the one that I am about to mention, the objective case is used:

> She knows <u>me</u> well.
> He has told <u>her</u> about me.
> You must go with <u>him</u>.

The exception is that the subjective case is also used for the subject complement. In these examples the complement follows the linking verb <u>be</u>:

> This is <u>he</u>.
> It is <u>I</u> who issued the order.

In informal style, however, the objective case is usual here too:

> It's <u>me</u>.

The masculine and feminine genders apply to human beings and also to other beings that are treated as persons, such as pets or perhaps some farm animals. The distinction between the two genders is made on the basis of natural distinctions in sex (but see section 8.6). Some other objects (such as ships or cars) or even personified abstractions (such as Death or Beauty) may be treated as if they were persons. Otherwise, the nonpersonal pronoun <u>it</u> is used. One exceptional use of <u>it</u> is for babies whose sex is unknown to the speaker.

The personal pronouns take modifiers to a limited extent:

> <u>you</u> <u>who</u> <u>know</u> <u>me</u>   <u>we</u> in <u>this</u> <u>country</u>
> <u>you</u> <u>there</u>   <u>they</u> <u>both</u>

═══════════════════ EXERCISE 5.19 ═══════════════════

Specify the person (first, second, or third), number (singular or plural), and case (subjective or objective) of each of the underlined pronouns.

EXAMPLE
<u>I</u> like foreign films. (*first person, singular, subjective*)

1. The instructor made <u>us</u> read for the entire period.
2. Economists now realize that <u>they</u> have a responsibility not just to the academic community but to the general public as well.
3. If <u>he</u> can fit it into his schedule, the man plans to visit New York.
4. The woman didn't give <u>him</u> a chance to speak.
5. While <u>she</u> was speaking, the politician was continually interrupted by hecklers.
6. The councilman knows that he must give <u>them</u> a chance to vote on the bill.
7. <u>We</u> realized that the effects of pollution would only increase over the years.
8. The promotion gave <u>me</u> a significant increase in pay.

5.17 POSSESSIVES

The possessives are the genitives of the personal pronouns. There are two sets. One set contains the **possessive determiners,** a subclass of determiners (cf. 5.24f). A possessive determiner is dependent on a noun:

> Here is your book.

The other set of possessives contains the **possessive pronouns,** a subclass of pronouns. A possessive pronoun functions independently:

> This book is yours.

The possessive determiners are not pronouns, but it is convenient to deal with them in this section because of the parallels between the two sets of possessives.
Nouns in the genitive case also have these two functions (cf. 5.7):

> Here is Geoffrey's book. [*determinative genitive*]
> This book is Geoffrey's. [*independent genitive*]

But unlike the nouns, most of the possessives have separate forms for the determiner and independent functions. The two sets of forms parallel the forms for the personal pronouns (5.16).

		determiner	**pronoun**
first person			
singular		my	mine
plural		our	ours
second person			
singular/plural		your	yours
third person			
singular	masculine	his	his
	feminine	her	hers
	nonpersonal	its	its
plural		their	theirs

=========================== **EXERCISE 5.20** ===========================

Indicate whether each underlined pronoun is a possessive determiner or a possessive pronoun.

EXAMPLE
    The boy gave his sister a very nice gift. (*possessive determiner*)

1. The governor spoke to the assembly about <u>its</u> desire to increase government pensions.
2. The book is <u>mine</u>, not the library's.
3. If <u>your</u> needs are not met in your childhood, you will grow up feeling isolated and deprived.
4. No one came to the police station to claim the jewelry as <u>his</u>.
5. <u>Ours</u> is the red car parked out back, not the blue one.
6. <u>Our</u> greatest desire is to see poverty eliminated from the United States within our lifetime.
7. The young girl claimed that the doll was <u>hers</u>.
8. The presidents of all of the state universities met to discuss <u>their</u> concerns over the drastic increases in tuition that the regents have proposed.
9. The candidate expressed <u>his</u> belief that taxes had to be raised to balance the budget.
10. Is the glass of water on the table <u>yours</u>?

5.18 REFLEXIVE PRONOUNS

The reflexive pronouns parallel the personal and possessive pronouns in person and number but have no distinctions in case. There are separate forms for the second person singular (<u>yourself</u>) and plural (<u>yourselves</u>), whereas there is only one form of the second person for the personal pronoun (<u>you</u>) and the possessive pronoun (<u>yours</u>).

first person
singular   <u>myself</u>
plural   <u>ourselves</u>

second person
singular   <u>yourself</u>
plural   <u>yourselves</u>

third person
singular masculine   <u>himself</u>
          feminine   <u>herself</u>
          nonpersonal   <u>itself</u>
plural   <u>themselves</u>

The reflexives have two main uses:

1. They refer to the same person or thing as the subject does:

<u>They</u> behaved <u>themselves</u> for a change.
<u>You</u>'ll hurt <u>yourself</u>.

2. They give emphasis to a noun phrase:

She herself spoke to me.
He wrote to me himself.
I appealed to the President himself.

=============== **EXERCISE 5.21** ===============

Fill in the blanks with the appropriate reflexive pronoun.

EXAMPLE
    The man gave *himself* credit for getting the work done on time.

1. The woman wrote _____ a message so that she wouldn't forget to stop at the store.
2. We congratulated _____ on a job well done.
3. John _____ is the person responsible for coordinating efforts to organize the benefit.
4. Save _____ an extra ten minutes to proofread your essay once you've written it.
5. I _____ wouldn't be able to finish the assignment in that short a span of time.
6. The surveyors gave _____ plenty of time to map out the lot on which the building was to be constructed.
7. All of you should take your time and allow _____ to enjoy the meal.
8. The horse hurt _____ when it broke out of the stall and jumped over the barbed wire fence.
9. We helped _____ to a cocktail and some food.
10. The man did the entire job by _____.
11. Each one of you should help _____ to some food and a beverage.

.19 DEMONSTRATIVE PRONOUNS

There are four demonstrative pronouns:

singular	this	that
plural	these	those

This is for you.
You may take those.

The demonstratives may also be determiners (cf. 5.24f):

This letter is for you.

═══════════════════ **EXERCISE 5.22** ═══════════════════

Specify whether each underlined word is a demonstrative pronoun or a demonstrative determiner.

EXAMPLE
This assignment is proving very hard to complete. (*demonstrative determiner*)

1. This happens to be the best meal I've eaten in quite some time.
2. These knives are useless because they need to be sharpened.
3. Please return this letter to the person who mailed it.
4. Those are the kindest remarks the president has received in quite some time.
5. That is the largest fish that I have ever seen.
6. That gift should not be opened until your birthday.
7. You should send these donations to the Catholic Relief Fund.
8. These will have to do until we receive the new shipment from the central office.

5.20 RECIPROCAL PRONOUNS

There are two reciprocal pronouns, and they have genitives:

> each other   one another
> each other's   one another's

The partners trusted each other fully.
My brother and I borrow one another's ties.

5.21 INTERROGATIVE PRONOUNS

One set of the interrogative pronouns has distinctions in gender and case:

	subjective case	objective case	genitive case
personal	who	whom	whose

It is normal to use <u>who</u> for both the subjective and objective cases and to reserve <u>whom</u> for formal style (cf. 8.18). The other interrogative pronouns, <u>which</u> and <u>what</u>, have only one form. <u>Whose</u> is a determiner, and <u>which</u> and <u>what</u> may also be determiners (cf. 5.24f).

We use <u>who</u> and <u>whom</u> when we refer to persons:

> <u>Who</u> is your favorite pop singer?
> <u>Who</u> (or <u>whom</u>) have they appointed?

<u>Which</u> can be either personal or nonpersonal:

> <u>Which</u> is your sister?
> <u>Which</u> (of the drinks) do you prefer?

<u>What</u> is normally only nonpersonal:

> <u>What</u> do you want?

===== **EXERCISE 5.23** =====

Specify whether the interrogative pronouns are personal or non-personal and whether they are in the subjective case, the objective case, or the genitive case. Ignore case labels for pronouns (such as <u>what</u>) that lack case distinctions.

EXAMPLE
> Which of the papers do you plan on reading at the conference? (*nonpersonal*)

1. Whom did you contact about the job interview?
2. Whose is the car that is blocking mine in the driveway?
3. What do you like on your salad?
4. Who is going to lead the session that meets next Tuesday?
5. Whom do they plan to issue the arrest warrant for?
6. Which of the two choices do you think would be the best to make?

5.22 RELATIVE PRONOUNS

Relative pronouns introduce relative clauses (cf. 4.5). They also have distinctions in gender and case:

	subjective case	objective case	genitive case
personal	<u>who</u>	<u>whom</u>	<u>whose</u>
nonpersonal	<u>which</u>	<u>which</u>	<u>whose</u>
	<u>that</u>	<u>that</u>	

As with the interrogative pronouns (cf. 5.21), who is the normal form for the subjective and objective cases, whereas whom is used only in formal style. The relative pronoun may be omitted in certain circumstances. The omitted pronoun is sometimes called the **zero relative pronoun**.

> the instructor who (or that) taught me freshman composition
> the house which (or that or zero) we bought
> the person whom (or, less formally, who or zero) they appointed.
> the student to whom you gave it [formal]
> the student who (or that or zero) you gave it to

Genitive whose is a determiner, like his or her (cf. 5.24f).

There is another set of relative pronouns that introduce **nominal relative clauses** (cf. 6.9); these are the **nominal relative pronouns**. In addition to who, whom, and which, they include whoever, whomever (in formal style), whichever, what, and whatever:

$$\text{You may take} \begin{Bmatrix} \text{which} \\ \text{whichever} \\ \text{what} \\ \text{whatever} \end{Bmatrix} \text{you wish}$$

> What I need is a period of peace and quiet.
> I'll speak to whoever is in charge.

Nominal relative pronouns correspond to a combination of a relative pronoun with a preceding antecedent (cf. 5.15):

> What I need . . . (the thing that I need)
> . . . to whoever is in charge (to the person who is in charge)

Some of these nominal relatives may also be determiners (cf. 5.24f).

========================= **EXERCISE 5.24** =========================

Rewrite the sentences below, deleting relative pronouns.

EXAMPLE
He was the man to whom we donated the gift.
(He was the man we donated the gift to.)

1. The senator of Maine was the man for whom we campaigned.
2. We spoke to the woman who we had sold girl scout cookies to.
3. Leaders of the country negotiated with the rebels with whom they had been fighting for over seven years.
4. This is the company that we had hoped to open an account with.
5. Ticket vendors had to turn away an angry crowd of people who they knew they wouldn't have enough tickets to sell to.
6. The team has tried to identify athletes who they think have a drug or alcohol problem.

EXERCISE 5.25

Indicate whether the relative pronouns introduce relative clauses or nominal relative clauses and specify whether the case of the relative pronoun is subjective or objective. Ignore case labels for relative pronouns (such as <u>whatever</u>) that lack case distinctions.

EXAMPLE
   We spoke to the clerk <u>who</u> was working at the time.
   (relative clause, subjective case)

1. The police located the individual <u>whom</u> they had been searching for since Saturday.
2. American car manufacturers have begun to make cars <u>that</u> last longer than a few years.
3. The contestant was allowed to select <u>whatever</u> she wanted.
4. The company for <u>which</u> I work will soon be declaring bankruptcy.
5. <u>Whoever</u> is elected president will need to work hard to avoid a major recession in the near future.
6. We must concentrate hard on electing an individual <u>who</u> meets all of the qualifications the position requires.
7. <u>What</u> is most urgent is that our elected officials find a solution to the problem of poverty in Central America that has existed for centuries.
8. The countries must negotiate a treaty <u>which</u> is fair to all parties involved.
9. We must cooperate fully with <u>whomever</u> the firm hires to do the job.
10. You are expected to attend the conference with <u>whoever</u> wishes to go.

5.23 INDEFINITE PRONOUNS AND NUMERALS

Indefinite pronouns are the largest group of pronouns. They refer to the presence (or absence) of a quantity. Most of the same words function as indefinite determiners (cf. 5.24f).

Here are some examples of indefinite pronouns:

> <u>Many</u> have replied to the advertisement and <u>several</u> have been interviewed.
> You take <u>one</u> and I'll take <u>the other</u>.
> <u>No one</u> was absent today.
> <u>More</u> will be arriving later.
> You can have <u>both</u>.
> <u>Either</u> will do for me.
> There are <u>fewer</u> here today.
> <u>Everybody</u> was pleased with the speech.

The <u>some</u>-set of indefinite pronouns contrasts with the <u>any</u>-set:

<u>some</u>	<u>any</u>
<u>someone</u>	<u>anyone</u>
<u>somebody</u>	<u>anybody</u>
<u>something</u>	<u>anything</u>

The <u>any</u>-set is normal in negative contexts. Contrast:

> She has <u>some</u> good grades.
> She doesn't have <u>any</u> good grades.

<u>Some</u> implies a specific quantity, though the quantity is not specified. <u>Any</u> does not imply a specific quantity; the quantity is without limit. The <u>any</u>-set is also normal in questions unless a positive reply is expected:

> Did <u>anyone</u> call for me?
> Did <u>someone</u> call for me?

Two uses of indefinite <u>one</u> deserve special mention:

1. <u>One</u> has the meaning "people in general":

> If <u>one</u> goes to medical school, <u>he</u> (or <u>one</u>) must be prepared to borrow vast sums of money.

2. <u>One</u> is a substitute for a noun:

> A: Do you want an ice cream?
> B: I guess I'll take a small <u>one</u>.

Unlike most pronouns, <u>one</u> in the response by B substitutes for a noun, not a noun phrase. It is the main word in the noun phrase <u>a small one</u>.

Many of the indefinite pronouns may be postmodified. <u>Of</u>-phrases are particularly common:

<u>somebody</u> else   <u>neither</u> of us
<u>several</u> in our group   <u>half</u> of your class
<u>something</u> quite funny   <u>a few</u> of my friends

Numerals may be used as pronouns. Here are two examples of **cardinal numerals** as pronouns:

<u>Twenty-two</u> were rescued from the sinking ship.
<u>Three</u> of the children wandered off on their own.

The **ordinal numerals** (<u>first</u>, <u>second</u>, <u>third</u>, . . .) combine with <u>the</u> in this function:

<u>The first</u> of my children is still in high school.

================= **EXERCISE 5.26** =================

Indicate whether the underlined pronouns are personal, possessive, reflexive, demonstrative, reciprocal, interrogative, relative, or indefinite.

EXAMPLE
  Individuals <u>who</u> buy their tickets early will receive a 10% reduction in price. (*relative*)

1. <u>We</u> as a society must become more concerned about preserving our natural environment.
2. We must take the initiative <u>ourselves</u> because our legislators are reluctant to act on their own.
3. Many legislators are too obligated to special interest groups <u>that</u> helped them get elected.
4. <u>These</u> are groups that exert much political clout.
5. <u>They</u> are a powerful lobbying group in Washington with lots of money.
6. Often they represent huge corporations <u>who</u> stand to lose money if they are forced to conform to pollution control laws.
7. As concerned citizens, however, we must stand up to <u>whoever</u> is in the way of cleaning up our natural environment.
8. We must communicate to <u>one another</u> our concern.
9. And we must communicate to <u>those</u> who are our legislators that we want a cleaner living environment.

10. What can we do?
11. We can write letters to our local representatives, saying that our interests are as great as theirs.
12. Nothing will be done unless someone takes the initiative to break the power of the lobby in Washington that seeks to continue to pollute the environment.

DETERMINERS

5.24 CLASSES OF DETERMINERS

Determiners introduce noun phrases. The three classes of determiners are defined by the order in which they come:

1. **predeterminers**
2. **central determiners**
3. **postdeterminers**

Here are examples with determiners from each class:

> all (1) those (2) other (3) problems
> once (1) every (2) two (3) weeks

Many words may be either determiners or pronouns:

pronoun:	Some have left.
determiner:	Some people have left.

pronoun:	I need more.
determiner:	I need more money.

pronoun:	All are forgiven.
determiner:	All faults are forgiven.

pronoun:	You may borrow this.
determiner:	You may borrow this pencil.

5.25 CENTRAL DETERMINERS

The central determiners fall into several subclasses. We cannot combine central determiners to introduce the same noun phrase.

1. **definite article** (cf. 5.26): the
2. **indefinite article** (cf. 5.26): a or (before a vowel sound) an

3. **demonstratives** (cf. 5.19): <u>this</u>, <u>that</u>, <u>these</u>, <u>those</u>
4. **possessives** (cf. 5.17): <u>my</u>, <u>our</u>, <u>your</u>, <u>his</u>, <u>her</u>, <u>its</u>, <u>their</u>
5. **interrogatives** (cf. 5.21): <u>what</u>, <u>which</u>, <u>whose</u>
<u>What</u> day is it?
<u>Whose</u> coat are you wearing?
6. **relatives** (cf. 5.22): <u>which</u>, <u>whose</u>, <u>whatever</u>, <u>whichever</u>, <u>who-soever</u>
. . . , at <u>which</u> point I interrupted him.
. . . , <u>whose</u> student I used to be.
You can use it for <u>whatever</u> purpose you wish.
7. **indefinites** (cf. 5.23): <u>some</u>, <u>any</u>, <u>no</u>, <u>enough</u>, <u>every</u>, <u>each</u>, <u>either</u>, <u>neither</u>

EXERCISE 5.27

Indicate whether the underlined words are definite articles, indefinite articles, demonstratives, possessives, interrogatives, relatives, or indefinites.

EXAMPLE
<u>Many</u> people dislike liver. (*indefinite*)

1. <u>Which</u> pair of shoes do you plan on buying?
2. We planned to visit <u>our</u> relatives in Cape Cod next week.
3. The children wanted <u>their</u> parents to buy them <u>some</u> toys.
4. <u>These</u> plans will have to be changed to accommodate the wishes of the planning committee.
5. The commander issued <u>a</u> direct order to his squadron.
6. You must report to <u>whichever</u> school is in need of a substitute teacher.
7. <u>Few</u> enlistees are able to serve a full term without any problems.
8. We hadn't anticipated <u>the</u> large number of people who attended the seminar.
9. <u>What</u> plans have you made for your upcoming vacation?
10. <u>This</u> week the students will be traveling to New York to visit a few art galleries.

---

26 THE ARTICLES AND REFERENCE

We can apply three sets of contrast in the reference of noun phrases:

1. generic and nongeneric
2. specific and nonspecific
3. definite and indefinite

Generic/Nongeneric Reference

Noun phrases are **generic** when they refer to a class as a whole:

> <u>Dogs</u> make good pets.

They are **nongeneric** when they refer to individual members of the class:

> Bring in <u>the dogs</u>.

For generic reference, the distinction between singular and plural is neutralized, and so is the distinction between the definite and indefinite articles. In their generic use, all of the following are roughly similar in meaning:

[1] <u>An American</u> works hard.
[2] <u>Americans</u> work hard.
[3] <u>The American</u> works hard.
[4] <u>The Americans</u> work hard.

Depending on the contrast, [3] and [4] can also be interpreted nongenerically to refer to individual Americans.

Specific/Nonspecific Reference

Noun phrases are **specific** when they refer to some particular person, place, thing, and so on. In [5] <u>a New Yorker</u> refers to a specific person (even if unknown to the speaker):

[5] Patrick has married <u>a New Yorker</u>. (some New Yorker)

In [6], on the other hand, <u>a New Yorker</u> does not refer to anybody specific:

[6] Patrick would not dream of marrying <u>a New Yorker</u>. (any New Yorker)

Sentence [7] is ambiguous between the two interpretations:

[7] Patrick intends to marry <u>a New Yorker</u>.

It may mean that Patrick has a specific person in mind (perhaps unknown to the speaker), or that he has the ambition to marry someone from New York though he has nobody in mind at present.

As we will shortly see, both the indefinite article <u>a</u> and the definite article the are readily available for specific reference. For nonspecific reference, indefinite a is usual but definite the also occurs:

[8]   Patrick intends to marry the first New Yorker he meets.

Generic reference is always nonspecific. Some nongeneric reference may also be nonspecific, as in [6] and [8].

Definite/Indefinite Reference

The definite article the is used to signal that a noun phrase is **definite.** Noun phrases are definite when they are intended to convey enough information to identify what they refer to. If they are not so intended, they are **indefinite.** The identification may come from several sources:

1.   The phrase refers to something uniquely identifiable by the speaker and hearer from their general knowledge or from their knowledge of the particular situation:

> the sun; the sea; the Church
> The President is addressing the nation this evening.
> I must feed the dog.
> The door is locked.
> The boss wants you.

2.   The phrase may refer to something mentioned previously:

> Nancy introduced me to a young man and his wife at the reception. The young man was her nephew.

At the first mention of the young man, the sentence refers to him by the indefinite phrase a young man.

3.   The information may be identified by modifiers in the noun phrase:

> I wonder whether you would mind getting for me the blue book on the top shelf.

Noun phrases may be definite even though they are not introduced by the definite article. For example, in a particular situation, personal pronouns (I, you, etc.) and names are uniquely identifiable, and so are the demonstrative pronouns (cf. 5.19). Other determiners, such as the demonstrative determiners (cf. 5.25), may also signal that the noun phrase is definite.

═══ EXERCISE 5.28 ═══

Indicate whether the underscored phrases are generic or nongeneric. If they are nongeneric, also indicate whether they are specific or nonspecific, and definite or nondefinite.

EXAMPLES

The dinosaur is now extinct.
(*generic*)
A woman walked into the store.
(*nongeneric*
specific
nondefinite)

1. The student of history will have a hard time finding a job after graduation.
2. I am planning on going to a movie tonight.
3. An unidentified man was reported to have robbed a liquor store last night.
4. Please pass the salt when you have a minute.
5. Teachers are often overcriticized and underpaid.
6. The gardeners chopped up the tree that was knocked down during the storm last night.
7. William Shakespeare is the greatest English dramatist.
8. The doctor gave the patient a large dose of penicillin.
9. A linguist is a scholar interested in the structure of human language.
10. You should not be too concerned if you aren't accepted into graduate school at Harvard.

═══ EXERCISE 5.29 ═══

Make up sentences that contain noun phrases or pronouns with the features given below.

EXAMPLE

plural generic noun phrase
Canadians often vacation in Maine.

1. nongeneric, specific, nondefinite noun phrase
2. nongeneric, nonspecific, nondefinite noun phrase

3. generic noun phrase headed by definite article <u>the</u>
4. nongeneric, specific, definite noun phrase
5. generic noun phrase headed by indefinite article <u>a</u> or <u>an</u>
6. nongeneric, specific, definite pronoun
7. plural generic noun phrase
8. nongeneric, nonspecific, definite noun phrase

5.27 PREDETERMINERS

There can also be predeterminers before the central determiners. These include the multipliers (<u>double</u>, <u>twice</u>, <u>three times</u>, ...) and the fractions (<u>half</u>, <u>one-third</u>, ...):

> <u>double</u> her fee
> <u>half</u> a loaf

They also include the words <u>all</u>, <u>both</u>, <u>such</u>, and <u>what</u>:

> <u>all</u> their problems
> <u>such</u> a mess
> <u>what</u> a good idea

These can also occur without a central determiner:

> <u>all</u> stations
> <u>both</u> children
> <u>such</u> jokes

<u>Such</u> is exceptional in that it can combine with other predeterminers (<u>all such jokes</u>) and can come after a central determiner (<u>no such jokes</u>) and even a postdeterminer (<u>many such jokes</u>).

5.28 POSTDETERMINERS

Postdeterminers come after the central determiners. They include the cardinal numbers and the ordinal numbers:

> the <u>three</u> largest rooms
> <u>our</u> <u>first</u> apartment

They also include <u>many</u>, <u>few</u>, and <u>little</u>:

> <u>my</u> <u>many</u> good friends
> <u>the</u> <u>little</u> furniture that I have

The ordinal and cardinal numerals can co-occur:

> the <u>first two</u> weeks

The postdeterminers can occur without other determiners:

> He has <u>few</u> <u>vices</u>.
> We saw <u>two</u> <u>accidents</u> on our way here.

_____ AUXILIARIES _____

5.29 CLASSES OF AUXILIARIES

Auxiliaries come before the main verb in a verb phrase. The **primary auxiliaries** are <u>be</u>, <u>have</u>, and <u>do</u>. They are different from each other and from the other auxiliaries. Their uses are:

1. <u>be</u> for (a) the **progressive:** <u>was playing</u> (cf. 4.14)
   (b) the **passive:** <u>was played</u> (cf. 4.15)
2. <u>have</u> for the **perfect:** <u>has played</u> (cf. 4.14)
3. <u>do</u> as the **dummy operator:** <u>did play</u> (cf. 4.17)

The remaining auxiliaries are the **modal auxiliaries** or, more simply, the **modals.** The central modals are:

present	<u>can</u>	<u>may</u>	<u>will</u>	<u>shall</u>	<u>must</u>
past	<u>could</u>	<u>might</u>	<u>would</u>	<u>should</u>	

Like other verbs, most of the modals have a tense distinction between present and past, but the past forms are often used for present or future time:

> We $\left\{ \begin{array}{c} \underline{may} \\ \underline{might} \end{array} \right\}$ come along after dinner.

> I $\left\{ \begin{array}{c} \underline{can} \\ \underline{could} \end{array} \right\}$ help you later.

30 MEANINGS OF THE MODALS

The modals express two main types of meaning:

1. human control over events, such as is involved in permission, intention, ability, or obligation:

   You <u>may</u> leave now. (I give you permission to . . .)
   I <u>could</u> speak Greek when I was young. (I knew how to . . .)
   You <u>must</u> go to bed at once. (I require you to . . .)

2. judgment whether an event was, is, or will be likely to happen:

   They <u>may</u> be on vacation. (It is possible that they are . . .)
   That <u>could</u> be your mother. (It is possible that it is . . .)
   It <u>must</u> be past midnight. (It is certainly the case that it is . . .)
   Joan <u>may</u> have heard the result by now. (It is possible that Joan has . . .)

=============================== **EXERCISE 5.30** ===============================

Paraphrase the meanings of the modals in the sentences below.

EXAMPLE
   I can speak three different languages.
   I have the ability to speak three different languages.

1. Students must be required to take a foreign language in college.
2. Many students cannot see the point of studying a foreign language.
3. They should realize, however, that multilingualism has many benefits.
4. Studying a foreign language can make them better job candidates upon graduation.
5. Studying a foreign language will also enhance their educational experiences.
6. In most foreign universities, students must study a foreign language.
7. In universities in the United States, in contrast, students can choose not to take a foreign language.
8. American society would benefit tremendously from multilingualism.

9. Study of a foreign language should therefore be required at the college level.
10. And such study might also be considered a requirement at lower grade levels, such as grade school or high school.

5.31   CONJUNCTIONS

There are two classes of conjunctions:

1. coordinators, or coordinating conjunctions
2. subordinators, or subordinating conjunctions

Coordinators link units of equal status. The central coordinators are and, or, and but:

> I enjoy novels and short stories best of all.
> I can and will speak!
> The device seals a plastic shopping bag and equips it with a handle.
> He was apologetic, but he refused to intervene.
> We demand government for the people and by the people.

The coordinators may be reinforced by **correlative** expressions: both . . . and; either . . . or; not only . . . but also:

> both Susan and her brother
> either tea or coffee
> Not only was the speech uninspiring, but it was also full of illogical statements.

The marginal coordinator nor may be reinforced by the correlative neither:

> I have neither seen the movie nor read the book.

Subordinators introduce subordinate clauses (cf. 6.9).

> The negotiations succeeded because both sides bargained in good faith.
> If you like the service, tell the manager.

Here are some common subordinators:

after	before	till	where
although	if	unless	while
as	since	until	
because	that	when	

Some subordinators consist of more than one word: <u>except that</u> and <u>as long as</u>, for example.

Some words are both subordinators and prepositions. If the word introduces a finite clause, it is a subordinator; if it introduces a phrase, it is a preposition:

subordinator   I saw her <u>after I had my interview</u>.
preposition   I saw her <u>after the interview</u>.

EXERCISE 5.31

Make up sentences containing the conjunctions listed below.

EXAMPLE
until
We weren't able to appreciate Salem until we visited the House of the Seven Gables.

1. after
2. either . . . or
3. because
4. although
5. not only . . . but
6. and
7. while
8. since
9. but
10. or
11. if
12. unless

EXERCISE 5.32

Specify whether the underlined constructions are coordinators, or subordinators.

EXAMPLE
<u>Because</u> we were late, we missed the first act of the play.
(*subordinator*)

1. <u>Although</u> businesses in the past did not hire humanities majors, this trend is changing.
2. Many companies are now actively recruiting humanities majors <u>or</u> at least requiring that the people they hire have some background in the humanities.
3. In the past, <u>when</u> an employer hired a worker, he or she looked for a specialist.
4. An accounting firm hired an accountant, <u>and</u> an engineering firm hired an engineer.
5. Unfortunately, these hiring practices gave companies employees who were competent <u>but</u> not creative.
6. <u>While</u> it is important that employees be able to perform their duties, it is also important that they be able to think creatively on the job.
7. Neither the company <u>nor</u> its customers benefits from employees who are only technicians.
8. <u>If</u>, however, employees can combine technical expertise with creative thinking, both company and customer will benefit tremendously.
9. <u>And</u> study in the humanities is an excellent way to instill creativity in prospective employees.
10. An architect, for instance, will benefit from study in both drafting <u>and</u> art history.
11. In the past, <u>although</u> companies failed to see the need for anything but a specialist, they now understand the importance of hiring people with diverse educational experiences.

5.32 PREPOSITIONS

Prepositions introduce a prepositional phrase and are followed by a prepositional complement (cf. 4.25). The preposition links the complement to some other expression. If it links the complement to the rest of the sentence or clause, the prepositional phrase may be placed in any of various positions:

> I had an argument *in a supermarket.*
> All the members of the team, *in my view,* contributed equally to the victory.
> *By that time* I was feeling sleepy.

It may also link the complement to a phrase:

> He became personal assistant *to the president of the company.*

The government suppressed all information *about the epi-demic.*

Here are some common prepositions:

about	at	despite	off	till
above	before	down	on	to
across	behind	during	out	toward
after	below	for	over	under
against	beside	from	past	until
among	between	in	since	up
around	but	inside	than	with
as	by	into	through	without

Some prepositions consist of more than one word; for example <u>because of</u>, <u>in spite of</u>, <u>in addition to</u>.

Many of the words listed as single-word prepositions are also adverbs or conjunctions.

═══════════════════ **EXERCISE 5.33** ═══════════════════

Indicate whether the underscored words are subordinators or prepositions.

EXAMPLE
I was quite ill <u>until</u> yesterday. (*preposition*)

1. <u>During</u> the blizzard of 1978, many New Englanders feared for their lives.
2. <u>Because</u> over two feet of snow fell, many cities were paralyzed for up to a week.
3. Many stores ran out of food a few days <u>after</u> the blizzard.
4. Many people panicked <u>because of</u> the food shortages that resulted.
5. Most roads could not be traveled on <u>unless</u> one had a vehicle that could plow through all of the snow.
6. Most people spent the week <u>in</u> their houses.
7. They listened to the radio <u>for</u> reports from the outside world.
8. They played games with their families <u>so that</u> they could get their minds off the snow.
9. A few people died <u>from</u> the blizzard.
10. Fortunately, however, most people survived the blizzard and now think of it <u>as</u> an event that they will never forget.

EXERCISE 5.34: Summary

Identify the part of speech of the underscored word in each sentence. Select the appropriate term from among the following and write it at the end of the sentence: noun, pronoun, determiner, adjective, adverb, main verb, auxiliary, preposition, conjunction.

A. 1. For nearly fifty years Alberta Hunter had been singing the blues in cabarets and <u>concert</u> halls.
   2. She had <u>made</u> dozens of recordings.
   3. <u>Then</u> her mother died.
   4. <u>The</u> shock made her change to a nursing career.
   5. After twenty years she very suddenly returned <u>to</u> the stage.
   6. Her <u>voice</u> was better than ever.
B. 1. <u>Fresh</u> water is expensive in Saudi Arabia.
   2. One Saudi is investigating a new source <u>of</u> fresh water.
   3. His company <u>will</u> be supplying fresh water from an Antarctic icepack.
   4. Seven tugboats will <u>haul</u> a 100 million-ton iceberg to Saudi Arabia.
   5. The iceberg will be <u>covered</u> with insulating plastic.
   6. The water from <u>the</u> iceberg will sell for 50 cents a gallon.
C. 1. Testifying in court can be <u>risky</u>.
   2. It <u>can</u> also be time-consuming and costly.
   3. <u>Witnesses</u> need better protection.
   4. <u>They</u> worry about retribution.
   5. <u>Intimidation</u> of witnesses is a major problem.
   6. The criminal justice system <u>depends</u> on civilian witnesses.
   7. <u>In</u> many instances, the loss of one key witness means no case.
   8. The reluctance of witnesses is <u>understandable</u>.
   9. Cross-examination by a defense lawyer is <u>often</u> a fearful experience.
  10. Speedier trials <u>and</u> stiffer bail can help.
  11. Written testimony by witnesses <u>before</u> the trial is another solution.
  12. The <u>death</u> of the witness would not prevent the use of his written testimony.

EXERCISE 5.35: Summary

At the end of each sentence you will find a label for a part of speech. Underline any words in the sentence that belong to that part of speech.

EXAMPLE
   <u>The</u> South Bronx is <u>a</u> symbol of urban failure. · <u>determiners</u>

A. 1. Building after building stands empty. · <u>nouns</u>
  2. Entire blocks are vacant lots strewn with rubble. · <u>adjectives</u>
  3. An organization of neighborhood residents has recently begun to reno-
     vate abandoned buildings. · <u>nouns</u>
  4. Most of the members are Hispanic and black South Bronx residents.
     <u>conjunctions</u>
  5. Only a few had done construction work before. · <u>main verbs</u>
  6. Most of them gave the organization their spare time and their energy.
     <u>determiners</u>
  7. Skilled craftsmen taught them their trades. · <u>nouns</u>
  8. They have already renovated one apartment building and are working
     on others. · <u>auxiliaries</u>
  9. They want to create an urban village. · <u>pronouns</u>
 10. They have made one small area of the South Bronx beautiful to look at.
     <u>adjectives</u>
B. 1. Advertising agencies spend enormous sums on the production of some
     television commercials. · <u>nouns</u>
  2. Some of those commercials portray a fantasy land. · <u>determiners</u>
  3. Their scenarios approach the clarity and speed of our dreams. · <u>nouns</u>
  4. They encourage us to imagine life the way children do. · <u>main verbs</u>
  5. Every commercial creates an artificial universe in which we have the mag-
     ical power to change our size and shape in any way we wish. · <u>adjectives</u>
  6. Commercials are a part of the entertainment on television. · <u>nouns</u>
  7. No television addict can escape their influence. · <u>auxiliaries</u>
  8. They may be America's most important product. · <u>main verbs</u>

CHAPTER SIX

Sentences and Clauses

6.1 SENTENCE TYPES

In 2.4 I listed the four major types of sentences that are associated with four major uses in communication:

1. declaratives for statements
2. interrogatives for questions
3. imperatives for directives
4. exclamatives for exclamations

Most of the sentences that we looked at so far have been declaratives. In the sections that follow we will examine the other three types of sentences.

6.2 QUESTIONS

There are two main types of interrogative sentences:

(1) **Yes-no questions** begin with a verb. They require **subject–operator inversion,** that is, a reversal of the order of subject and verb (the order that is normal in declaratives). The verb that appears before the subject is an operator (cf. 3.3f).

> <u>Should</u> (op) <u>the Federal Government</u> (S) cut income taxes?
> <u>Does</u> (op) <u>this store</u> (S) open twenty-four hours every day?

They are called <u>yes</u>-<u>no</u> questions because they expect the answer <u>yes</u> or <u>no</u>. They may in fact be answered in other ways; for example, <u>Certainly</u>; <u>Perhaps</u>; <u>I don't know</u>; <u>What do you think</u>?

(2) **Wh-questions** begin with an interrogative word or phrase:

> <u>Why</u> should the Federal Government cut income taxes?
> <u>On which days</u> does this store open twenty-four hours?

They are called <u>wh</u>-questions because most of the interrogative words begin with <u>wh</u>- (the exception is <u>how</u>). The interrogative phrases contain an interrogative word such as <u>which</u> in <u>On which days</u>. The interrogative word in <u>wh</u>-questions represents a missing piece of information that the speaker wants the hearer to supply.

Wh-questions generally require subject-operator inversion too. The exception occurs when the interrogative word or phrase is the subject; in that case the normal subject-verb order applies:

> <u>Who</u> has taken my car?
> <u>Which bus</u> goes to Chicago?

There are also several other types of questions.

(3) **Declarative questions** have the form of a declarative sentence but the force of a question. They are signaled by a rising intonation in speech and by a question mark in writing:

> You know my name?
> He's got the key?

(4) **Alternative questions** present two or more choices, and the hearer is expected to reply with one of them. One type of alternative question resembles the form of <u>yes</u>-<u>no</u> questions:

> Should the government reduce the federal deficit by raising
> income taxes or by cutting expenditure?

The other type resembles <u>wh</u>-questions:

> Which do you want, coffee or tea?

(5) **Tag questions** are attached to sentences that are not interrogative. They invite the hearer to respond in agreement with the speaker:

> The Federal Government should cut income taxes, <u>shouldn't</u>
>   <u>it</u>?
> You haven't said anything yet, <u>have you</u>?

Tag questions have the form of <u>yes</u>-<u>no</u> questions. They consist of an operator and pronoun subject that echo the subject and operator of the sentence. The tag question is usually negative if the sentence is positive, and positive if the sentence is negative. Tag questions can be attached to imperative sentences; generally in these the subject is <u>you</u> and the operator is <u>will</u>:

> Don't tell him, <u>will you</u>?
> Make yourself at home, <u>won't you</u>?

(6) **Rhetorical questions** do not expect a reply since they are the equivalent of forceful statements. If the rhetorical question is positive it has negative force, and if it is negative it has positive force. The questions may resemble either <u>yes-no</u> questions or <u>wh</u>-questions:

> Is there anything more American than apple pie? (Surely
> there isn't . . .)
> Haven't you eyes? (Surely you have eyes.)
> Who could defend such a view? (Surely no one could . . .)

═══════════════════════ **EXERCISE 6.1** ═══════════════════════

Specify whether the sentences below are yes/no questions, wh-questions, declarative questions, alternative questions, or rhetorical questions, or have tag questions attached to them.

EXAMPLE
   Would you kindly move your car so that I can move mine? (*yes/no question*)

1. Should peace in Central America be achieved through diplomacy or through war?
2. Which tax form should I file if I wish to deduct my new computer?
3. The book hasn't been published yet, has it?
4. Should prisoners be released from prison simply because we've run out of cells to house them in?
5. Joan borrowed some money and wouldn't repay it?
6. What kind of dictionary is most useful for translating from English to French?
7. Should laws be passed that protect the rights of some but not others?
8. How many people do you think will attend the conference, twenty or thirty?
9. It's been a lovely day, hasn't it?
10. You say that he took your car without having your permission to do so?

======================= **EXERCISE 6.2** =======================

Rewrite each sentence, turning it into the type of question specified in parentheses.

EXAMPLE
>   We will be very lucky to arrive at the restaurant on time. (wh-question based on <u>at the restaurant</u>)
>   *Where will we be very lucky to arrive on time?*

1.   The budget can be balanced by raising taxes or cutting expenditures. (alternative question)
2.   You haven't seen the movie yet. (tag question)
3.   The voting rights bill will be passed at the next legislative session. (wh-question based on <u>The voting rights bill</u>)
4.   We must continue to protest against discrimination until it is no longer present in the United States. (rhetorical yes/no question)
5.   You said that our papers are due next month. (declarative question)
6.   Many professors at American universities must publish or run the risk of losing their jobs. (yes/no question)
7.   We've received numerous inquiries about the new treatment being offered for the disease. (tag question)
8.   Most of the students are absent because of the flu epidemic. (yes/no question)
9.   Many young children do not understand the importance of an education. (wh-question based on <u>the importance of an education</u>)
10. The group wanted to rent an expensive house on Martha's Vineyard. (declarative question)

6.3 IMPERATIVES

Imperative sentences usually do not have a subject. If there is no auxiliary, the verb has the base form:

>   <u>Take</u> a seat.
>   <u>Pass</u> me a coke.
>   <u>Make</u> us an offer.

Modal auxiliaries do not occur with imperatives, and the only auxiliary that occurs with any frequency is passive <u>be</u> (usually in the negative):

Don't be carried away with the idea.

<u>You</u> may be added as a second person subject:

<u>You</u> make us an offer.

Occasionally, a third person subject is used:

<u>Somebody</u> make us an offer.
<u>Those in the front row</u> sit down.

First and third person imperatives may be formed with <u>let</u> and a subject:

<u>Let us</u> go now.
<u>Let's</u> not tell him.
<u>Let me</u> think what I should do.
<u>Let nobody</u> move.

EXERCISE 6.3

Rewrite each sentence, turning it into an imperative sentence.

EXAMPLE
You should not stay out later than midnight.
Don't stay out later than midnight.

1. We should try to be as polite as possible to the visiting dignitaries.
2. You might offer to let them spend the night.
3. The boss requests that you work until 7:30.
4. You should try not to break any of the delicate glassware in the store.
5. Nobody can leave until the police have searched the building.
6. You should help yourself to a drink while I get dressed.
7. I'd be most happy if you'd pass me the salt.
8. We should take great care to do the best job we can.

6.4 EXCLAMATIVES

Exclamatives begin with <u>what</u> or <u>how</u>. <u>What</u> introduces noun phrases; <u>how</u> is used for all other purposes. The exclamative word or (more commonly) phrase is fronted:

What <u>a</u> <u>good</u> <u>show</u> it was! (It was an extremely good show.)
What <u>a</u> <u>time</u> we've had!
How <u>hard</u> she works!
How <u>strange</u> they look!
How <u>time</u> flies! (Time flies extremely fast.)

Exclamative sentences express strong feeling. More specifically, they indicate the extent to which the speaker is impressed by something. <u>What</u> and <u>how</u> are intensifiers expressing a high degree.

═══════════════════ **EXERCISE 6.4** ═══════════════════

Rewrite each sentence, turning it into an exclamation based on the underscored words.

EXAMPLE

We've had <u>a nice</u> time during our visit.
What a nice time we've had during our visit!

1. The paintings look <u>peculiar</u>.
2. The performance was <u>delightful</u>.
3. It's been <u>a long time</u> since we've had so much fun.
4. He's been acting <u>foolish</u> for the past few weeks.
5. My wife sent me <u>a lovely collection of antique glasses</u>.
6. The man looks <u>very unkempt</u> when he shows up for work.
7. It's been <u>extremely cold</u> all week.

6.5 SPEECH ACTS

When we say or write something, we are performing an action. This action expressed in words is a **speech act.** The intended effect in a speech act is the communicative purpose of the speech act.

In section 2.4 I referred to four major communicative uses associated with the four major types of sentences. We have already seen (cf. 6.2) that a sentence type may have a communicative use other than the one normally associated with it: A declarative question is a declarative sentence with the force of a question; a rhetorical question, on the other hand, is an interrogative sentence with the force of a statement.

There are many more than four types of communicative purpose. Directly or indirectly, we may convey our intention to promise, predict, warn, complain, offer, advise, and so on. The communicative purpose of a speech act depends on the particular context in which the act is performed. Here are some sentences, together with plausible interpretations of their purpose if they are uttered as speech acts:

> It's getting late. [*request for someone to leave with the speaker*]
> Tell me your phone number. [*inquiry—request for information*]
> There is a prospect of heavy thunderstorms later in the day. [*prediction*]
> I'm afraid that I've broken your vase. [*apology*]
> Break it, and you'll pay for it. [*warning*]
> Do you want a seat? [*offer*]
> I nominate Tony Palmer. [*nomination*]
> Enjoy yourself. [*wish*]
> Don't touch. [*prohibition*]
> I won't be late. [*promise*]
> It would be a good idea to send a copy to the manager. [*advice*]

The purpose may be merely to make a friendly gesture, where silence might be interpreted as hostility or indifference:

> It's a nice day, isn't it? [*ostensibly information*]
> How are you? [*ostensibly an inquiry*]

═══ EXERCISE 6.5 ═══

We speak or write for many different purposes; for example, to inform, promise, predict, warn, request, complain, boast, ask for information, ask for advice, be friendly. Explain what might be the communicative purpose of the following sentences. Select at least one plausible purpose.

1. It looks as if Spring is here at last.
2. Do you mind changing seats?
3. The new Certificate has some special features that other banks will not be offering.
4. Showers are likely on Wednesday.
5. Did you bring your car?
6. Help yourself to a drink.
7. Do you have any dimes on you?
8. The Soviets have made major advances in electronic warfare technology.

9. Break it, and you pay for it.
10. Do you have a light?

6.6 COMPOUND SENTENCES

A **multiple sentence** is a sentence that contains one or more clauses (structures that can be analyzed in terms of sentence elements such as subject). If the multiple sentence consists of two or more coordinated clauses, it is a **compound sentence.** The coordinated clauses are normally linked by a coordinator (or coordinating conjunction). The central coordinators are <u>and</u>, <u>or</u>, and <u>but</u>:

[1] She is a superb administrator, and everybody knows that.

[2] Lawns are turning green, flowers are blooming, and daylight savings time is returning.

[3] Send it to me by mail or bring it around yourself.

[4] They have played badly every year since 1980, but this year may be different.

Compound sentences have two or more **main clauses,** each with independent status. We cannot therefore speak of, say, "the subject of the sentence." In [1] for example, there is no subject of the sentence as a whole: the subject of the first main clause is <u>she</u> and the subject of the second main clause is <u>everybody</u>. In [2] there are three subjects of main clauses: <u>lawns</u>, <u>flowers</u>, and <u>daylight savings time</u>.

Instead of linking main clauses with a coordinator, we can often juxtapose them (place them side by side), and link them with a semicolon:

[1a] She is a superb administrator; everybody knows that.

[4a] They have played badly every year since 1980; this year may be different.

If we put a period between them, we have two orthographic sentences.

We sometimes avoid repeating identical expressions across coordinated clauses by **ellipsis** (the omission of essential grammatical units that can be supplied by the hearer from the context):

The adults ate rib steaks, the teenagers hamburgers, and the youngest children hot dogs. [*The verb* <u>ate</u> *is ellipted in the second and third clauses.*]

Last year we spent a vacation in Oregon, the year before in Colorado. [*The expression* <u>we spent a vacation</u> *is ellipted in the second clause.*]

========================= **EXERCISE 6.6** =========================

Join each pair of sentences with the conjunction given in parentheses. Wherever possible, eliminate redundancy by deleting words or using pronouns.

EXAMPLE

We arrived at the airport a little before 9:00. We soon afterwards took a taxi downtown to our hotel. (and)
We arrived at the airport a little before 9:00 and soon afterwards took a taxi downtown to our hotel.

1. Road construction in the long run improves driving conditions. In the short run, road construction causes great inconveniences for drivers. (but)

2. Drivers must endure traffic gridlocks. Traffic police must endure the stress that such delays cause. (and)

3. In most cities, road delays occur only during rush hour. In cities whose roads are under construction, road delays can occur at any time. (but)

4. This unpredictability makes driving very frustrating. Drivers often take out their anger on other drivers. (and)

5. Drivers honk their horns in frustration. Drivers cut off cars whose drivers they are angry at. (or)

6. This kind of behavior can lead to unnecessary accidents. This kind of behavior can lead to serious injury, even death. (and)

7. Drivers must realize that there is nothing they can do about traffic jams. Drivers must accept the fact that their trip home will be delayed a bit. (and)

8. Driving should be a pleasant experience for people. At the very least, driving should be an uneventful experience. (or)

6.7 COMPLEX SENTENCES

A **complex sentence** is a multiple sentence in which are embedded one or more **subordinate clauses**:

[1] Everybody knows that she is a superb administrator.

[2] He saw the trouble that idle gossip can cause.

[3] I am happy that you are joining our company.

In [1] the clause functions as a sentence element: the direct object. In [2] it is a modifier in a phrase: the postmodifier of the noun trouble. In [3] it is a complement in a phrase: the complement of the adjective happy.

Subordinate clauses are often introduced by a subordinator (or subordinating conjunction, cf. 5.31), particularly if the clauses are finite.

A complex sentence can be analyzed in terms of sentence elements such as subject and verb. In [1] the subject is <u>Everybody</u>, the verb is <u>knows</u>, and the direct object is the subordinate <u>that</u>-clause. In the subordinate clause, which is introduced by the subordinator <u>that</u>, <u>she</u> is the subject, <u>is</u> is the verb, and <u>a superb administrator</u> is the subject complement.

6.8 NONFINITE AND VERBLESS CLAUSES

Nonfinite and verbless clauses are generally subordinate clauses. **Nonfinite clauses** have a nonfinite verb (cf. 4.18); **verbless clauses** are without a verb.

There are three types of nonfinite clauses, depending on the form of the first verb in the verb phrase:

1. -<u>ing</u> clauses (or -<u>ing</u> participle clauses)

    [1] <u>Just thinking about the final round</u> put him in a combative mood.

2. -<u>ed</u> clauses (or -<u>ed</u> participle clauses)

    [2] <u>Dressed in street clothes</u>, the patient strolled in the garden.

3. infinitive clauses
    (a) with <u>to</u>

    [3] They wanted <u>to pay for their meal</u>.

    (b) without <u>to</u>

    [4] We helped <u>unload the car</u>.

Here are two examples of verbless clauses:

    [5] <u>Though fearful of road conditions</u>, they decided to go by car.
    [6] <u>Weary and almost out of money</u>, we drove into a gas station off the highway.

Nonfinite and verbless clauses can be regarded as reduced clauses, reduced in comparison with finite clauses. They often lack a subject, and verbless clauses also lack a verb. However, we can analyze them in terms of sentence elements if we reconstruct them as finite clauses, supplying the missing parts that we understand from the rest of the sentence:

[2]   Dressed in street clothes, . . . (V + A)
[2a]   They were dressed in street clothes. (S + V + A)

[4]   . . . unload the car. (V + dO)
[4a]   We unloaded the car. (S + V + dO)

[5]   Fearful of road conditions, . . . (SC)
[5a]   They were fearful of road conditions. (S + V + SC)

Nonfinite and verbless clauses may have their own subject:

> He nervously began his speech, **his voice** (S) <u>trembling</u> and **his face** (S) <u>flushed</u>.
> They trudged by the river in the deep snow, **their heads and their hands** (S) <u>bare</u>.

If they do not have a subject, their subject is generally interpreted as being identical in its reference with that of the subject of the sentence or clause in which they are embedded. This rule applies to sentences [2]–[6]. For [1] we deduce that the reference of the subject of <u>thinking</u> is identical with that of the object <u>him</u>.

Nonfinite and verbless clauses are sometimes introduced by subordinators (cf. 4.18). In sentence [5] the subordinator <u>though</u> introduces the verbless clause.

We saw earlier (3.7–12) that the choice of the verb determines the choice of other sentence elements. For example, a transitive verb requires a direct object. The verb also determines the form of the element, including whether it allows a clause and what type of clause. For example, the transitive verb <u>like</u> may have as its direct object a noun phrase, an infinitive clause, or an <u>-ing</u> clause:

I like
- vanilla ice cream.
- to shop at Macy's.
- shopping at Macy's.

The transitive verb <u>prefer</u>, on the other hand, takes as a direct object a noun phrase, an infinitive clause, an <u>-ing</u> clause, or a <u>that</u>-clause:

I prefer
- vanilla ice cream.
- to shop at Macy's.
- shopping at Macy's.
- that we shop at Macy's.

EXERCISE 6.7

Specify whether the underlined clauses are -ing clauses, -ed clauses, infinitive clauses, or verbless clauses.

EXAMPLE

Having finished their homework, the students went to a movie. (*-ing clause*)

1. Unhappy with his life, the man decided to change jobs.
2. Working as a manual laborer no longer appealed to him.
3. To better his condition in life, he decided to return to school.
4. Attending school, he met many people in situations similar to his.
5. Dissatisfied with their jobs, they too had decided to obtain college degrees.
6. They wanted to get better paying jobs.
7. The man diligently attended school for a year, hoping that he would find an area to major in that interested him.
8. After attending college for a year, he decided to major in business.
9. Convinced he would succeed, he studied hard for four years.
10. In four years he graduated, his degree in business giving him many career options.

EXERCISE 6.8

Join the sentences in each pair, making one of the sentences a subordinate clause. The subordinate clause should be of the form given in parentheses.

EXAMPLE

We took a bus to the convention. We couldn't afford to travel by plane. (finite clause with because)
Because we couldn't afford to travel by plane, we took a bus to the convention.

1. Writing is a process. It involves planning, drafting, and revising an essay. (finite clause with since)
2. Writers must discover their own personal writing processes. This is necessary to become a proficient writer. (nonfinite to infinitive clause based on become)
3. Some writers find it necessary to plan their essays in detail. Other writers like to sit down and simply begin writing. (finite clause with while)
4. Many beginning writers are not familiar with their writing proc-

esses. Many beginning writers do not write up to their abilities. (verbless clause headed by <u>not familiar</u>)

5. These writers will continue to find writing difficult and frustrating. They must discover a process of writing that works for them. (finite clause with <u>until</u>)

6. Most writers find writing difficult. With practice it becomes more enjoyable. (finite clause with <u>although</u>)

7. They learn to become more comfortable with their writing. They find writing quite rewarding and satisfying. (nonfinite ·ing clause based on <u>learn</u> and headed by <u>after</u>)

8. Many people may not write professionally for a living. Writing is a useful skill. (finite clause headed by <u>even though</u>)

9. There are so many uses for writing. These uses range from keeping a writing journal to writing formal essays. (non-finite ·ing clause based on <u>range</u>)

10. People need to take the time to learn how to write. This could prove to be a very satisfying and rewarding experience. (non-finite ·ing subject based on <u>take</u>)

6.9 FUNCTIONS OF SUBORDINATE CLAUSES

Subordinate clauses have three main sets of functions:

1. **Nominal clauses** have a range of functions similar to those of noun phrases (cf. 4.10). For example:

subject	<u>Saving energy</u> will help our balance of payments.
subject complement	The only problem in design is <u>to relate design to people's needs</u>.
direct object	I believe <u>that a hot, humid summer has benefited the movie business</u>.
prepositional complement	I listened to <u>what the candidates had to say</u>.

Nominal relative clauses are clauses that are introduced by nominal relative pronouns (cf. 5.22). Whereas relative clauses postmodify nouns, nominal relative clauses have the same functions as noun phrases:

He gave his children <u>what they wanted</u> (dO).
<u>Whoever said that</u> (S) does not understand the question.

2. **Modifier** and **complement clauses** function as modifiers and complements in phrases.

One common kind of modifier is the **relative clause** (cf. 4.5), which post-modifies a noun:

> <u>Drugs</u> <u>that are used in chemotherapy</u> damage a patient's healthy cells as well.

Nonfinite clauses function as reduced relative clauses:

> The townfighters battled an <u>inferno</u> <u>fueled by toxic chemicals at an illegal stockpile</u>. (that was fueled by . . .)
>
> Scientists found no <u>evidence</u> <u>to suggest that neutrinos have mass</u>. (that would suggest that . . .)
>
> I was engaged in a program of laborious <u>research</u> <u>involving many chemical reactions</u>. (that involved . . .)

A common kind of complement is the **comparative clause** introduced by <u>than</u> or <u>as</u>:

> She is a better doctor <u>than I am</u>.
> He spoke more rashly <u>than he used to do</u>.
> Norman plays as fiercely <u>as I expected</u>.

Another kind is the complementation of an adjective:

> Roger was afraid <u>to tell his parents</u>.

3. **Adverbial clauses** function as the adverbial element in sentence or clause structure (cf. 3.10):

> <u>If a heart attack occurs</u>, the electronic device automatically orders charges of electricity <u>to jolt the heart back into a normal rhythm</u>.
> <u>Reflecting on the past three years</u>, she wondered whether she could have made better choices.
> <u>When in Rome</u>, do as the Romans do.

═══════════════ **EXERCISE 6.9** ═══════════════

Specify whether the italicized constructions are nominal clauses, nominal relative clauses, relative clauses, reduced relative clauses, comparative clauses, or adverbial clauses.

EXAMPLE
> We spoke with the physician <u>who was treating our father</u>.
> (*relative clause*)

1. People know that it's spring <u>when the baseball season starts</u>.
2. Every season baseball teams travel to warm climates <u>where they can practice for the regular baseball season</u>.
3. <u>Starting in the spring</u> enables teams to prepare for the regular season.
4. <u>Because the regular season is so long</u>, players need the spring to get in good shape.
5. In addition, baseball is a sport <u>requiring much skill and talent</u>.
6. Players use spring training to develop these skills, <u>which they will use all season long</u>.
7. In spring training, some teams perform better <u>than others</u>.
8. In exhibition games, they will beat <u>whatever teams they play</u>.
9. <u>Although it's important to win in exhibition games</u>, most teams use spring training to discover who has talent on the team and who doesn't.
10. Managers know <u>that they have to field the best team that is possible</u>.
11. Consequently, they are more concerned with discovering their starting lineups than <u>winning every exhibition game they play</u>.
12. Many times teams have had bad exhibition records in spring training and go on to win the divisions <u>that they play in during the regular season</u>.
13. Other teams have won many exhibition games and have gone on to lose games <u>played during the regular season</u>.

===

EXERCISE 6.10

Make up sentences containing the subordinate clauses given below.

EXAMPLE
   clause headed by subordinator and functioning as adverbial
   After we attended the workshop, we went for a walk.

1. <u>to</u> infinitive clause functioning as subject
2. <u>-ing</u> clause functioning as adverbial
3. <u>-ed</u> clause functioning as adverbial
4. clause headed by subordinator and functioning as direct object
5. clause headed by subordinator and functioning as complement of an adjective
6. <u>-ing</u> clause functioning as subject complement
7. <u>to</u> infinitive clause functioning as postmodifier of a noun
8. verbless clause functioning as an adverbial

10 SENTENCE COMPLEXITY

The earlier division of multiple sentences into compound sentences and complex sentences (cf. 6.6–7) is an oversimplification. It indicates at the highest level within the sentence a distinction between coordination and subordination of clauses. But these two types of clause linkage may mingle at lower levels. A compound sentence may have subordination within one of its main clauses. In this compound sentence, the second main clause is complex:

> [1] Mite specialists have identified thirty thousand species of mites, <u>but</u> they believe <u>that</u> these represent only a tenth of the total number.

In [1], <u>but</u> introduces a main clause and <u>that</u> introduces a subordinate clause within the main clause. The <u>that</u>-clause is subordinate to the <u>but</u>-clause and not to the sentence as a whole: the <u>but</u>-clause is <u>superordinate</u> to the subordinate <u>that</u>-clause.

A complex sentence may contain a hierarchy of subordination:

> [2] They refused (A) <u>to say</u> (B) <u>what they would do</u> (C) <u>if the strikers did not return to their jobs</u>.

In [2] each of the subordinate clauses extends from the parenthesized letter that marks it to the end of the sentence: (A) is a direct object that is subordinate to the sentence as a whole and superordinate to (B); (B) is a direct object that is subordinate to (A) and superordinate to (C); (C) is an adverbial clause that is subordinate to (B).

The next example is a complex sentence whose subordinate clauses are coordinated:

> [3] They claimed <u>that the streets are clean, the trash is promptly collected, and the crime rate is low</u>.

In [3] the three coordinated subordinate clauses together constitute the direct object of the sentence.

In the final example, the compound sentence has both subordination and coordination at lower levels:

> [4] The Great Lake states warned pregnant women and nursing mothers to avoid eating certain Great Lakes fish <u>and</u> they advised the rest of us to avoid certain large fatty species and to limit the consumption of other fish.

The two main clauses are linked by <u>and</u> (underlined in the sentence). The first main clause contains a nonfinite subordinate clause (beginning <u>to</u> <u>avoid</u>) in which is embedded another nonfinite subordinate clause (<u>eating . . . fish</u>). The

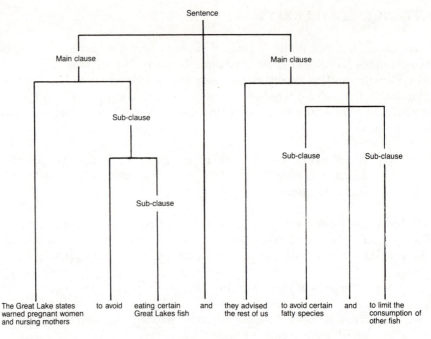

FIGURE **6.1**

second main clause contains two coordinated nonfinite subordinate clauses (to
avoid . . . and to limit . . .). The relationship of coordination and subordination
in [4] is represented in Figure 6.1.

6.11   THERE-STRUCTURES

In the remaining sections of this chapter we will examine some common structures that depart from the basic sentence patterns.

The first is the **there-structure.** There is put in the subject position and the
subject is moved to a later position:

> There is nobody outside. [*Compare:* Nobody is outside.]
> There are some topics that are best discussed in private.
>   [*Compare:* Some topics are best discussed in private.]
> There are several countries that have asked the Secretary-
>   General for an emergency session of the Security Council.
> There is somebody knocking on the door.

The effect of this structure is to present the postponed subject and the rest of
the sentence as new information and thereby to give the sentence (in particular
the subject) greater prominence. The postponed subject is normally an indefinite pronoun (cf. 5.23) or a noun phrase with an indefinite determiner (cf. 5.25).

===================== **EXERCISE 6.11** =====================

Convert the sentences below into sentences containing There-structures.

EXAMPLE

Nobody is in the room.
There is nobody in the room.

1. Many individuals do not take the time to eat well and exercise.
2. A dog in our neighborhood is constantly loose and always wander-
   ing into people's yards.
3. Many countries in the world do not give women the same rights
   as men.
4. A number of universities in the United States are worried about
   declining enrollments.
5. Somebody is at the door trying to get inside.
6. Nothing can be done about the excessive noise that comes from
   that house.
7. Many individuals give generously to their favorite charities.
8. A large park is within walking distance of our house.

6.12 CLEFT SENTENCES

In **cleft sentences** the sentence is divided into two and one part is given greater
prominence:

> It was Thomas Edison that (or who) invented the electric
> lamp. (*Compare*: Thomas Edison invented the electric lamp.)

In a cleft sentence, the subject is it, the verb is a form of be, and the emphasized
part comes next. The rest of the sentence is usually introduced by that:

> It was an American flag that he was waving.
> It was in 1939 that (or when) the Second World War started.
> It was after I spent a summer working for the Humane Soci-
>   ety that I decided to become a vegetarian.
> It was in San Francisco that Bob and Fiona fell in love.

Pseudo-cleft sentences have a similar purpose, but the emphasized part
comes at the end. The first part is normally a nominal relative clause (cf. 6.9)
introduced by what. The verb be links the two parts of this SVC structure:

> What I want is a good sleep.
> What he did was open my letters.
> What I'm going to do is see the principal.

═══════════════ EXERCISE 6.12 ═══════════════

Convert each sentence into a cleft or pseudo-cleft sentence that focuses the underlined words.

EXAMPLE

> Last week we visited the Museum of Fine Arts. (cleft)
> *It was last week that we visited the Museum of Fine Arts.*

1. We read a novel by Jonathan Swift in English class last week. (cleft)
2. Swift is one of the better English satirists. (cleft)
3. "A Modest Proposal" makes Swift appear vicious and cruel. (pseudo-cleft)
4. However, the essay is a satire. (pseudo-cleft)
5. Swift is not advocating that people eat their children. (pseudo-cleft)
6. Rather, he is dramatizing the bad conditions that existed in Ireland during this period. (cleft)
7. Many people misunderstand Swift. (cleft)
8. They mistakenly think that he is a misanthrope. (pseudo-cleft)
9. On the contrary, he was an individual deeply concerned about mankind. (pseudo-cleft)

6.13 ANTICIPATORY IT

It is unusual to have a nominal clause as the subject of the sentence:

[1] That the season has started so early seems a pity.

Instead, the subject is usually moved to the end (the "postponed subject") and its position is taken by it (the "anticipatory subject"):

[1a] It seems a pity that the season has started so early.

Here are some other examples:

> It is likely that we'll be moving to San Diego.
> It doesn't matter to me who pays my ticket.
> It's impossible to say when they are arriving.
> It has not been announced whether negotiations between the employers and the strikers have broken down.

The exception is that nominal -<u>ing</u> clauses are natural in the normal subject position:

> <u>Having a good self-image</u> keeps me sane.
> <u>Finding rattlesnake dens</u> provided rare excitement.

════════ EXERCISE 6.13 ════════

Convert the sentences below into sentences containing anticipatory <u>It</u>.

EXAMPLE

> That it will rain today is unlikely.
> *It is unlikely that it will rain today.*

1. Whether the contest is held here or in Hingham doesn't matter.
2. That I arrived late is not true.
3. That the strikers plan to come back to work soon is unlikely.
4. To submit a lengthy resume is unnecessary.
5. That the man graduated from college is remarkable.
6. Whether you finish the painting or not is irrelevant.
7. That U.S. forces have been moved into the region is more than a possibility.
8. To become mature and healthy adults is possible for children from divorced households.

════════ EXERCISE 6.14: Review ════════

Identify the function of the underlined subordinate clause by writing at the end of the sentence an appropriate abbreviation: S (subject), SC (subject complement), dO (direct object), iO (indirect object), OC (object complement), A (adverbial), oP (object of preposition), mN (modifier of noun phrase), m Adj (modifier of adjective phrase), or m Adv (modifier of adverb phrase).

EXAMPLE

> <u>Working for a newspaper</u> is a very rewarding career. S

1. Congress directed <u>that production of an American tank should start as planned.</u>
2. The Social Security Administration says that security has been heightened <u>since investigators visited field offices.</u>
3. A report has stated <u>that files are left around.</u>

4. The computer system allows employees to change files <u>if they wish</u>.
5. One employee told the computer that a beneficiary had moved <u>although in fact he had died</u>.
6. The embassy is a fitting accessory to the role <u>performed by U.S. envoys</u>.
7. The next decade should be economically smoother <u>than the one we have just been through</u>.
8. <u>Having a good self-image</u> keeps me sane and happy.
9. Metal-particle tapes accept and hold high-frequency magnetic pulses much more readily <u>than do metal-oxide tapes</u>.
10. She accused him of <u>wasting his talents</u>.
11. The factory <u>that had provided employment</u> was about to close.
12. His first job had been <u>selling insurance</u>.
13. Attempts <u>to duplicate the Tennessee Valley Authority's regional water management</u> have been made at home and abroad.
14. The visit of American scientists to China was announced after many American scientists decided <u>to discontinue their cooperation with Russian scientists</u>.
15. A presidential spokesman said <u>the China visit was not intended to play the Russians and Chinese off against each other</u>.
16. One theory of climate <u>that has gained wide acceptance</u> is used to predict the duration of periodic changes in climate.
17. When food is withdrawn from their stomach <u>after a meal is finished</u>, rats will compensate for the amount withdrawn.
18. We asked the Senate committee to postpone <u>considering the proposed legislation</u>.

=========== **Exercise 6.15: Review** ===========

Indicate whether each sentence is a statement, a question, a directive, or an exclamation.

EXAMPLE
Please leave immediately.
(*directive*)

1. Have you been able to see a game at Fenway Park yet this year?
2. Ask for some help carrying the table if you think you'll need it.
3. The visitors to the city decided to cancel their tour of the museum.
4. What a great time we had on our vacation!

5. Be sure to enclose a self-addressed stamped envelope with your order.
6. How much weight you've gained since I last saw you!
7. Is it too late to sign up for summer school?
8. Temperatures have been in the 50's most of the week.
9. Take one more step and you'll regret it.
10. What an enormous city New York is!

Exercise 6.16: Review

Indicate whether each sentence is compound or complex.

EXAMPLE

We've completed our part of the job, but the construction company hasn't as yet finished its part. (*compound*)

1. Society must adapt to people's needs, or people will not live happy lives.
2. The United States is a country whose buildings contain round doorknobs instead of levers.
3. Many handicapped people cannot open doors with round doorknobs, but they can open doors with levers.
4. Doorknobs are an inconvenience for the handicapped because they cannot be easily gripped.
5. Levers, in contrast, are much easier to hold, and therefore they are much easier to turn.
6. In general, many places are accessible only to those who are in good health.
7. While curbs pose little problem to the average person, to the handicapped they are an insurmountable obstacle.
8. An unshoveled sidewalk is a nuisance to the average person, but to the elderly it can cause pain and injury.
9. Our society must become more sensitive to the needs of the disabled and elderly, or we will cause this segment of society much hardship and inconvenience.

PART II

Applications

CHAPTER SEVEN

Punctuation

7.1 PUNCTUATION RULES

The rules for punctuation are conventions that have been developed by printers and publishers. In large part, punctuation helps the readers to understand the written communication by breaking it down into smaller components. The conventions also contribute to the appearance of the printed page, notably through paragraphing.

The conventions establish a measure of consistency for writers. Some conventions are obligatory: if we break them, we have made mistakes in punctuation. Others are optional: we can make better or worse choices in particular circumstances, depending on the effects we wish to convey. To that extent, punctuation is an art.

Some punctuation marks are intended to represent pauses that we should make in our reading. In [1] below, the author has chosen to enclose two words in commas to indicate that they are to be read with pauses on either side. The effect of the separating pauses is rhetorical: they emphasize the addition of and useful.

> [1] There is a very high probability that whatever astonishes us in biology today will turn out to be usable, and useful, tomorrow. [Lewis Thomas, The Medusa and the Snail, p. 172. New York: The Viking Press, 1979]

We do not always insert punctuation marks where we pause in speech, however. We would be likely to read or speak the sentence in [2] with a pause (or a break in our intonation) after the word agencies:

> [2] Funding of scientific research projects by federal agencies is an important channel for federal financial support of the universities.

The punctuation system, however, does not allow a comma after <u>agencies</u>. There is a punctuation rule that forbids a comma between the subject and predicate unless the comma is the first of a pair of commas, as in [2a]. Here the parenthetic <u>on the other hand</u> is separated by a pair of commas:

[2a]   Funding of scientific research projects by federal agencies, <u>on the other hand</u>, is an important channel for federal financial support of the universities.

The rule forbidding a comma after <u>agencies</u> in [2] depends on the grammar of the sentence: the analysis of the sentence into subject and predicate. Some punctuation rules involve grammar and others involve meaning. We will be looking at such rules in the sections that follow.

EXERCISE 7.1

Read the following paragraph and mark where you pause. How many of the places where you paused have punctuation marks and how many do not? You will find it convenient to use a tape recorder for this exercise.

It seems to me that the safest and most prudent of bets to lay money on is surprise. There is a very high probability that whatever astonishes us in biology today will turn out to be usable, and useful, tomorrow. This, I think, is the established record of science itself, over the past two hundred years, and we ought to have more confidence in the process. It worked this way for the beginnings of chemistry; we obtained electricity in this manner; using surprise as a guide, we progressed from Newtonian physics to electromagnetism, to quantum mechanics and contemporary geophysics and cosmology. In biology, evolution and genetics were the earliest big astonishments, but what has been going on in the past quarter century is simply flabbergasting. For medicine, the greatest surprises lie still ahead of us, but they are there, waiting to be discovered or stumbled over, sooner or later.

[Lewis Thomas, <u>The Medusa and the Snail</u>, pp. 172–3. New York: The Viking Press, 1979]

7.2   SENTENCE FRAGMENTS AND FRAGMENTARY SENTENCES

Sentence Fragment

A **sentence fragment** is a set of words that is punctuated as a sentence even though it is not grammatically an independent sentence. Experienced writers can set a tone in their writing that allows them to violate the rules of punctuation through their intentional use of sentence fragments. When inexperienced writers violate these rules, their readers are given the impression that the writers do not know the rules. On the whole, it is safer for writers to avoid using fragments in formal writing until they are experienced enough to sense when it is appropriate to use them. Here are three types of sentence fragments to avoid:

1. subordinate clauses

Japanese students spend a mere 100 hours a year on mathematics in the seventh grade. While American students spend as much as 145 hours. [*Replace the period with a comma.*]

The letter grading system is better than the pass/fail system. Because the grades motivate students to work harder. [*Omit the period or replace it with a comma.*]

I woke up late the next morning. My head throbbing and my stomach burning. [*Replace the period with a comma or a dash.*]

2. loosely joined phrases

She noticed some pieces of paper on the floor of the car. Apparently receipts from a used car lot. [*Replace the period with a comma or a dash.*]

Our class was rowdy during the senior year. Especially during the last two months. [*Replace the period with a comma or a dash.*]

The legislators have made an effort to deal with the problem of teenage alcoholism. An effort that with the support of school officials can help the police to enforce the ban on the legal drinking age. [*Replace the period with a comma or—perhaps because it is a long appositive (cf. 4.7)—with a colon.*]

3. coordinated expressions

Some of his students became interested in environmental problems. And later helped to reduce the environmental price of progress and prosperity. [*Replace the period with a comma.*]

They have abandoned their homes. And taken all their possessions with them. [*Replace the period with a comma.*]

He gossiped about other people's relationships. And even his own. [*Replace the period with a comma or a dash.*]

Sentence fragments are occasionally used in print, particularly in advertising, to suggest a dramatic pause or an afterthought:

> You'll enjoy the taste of this wine. Because we care for our grapes as if they are children.

Fragmentary Sentences

Fragmentary sentences are sentences that are grammatically incomplete but can be completed from the verbal context (cf. 2.2). In written dialogue they are particularly common for responses, and their use in such contexts is perfectly appropriate.

> A: What did she tell you?
> B: To help myself to food. (She told me to help myself to food.)
>
> A: I heard you passed your driving test.
> B: After failing three times. (I passed it after failing three times.)

Fragmentary sentences are also common and appropriate in fictional description and narration, representing informal speech:

> My hole is warm and full of light. Yes, full of light.
> [Ralph Ellison, Invisible Man, p. 6. New York: Vintage Books, 1947]

In the next example (from a novel), all the sentences except the first are fragmentary. The first sentence (ending in a semicolon) provides the clue to their interpretation. For most of them we would supply an initial She was, She had, or She had a to make them grammatically complete.

> Dr von Haller looked younger than I; about thirty-eight, I judged, for though her expression was youthful there was a little gray in her hair. Fine face; rather big features but not coarse. Excellent nose, aquiline if one wished to be complimentary but verging on the hooky if not. Large mouth and nice teeth, white but not American-white. Beautiful eyes, brown to go with her hair. Pleasant low voice and a not quite perfect command of colloquial English. Slight accent. Clothes unremarkable, neither fashionable nor dowdy, in the manner Caroline calls "classic." Altogether a person to inspire confidence.
> [Robertson Davies, The Deptford Trilogy, p. 282. Harmondsworth, Middlesex: Penguin Books, 1977]

These final examples of fragments appear in a paragraph by a writer of popular science:

Our variation displays all the difficulties that make taxonomists shudder (or delight in complexity) and avoid the naming of subspecies. Consider just three points. <u>First, discordance of characters</u>. We might make a reasonable division on skin color, only to discover that blood groups imply different alliances. When so many good characters exhibit such discordant patterns of variation, no valid criterion can be established for unambiguous definition of subspecies. <u>Second, fluidity and gradations</u>. We interbreed wherever we move, breaking down barriers and creating new groups. Shall the Cape Colored, a vigorous people more than two million strong and the offspring of unions between Africans and white settlers (the ancestors, ironically, of the authors of apartheid and its antimiscegenation laws), be designated a new subspecies or simply the living disproof that white and black are very distinct? <u>Third, convergences</u>. Similar characters evolve independently again and again; they confound any attempt to base subspecies on definite traits. Most indigenous tropical people, for example, have evolved dark skin.

[Stephen Jay Gould, <u>The Flamingo's Smile</u>, p. 194.
Harmondsworth, Middlesex: Penguin Books, 1986]

========================= **EXERCISE 7.2** =========================

Rewrite the following sentences to avoid sentence fragments.

1. People buy electric kitchen gadgets that they do not need. For example hot dog cookers.
2. The smaller skulls were found near primitive shelters. Whereas the larger skulls were found in the hunting grounds.
3. For the last month, he has been drinking more heavily. Quarreling with his wife. Trying to make up his mind what to do.
4. Nothing has ever happened in this town. No triumphs. No tragedies.
5. Watching television, you see election meetings far away. In farmhouses in Iowa. And in schoolhouses in New Hampshire.
6. It is important to eat fresh fish. Because previously frozen fish can be rubbery and very untasty.
7. If individuals do not take the time to exercise regularly, they run the risk of becoming obese. And having a heart attack.
8. We stayed for the entire concert. Even though we thought it was too long and not especially good.
9. I visited them in their new home. A condo in the Back Bay.
10. Students should take school seriously. And attend class as regularly as possible.

═══════════════════════ **EXERCISE 7.3** ═══════════════════════

This paragraph contains several sentence fragments. Correct the punctuation to remove the sentence fragments. Attach them to the previous sentence or change them into sentences.

> Science is a way of thinking. Much more than it is a body of knowledge. Its goal is to find out how the world works. To seek what regularities there may be. To penetrate to the connections of things. From subnuclear particles, which may be the constituents of all matter, to living organisms, the human social community, and thence to the cosmos as a whole. Our intuition is by no means an infallible guide. Our perceptions may be distorted. By training or prejudice or merely because of the limitations of our sense organs. Which, of course, perceive directly but a small fraction of the phenomena of the world. Even so straightforward a question as whether in the absence of friction a pound of lead falls faster than a gram of fluff was answered incorrectly by Aristotle. And almost everyone else before the time of Galileo. Science is based on experiment. On a willingness to challenge old dogma. On an openness to see the universe as it really is. Accordingly, science sometimes requires courage. At the very least the courage to question the conventional wisdom.
>
> [adapted from *Broca's Brain* by Carl Sagan, p. 13.
> New York: Random House, 1974.]

7.3 RUN-ON SENTENCES AND COMMA SPLICES

In [1] we have two separate sentences:

> [1]   I used to be afraid of him. I have since gotten to know him well.

We can join them into one sentence by simply putting a semicolon between them:

> [1a]   I used to be afraid of him; I have since gotten to know him well.

The general rule is that if we juxtapose sentences, as in [1] and [1a], we must use a major punctuation mark. The major punctuation marks are periods, question marks, exclamation marks, colons, semicolons, and dashes. If we fail to use any mark at all, the resulting error is a **run-on sentence,** as in [1b]:

> [1b]   I used to be afraid of him I have since gotten to know him well. [*Correct by inserting a major punctuation mark after* afraid of him.]

If we use a comma instead of a major mark, the resulting error is a **comma splice,** as in [1c]:

[1c] I used to be afraid of him, I have since gotten to know him well. [*Replace the comma with a major punctuation mark.*]

Here are further examples of run-on sentences:

It did not matter to me whether or not I had made an impact on the world I just wanted to learn as much as possible. [*Insert a major punctuation mark after* the world.]

Ask the first person you see if they will help you I am sure they will. [*Insert a major punctuation mark after* help you.]

And here are further examples of comma splices:

I visited them in their new home, it was a large apartment with a living room, kitchen, dining alcove, and two bedrooms. [*Replace the comma after* home *with a major punctuation mark.*]

To attract tourists Indianapolis set out to become a sports center, it poured more than 180 million dollars into world-class sports facilities. [*Replace the comma after* small *with a major punctuation mark.*]

Comma splices are most likely to occur when a linking adverb (e.g., therefore, nevertheless) or a linking prepositional phrase (e.g., in spite of that, as a result) comes between the two sentences. A semicolon is the normal major punctuation mark if the two sentences are combined:

[2] They lost the battle, nevertheless they were determined to continue the war. [*Correct by replacing the comma with a major punctuation mark.*]

[3] The states supervise those programs, as a result the federal government has no responsibility for their efficiency. [*Correct by replacing the comma with a major punctuation mark.*]

These linking expressions do not have to come between the two sentences. They can be moved elsewhere in the second sentence, as in [2a] and [2b]:

[2a] They lost the battle; they were determined, nevertheless, to continue the war.

[2b] They lost the battle; they were determined to continue the war nevertheless.

There is one exception to the general rule. We may use commas between juxtaposed sentences if they are short and are similar in their structure. Usually, there is a set of three sentences, as in [4] and [5]:

[4] Most of the wealthy people who have put up their money for college tuitions have become involved with the schools they adopted and the kids who attend them. They counsel, they mediate, they encourage. [Richard Cohen in International Herald Tribune, 15 July 1987, p. 5; reprinted from The Washington Post]

[5] His round face was mournful, his shoulders slumped, his belly sagged. [Tom Wicker, A Time to Die, p. 92. New York: Ballantine Books, 1975]

But the sentence may consist of just two parallel clauses involving a kind of comparison, as in [6] and [7]:

[6] The sooner he finishes, the better he will feel.

[7] The more they earned, the more they wanted.

EXERCISE 7.4

Correct the errors in run-on sentences and comma splices.

1. One of the more popular methods of reducing waste is by incineration, this method is used where land is scarce for burial.
2. It is not clear if these small high schools are intended for disruptive students, if they are, I am not in favor of them.
3. We took the early bus to school our younger brother stayed home because he was ill.
4. Ask the first persons you see if they can help you I am sure they will.
5. Society may have to put restrictions on medical care, otherwise the medical system will break down.
6. He is not the world's leading authority on coins, however, he is often consulted by foreign buyers.
7. Linda was four years old she could write her own name.
8. The President's approval rating was dropping toward 25 percent, as a result the White House increased the campaign staff.
9. Teenagers are less likely than adults to exercise restraint, therefore their drinking can lead to damaging results.
10. The talk was held on Friday not many people attended it.

7.4 COORDINATED MAIN CLAUSES

Instead of juxtaposing sentences, we can often link them with a coordinator as two main clauses within one sentence. When we use a coordinator, we can put merely a comma between the clauses. In [1d] below, the coordinator <u>but</u> follows a comma:

[1d] I used to be afraid of him, but I have since gotten to know him well.

The central coordinators are <u>and</u>, <u>or</u>, and <u>but</u>. The marginal coordinators, which resemble the central coordinators in that they must come between the clauses, can also be used merely with a preceding comma: these are <u>for</u>, <u>nor</u>, <u>so</u> ("therefore"), and <u>yet</u>. Here are examples with the three central coordinators and the other linking words.

They were highly successful in the competition for grant support, <u>and</u> each grant provided jobs for technicians and other workers.

He ought to admit that he is responsible for what he is doing, <u>or</u> he ought not to do it all.

A loud quarrel was going on, <u>but</u> they could not hear the details from outside.

Peace is by no means assured, <u>for</u> several cabinet ministers are opposed to key paragraphs in the draft treaty.

He will not survive long if the revolution comes, <u>nor</u> does he wish to.

A storm damaged their radio, <u>yet</u> they were able to send messages.

She was refused admission, <u>so</u> she complained to the manager.

The central coordinators may also link clauses without a punctuation mark, particularly if the clauses are short:

The Administration's plan will help the balance of payments <u>and</u> it will heighten confidence in the dollar.

We may want to use major punctuation marks between coordinated main clauses because they are long, because we want to emphasize that each clause is a separate unit, or because one or more of the clauses has internal commas:

They're bored with TV; <u>and</u> they're bored with movies; <u>and</u> they're bored with stereo systems; <u>and</u> they're bored with athletics.

She is now president of the company, a position she had long waited for; her two sons have graduated from major universities; and to her great joy, she has recently become a grandmother.

On the other hand, we should not use a period or a semicolon to separate a subordinate clause from the main clause. Using a period results in a sentence fragment (cf. 7.2), and a similar mistake results from using a semicolon:

He told a social security investigator that she had moved; although in fact she had died. [*Replace the semicolon with a comma.*]

EXERCISE 7.5

Insert commas to separate main clauses joined by central and marginal coordinators.

1. The woman was very anxious about her upcoming job interview and she spent many hours worrying about it.
2. She had always wanted to be a stockbroker but she was still nervous about changing jobs.
3. Presently she was employed as a legal secretary for a law firm and she knew that at this job she was very underemployed.
4. She knew she had to change jobs yet she was afraid of not being hired as a stockbroker.
5. She woke up early the morning of her interview for she wanted to have plenty of time to get ready for it.
6. Her alarm went off promptly at 7:00 and she walked sleepily into the bathroom to take a shower.
7. After showering, she ate breakfast but she wasn't very hungry.
8. She knew that she had to eat something or she would be tired by early afternoon.
9. She prepared herself a couple of eggs so she would have sufficient strength to endure the interview.
10. She didn't want to eat the eggs nor did she want to be hungry later.
11. However, she forced herself to eat the eggs and she felt much better after doing so.

7.5   DIRECT SPEECH

We use **direct** speech when we report the actual words that somebody has said or written. It is normal to enclose direct speech in two pairs of double quotation marks, an opening pair and a closing pair.

In dialogue, direct speech often comes with a **reporting clause,** such as she said. Sentences [1]–[3] illustrate the usual punctuation of direct speech with a reporting clause when the direct speech is a declarative sentence. The reporting clause can appear in one of three positions:

> [1]   He said to us, "The solution is in your hands."
> [2]   "The solution is in your hands," he said to us.
> [3]   "The solution," he said to us, "is in your hands."

When we report the original in our own words, we use **indirect speech:**

> He told us that the solution was in our hands.

Rules for Punctuating Direct Speech

The following are the rules for punctuating direct speech with a reporting clause.

(a)   initial reporting clause, as in [1]

It is usual to put a comma after the reporting clause and before the initial quotation marks:

> [4]   She told them, "We should not waste food when millions are starving."

We may use a colon instead of a comma, particularly if the direct speech contains more than one sentence:

> [5]   As one man put it after the expedition: "When you are on the side of a volcano watching blocks of lava careening down a gully in front of you, so close that you can feel the heat from them, you get an impression that never leaves your mind."

If, as in [5], the quotation is centered, it is not necessary to use quotation marks, since the layout is a sufficient indication of direct speech.

If the quotation ends the sentence, we put a period, a question mark, an exclamation mark, or a dash before the final quotation marks. The period is illustrated in [1], [3], and [4]. The other three marks are illustrated in [6]–[8]:

[6]   The reporter asked, "Has the general arrived?"

[7]   The crowd cried, "Long live the President!"

[8]   She said, "I have done my share, but you—"

The dash in [8] indicates that the speaker has stopped in mid-sentence.

   If the question mark or exclamation mark belongs to the sentence as a whole (not to the direct speech), it goes outside the closing quotation marks:

[9]   Did she say, "It is against my religious principles"?

[10]   He actually said, "I am too busy to see you"!

In the rare situation when the question mark or exclamation mark belongs both to the sentence and to the direct speech, use only one mark and put it before the quotation marks:

   Did she say, "Is it against your religious principles?"

(b) final reporting clause, as in [2]

If the direct speech sentence would ordinarily end in a period, put a comma before the quotation marks:

[11]   "I'm not yet ready," he replied.

Otherwise, use a question mark or exclamation mark as appropriate:

[12]   "Do you know the way?" she asked.

[13]   "Lights!" he screamed.

   The sentence may continue after the reporting clause:

[11a]   "I'm not yet ready," he replied, and put down the telephone.

[11b]   "I'm not yet ready," he replied; then he picked up the telephone.

(c) medial reporting clause, as in [3]

The medial clause combines punctuation features associated with the initial and final reporting clause. The punctuation <u>before</u> the medial clause is the same as for the final reporting clause:

[14]   "I'm not yet ready," he replied. "You go ahead without me."
         [cf. [11]]

[15]   "Do you know the way?" she asked. "I'm lost." [cf. [12]]

[16]   "Lights!" he screamed. "Give me lights!" [cf. [13]]

If the reporting clause interrupts a sentence, use a comma even if the sentence would ordinarily have no punctuation:

[17]   "When you are ready," he said, "let me know." [*cf*: When you are ready, let me know.]

[18]   "I know," he said, "that they suspect me." [*cf*: I know that they suspect me.]

The punctuation after the medial reporting clause depends on whether the first part is an independent sentence. If it is, a period follows the reporting clause, as in [14]–[16]. If the reporting clause interrupts the sentence, where the sentence would ordinarily have either a comma or no punctuation, as in [17] and [18], then a comma follows the clause. If the reporting clause is placed where the sentence would ordinarily have a semicolon, the semicolon follows the reporting clause:

[19]   "The first two attempts to amend the constitution by convention succeeded," the senator said; "the next two attempts failed."

The punctuation at the end of the sentence is the same as for the initial reporting clause. Thus we have a period before the final pair of closing quotation marks in [14]–[15] and in [17]–[19], and an exclamation mark in [16]. Here are two further examples:

[20]   "Did you say," she asked, "that she would see me now?"

[21]   "I have done my share," she said, "but you—"

It is normal to start a new paragraph when there is a change of speaker, whether or not the direct speech is accompanied by a reporting clause:

"What was written in the letter?" she asked.
"I can't tell you. I couldn't read it."
"Why not?"
"It was in Spanish."

Use single quotation marks for a quotation within a quotation:

"I said I'd take the job. Then I went to bed and thought, 'What am I doing?' I don't want my kids to say, 'He was a good football coach.' I want them to think that I tried to do more than that."

=========================== **EXERCISE 7.6** ===========================

Insert quotation marks where necessary.

1. Do you like it here? asked Bob Portman.
2. I have lived here all my life, said Sally Mason with pride.
3. You have lived here all your life! he said.
4. I was born here, and my father before me, and my grandfather, and my great-grandfathers. She turned to her brother. Isn't that so?
5. Yes, it's a family habit to be born here! the young man said with a laugh.
6. Your house must be very old, then, said Bob.
7. How old is it, brother? asked Sally.
8. It was built in 1783, the young man replied. That's old or new, according to your point of view.
9. Your house has a curious style of architecture, said Bob.
10. Are you interested in architecture? asked the young man.
11. Well, I took the trouble, this year, said Bob, to visit about fifty churches. Do you call that interested?
12. Perhaps you are interested in theology, said the young man ironically.
13. Not particularly, said Bob.
14. The young man laughed and stood up. Good, he exclaimed. I'll show you the house.
15. Sally grasped Bob's arm. Don't let him take you, she said; you won't find it interesting. Wouldn't you prefer to stay with me?
16. Certainly! said Bob. I'll see the house some other time.

7.6 CITATIONS

We use words in a special way when we refer to them as words. Compare [1] with [2]:

[1] They are in love.

[2] *Love* can be either a verb or a noun.

In [1] *love* is used in the normal way. In [2] it is the word *love* that is being discussed. When a word or phrase is cited—quoted or mentioned rather than used in the normal way—it is either put in double quotation marks or underlined. (Underlining in writing is the equivalent of italics in print.) If you are going to use many such citations or if you need quotation marks for other purposes, it would be clearer to use underlining rather than quotation marks. Definitions and translations of words and phrases are usually in single quotation marks:

> *Perennial* 'perpetual' or 'recurring' has its roots in the Latin *per* ('through') and *annus* ('year').

Titles of works are also a special use of language. If the works are published or produced separately (for example, books, magazines, movies, musical compositions), they are underlined. But if the titles are for part of a larger work (for example, articles, chapters, short stories, songs), they are enclosed in double quotation marks:

> I read the report in the *New York Times*.
> You can find that character in *A Streetcar Named Desire*.
> My favorite Beatles song is "Eleanor Rigby."

Contrast:

> *Hamlet* is a complex play.
> Hamlet is a complex character.

EXERCISE 7.7

Insert underlining and quotation marks where necessary.

1. She was in Cambodia as a reporter for the Sunday Times, a London newspaper.
2. Henry Green's first novel, Blindness, is divided into three parts: Caterpillar, Chrysalis, and Butterfly.
3. Do you like Frank Sinatra's song Tennessee Newsboy?
4. Words like doctor and lawyer can be used for both sexes.
5. Alex Haley's book Roots was made into a powerful television serial.
6. Natural History is the official magazine of the American Museum of Natural History in New York.
7. Monsoon comes from the Arabic mansim, meaning season.
8. You can find the story in Sports Illustrated.
9. Your article Were the Vikings the First to Arrive? is not accurate.
10. Some people avoid using die, preferring a euphemism like pass on.

7.7 QUESTIONS

The general rule is that a question mark comes at the end of an interrogative sentence:

> Is our nation prepared for further sacrifices?

The rule also applies to tag questions (cf. 6.2):

> There is nothing more American than apple pie, <u>is there</u>?

It extends to declarative questions, which have the structure of a declarative sentence but function as a question (cf. 6.2):

> You know the rules?

It is usual to put an exclamation mark at the end of an exclamatory question to ensure that it is read as an exclamation:

> Haven't you grown!
> Am I thirsty!

It is usual to put a period at the end of a question beginning <u>Would you</u> that is intended as a polite request, particularly if the sentence is long. This usage is common in official letters. In this context the writer expects the fulfilling of the request, not a reply to the question:

> Would you please send me a copy of the instructional book that should have been enclosed with the microwave oven.

Do not use a question mark for an indirect question, that is, a question in indirect speech. Contrast the direct question in [1] with the indirect question in [2]:

[1] He asked, "Who wants to speak?"
[2] He asked who wanted to speak.

==================== **EXERCISE 7.8** ====================

Some of the sentences below contain unnecessary question marks. Eliminate the question marks that are not needed.

1. Are Americans ready to pay higher taxes to balance the national budget?

2. Would you please include payment for the magazines along with your subscription form?

3. The instructor inquired whether we had finished our essays yet?

4. The instructor inquired, "Have you finished your essays yet?"

5. It's time to leave now, isn't it?

6. Will foreign governments continue to tolerate American intervention in their foreign affair policies?

7. Would you kindly respond to this letter within three days of receiving it?

8. My mother asked us whether we were coming over for dinner on Saturday?

9. We don't have any reason to go to school today, do we?

10. The homeless man asked, "Do you have a spare quarter that I could have?"

7.8 RESTRICTIVE AND NONRESTRICTIVE RELATIVE CLAUSES

Relative clauses postmodify nouns (cf. 4.5):

[1] the house that they bought last year
[2] a student who belongs to our group
[3] the place where we first met

The three examples above are **restrictive** relative clauses. Restrictive clauses identify more closely what the nouns refer to. The house in [1] might be in contrast with the house that they used to live in. The student in [2] might be in contrast with a student who belongs to another group. The place in [3] might be in contrast with a place where we met last week.

Nonrestrictive relative clauses do not identify. They offer additional information:

[4] their present house, which they bought last year,
[5] Jean, who belongs to our group,
[6] San Francisco, where we first met,

The house in [4] is identified by their present. The person in [5] and the place in [6] are identified by their names. Names rarely need further identification, but it is possible to use a restrictive clause if further identification is necessary, as in [7]:

[7] The Jimmy Robinson who was in my high school senior class has just graduated from college.

Restrictive clauses should not be punctuated. Nonrestrictive clauses, on the other hand, should be enclosed in punctuation marks. The usual punctuation is a pair of commas, as in [8], unless a major punctuation mark (cf. 7.3) would ordinarily appear at the end of the nonrestrictive clause, as in [9] and [10]:

[8] The regulations, <u>which took effect last fall</u>, list over five hundred industrial processes and materials as hazardous.

[9] Americans are becoming like Europeans, <u>who prefer to buy goods that last a long time</u>.

[10] I had grown tired of my old stereo, <u>which I had bought twelve years ago</u>; however, I could not afford to buy a new one.

Dashes or parentheses are sometimes also used to enclose nonrestrictive clauses. Dashes indicate dramatic pauses and parentheses separate the clause more distinctly.

Nonrestrictive clauses may refer back not only to a noun, but also to a previous part of the sentence:

He had failed his driving test, <u>which must be discouraging</u>.
(His having failed . . . must be discouraging.)

She reads financial publications and studies the daily market tabulations, <u>which is unusual for a fifteen-year-old</u>. (Reading financial publications and studying is unusual for a fifteen-year-old.)

The distinction between restrictive and nonrestrictive applies also to reduced relative clauses—nonfinite clauses that correspond to relative clauses. Contrast the restrictive clause in [11] and the nonrestrictive clause in [12]:

[11] research <u>involving chemical reactions</u>
[12] his recent research, <u>involving chemical reactions</u>,

Here are further examples of restrictive clauses:

Industries <u>that deal with wood products</u> have been replacing oil-guzzling driers and kilns with devices <u>that burn scrap wood</u>.

There are many voters <u>that oppose the Administration's policies on Central America</u>.

You must meet the people <u>arranging the party</u>.

They checked earlier measurements <u>made by federally funded laboratories</u>.

These are the best courses <u>to register for</u>.

Here are further examples of nonrestrictive clauses:

The Brady cactus, <u>which is small and single-stemmed</u>, retracts its head into the soil during dry hot spells.

The technology has opened up astonishing new possibilities, <u>many of which are already being exploited</u>.

Human infants pass through a critical period, <u>lasting a few years</u>, during which they acquire language.

My sister, <u>now retired</u>, lives in the San Francisco area.

EXERCISE 7.9

Leave the restrictive clauses below unpunctuated. Punctuate the nonrestrictive clauses with commas.

1. She phoned the Women's Crisis Service which advised her to call the police.
2. Our yearly salvage operation scheduled to last six months has just begun.
3. Teenagers who drive while under the influence of alcohol should have their driver's licenses revoked.
4. Americans came to accept the theories of John Locke who wrote widely on child rearing.
5. I hate attending meetings which last longer than an hour.
6. The FBI which at one time gloried in stopping bank robbers is now turning its attention toward the bigger-money white-collar crimes.
7. All people living in the Boston area have to pay quite a bit of money to live comfortably.
8. This VC engine redesigned since last year has grown smoother and quieter.
9. Mr. Smith puffing heavily on a cigar was shoveling snow from his sidewalks.
10. You can't trust customers who refuse to place a down payment on products that they buy.

7.9 RESTRICTIVE AND NONRESTRICTIVE APPOSITION

Apposition expresses a relationship of some equivalence between two units (cf. 4.6f):

> The civil servants often switch from English, the official language, to their native languages.

The relationship can be demonstrated by linking the two units with the verb be:

> English is the official language.

The second unit is generally appositive to the first.

Like relative clauses (cf. 7.8), appositives are restrictive or nonrestrictive: restrictive appositives identify more closely the preceding noun, whereas nonrestrictive appositives offer additional information. And as with relative clauses, restrictive appositives are not punctuated, whereas nonrestrictive appositives are enclosed in punctuation marks, normally a pair of commas but occasionally dashes or parentheses. Appositives may be either noun phrases or clauses.

Here are examples of restrictive appositives:

> My brother Tom is an architect.
> Do you know the meaning of the word "perjorative"?
> I heard on the radio the news that the President had been reelected.
> The fact that she likes the job suggests that she will remain here for a long while.

Here are examples of nonrestrictive apposition:

> The genuine American hamburger, a ground beef patty served on a bun, was invented at the beginning of the twentieth century.

> The most reliable indication of Islam's revival is the observance of the hajj, the pilgrimage to Mecca that devout Muslims are expected to make at least once in their lifetime.

> Scientists have discovered two sets of hydrothermal vents (ocean hot springs).

> Retail prices were beginning to rise, an early warning of inflation.

The agency ignored <u>their objection</u>, <u>that the antipollution measures would greatly increase the cost of the products</u>.

Berkeley scientists have finally realized <u>the medieval alchemist's dream</u>: <u>transmuting a base metal into gold</u>.

Like nonrestrictive relative clauses, nonrestrictive appositives can refer back to a previous part of the sentence, not merely to a noun phrase:

The scientists wanted their research to be useful, <u>an indication of their desire to work for the benefit of humanity</u>.

═══════════════ **EXERCISE 7.10** ═══════════════

Leave the restrictive appositives below unpunctuated. Punctuate the nonrestrictive appositives with commas.

1. The committee objected strongly to the recommendation that low-income students be charged higher tuition rates.
2. A good friend of mine Bill Harris asked that I join him for dinner on Friday.
3. Pollution has two primary sources individuals and corporations.
4. The expression "A penny saved is a penny earned" is a worn out cliche.
5. We vacationed last winter in Arizona one of the nicest places to visit when the weather is cold and snowy.
6. The president liked the idea that the Soviets wanted to negotiate arms reductions.
7. The northeast a part of the country experiencing an economic resurgence is a pleasant place to live.
8. All written essays must contain three components an introduction, a body, and a conclusion.
9. We admire Shakespeare the poet and Shakespeare the dramatist.
10. We enjoyed the play a real tour de force.

.10 ADVERBIAL CLAUSES

Clauses that function as adverbials in sentence structure are **adverbial clauses** (cf. section 6.9). Adverbial clauses occur initially, medially, and finally. Medial position—the position between the subject and the verb—occurs relatively infrequently.

*4 Nonfinite and verbless clauses are generally enclosed in commas, whatever their position:

> When asked to speak, he complained about the poor service.
> Though somewhat unpleasant, the procedure was simple.
> My parents, needing money for extensive house repairs, applied for a second mortgage.
> It is peaceful to float down a river, carried effortlessly by the current.
> He weighed the deer, calling out its weight in a clear voice.
> Military preparations were going forward, though on a much smaller scale.

Medial finite clauses are always punctuated:

> The members of the committee, when they read his report, demanded his resignation.

Initial finite clauses are generally punctuated:

> If the negotiations are held in public, they are likely to fail.
> As the canoe drew near, the design on its prow became visible.

The punctuation of final finite clauses depends on their relationship to the rest of the sentence. If they specify the circumstances of the situation, they are not punctuated:

> Call me if you decide not to come with us.
> Security has been heightened since a janitor was mugged.
> I recognized her talents before anyone else.

If they provide additional information or a comment, they are punctuated:

> She walked fast, so that she arrived before us.
> They expelled him from the country, although he had not been charged with a crime.
> I have been studying every day past midnight, since I want to graduate this year.
> He was self-conscious in his casual clothes, as if he had appeared without socks for a formal reception.
> It's too large, if I may say so.

If the sentence is negative, the absence of punctuation indicates that the negation includes the adverbial clause. The distinction is particularly sharp for a because-clause:

[1]   He didn't go there <u>because his sister was going to be there</u>.

The absence of a comma before the <u>because</u>-clause in [1] suggests the interpretation "He did go there, but not because his sister was going to be there." On the other hand, the presence of a comma stops the negation from applying to the <u>because</u>-clause, as in [2]:

[2]   He didn't go there, <u>because his sister was going to be there</u>.

The interpretation of [2] is "He did not go there, and he decided not to because his sister was going to be there". The same interpretation applies if the <u>because</u>-clause is fronted:

[2a]   <u>Because his sister was going to be there</u>, he didn't go there.

Adverbials other than clauses are often separated by commas if they provide a comment or have a linking function:

> <u>Unfortunately</u>, we were unable to attend your party.
> It was, <u>quite frankly</u>, a very boring speech.
> She was, <u>in fact</u>, a mathematical genius.
> None of the children liked the puppet show, <u>to my surprise</u>.
> Do you know her, <u>by the way</u>?
> His opinion, <u>however</u>, does not carry any weight.
> Rhetoric has started wars; <u>on the other hand</u>, rhetoric has stopped wars.
> <u>In summary</u>, his idea was neither original nor correct.

═══════════════ EXERCISE 7.11 ═══════════════

In the sentences below, punctuate the adverbials that require punctuation.

1. Because it requires little intellectual activity many people dislike television.
2. Fed up with the banality of television they have taken to reading.
3. Although books require quite a bit of mental energy on the part of the reader they are ultimately more satisfying than television.
4. Scholarly books for instance require their readers to think about what they read.
5. Less scholarly books while easier to read still require the reader to become actively engaged with the text.
6. Television will never replace books even though there is a whole generation of children being raised on television.

7. So that the children of this generation do not lose total contact with books parents and teachers should encourage reading.
8. In addition they should reward students who show an active interest in reading.
9. To encourage interest in reading some schools give out certificates to students for each book they read.
10. Redeemable at local fast food restaurants these certificates demonstrate effectively to students that reading has its rewards.

7.11 VOCATIVES AND INTERJECTIONS

Vocatives are phrases—commonly names—that directly address the person spoken to. They resemble adverbials in their range of positions and are always separated with commas:

> Can you tell me, Caroline, what I have to do next?
> Mr. President, we are again facing a dangerous situation in the Middle East.

Similarly, interjections and other reaction expressions are isolated by commas:

> Oh, we didn't expect to see you so soon.
> Well, what's your explanation?
> Yes, the finals will be next week.
> Heck, I didn't notice.
> OK, we're ready.

EXERCISE 7.12

Punctuate the vocatives and interjections in the sentences below.

1. Dave you don't know what you're doing.
2. Oh I wasn't aware that the end of the line was back there.
3. Yes Mr. Patton I'm ready.
4. Is that you Shirley?
5. Hey make sure that you replace any pieces of glass that you break.
6. Navigation officers report to your positions immediately.
7. It may be sir that we are running out of fuel.

8. Yes you may leave the class when you finish taking the exam.
9. What's the verdict Dr. Ronson?
10. Give the package to Dorothy Gloria.

7.12   AVOIDANCE OF MISUNDERSTANDING

Commas may be needed to prevent readers from misunderstanding the sentence, even if only momentarily:

> After almost a decade of trimming fat, private colleges face the prospect of still deeper cuts. [*Not* fat private colleges]
> In short, discrimination is ethically indefensible. [*Not* short discrimination]
> With quantities low, prices will continue to rise. [*Not* low prices]
> When architectural changes occur, clearly society is changing. [*Not* occur clearly]
> In most parts of the country you replaced thou, and ye was rarely used. [*Not* you replaced thou and ye]

If the same verb appears twice, a comma is inserted between the two verbs:

> What she thinks her role on the committee is, is likely to influence her decisions.

═══════════ EXERCISE 7.13 ═══════════

Insert commas where they help to make the meaning clear.

1. Above all discrimination is ethically indefensible.
2. As the new year opens stores are putting on their annual sales.
3. When architecture changes occur clearly society is changing.
4. Although 92% Catholic Mexico lacks formal diplomatic ties with the Vatican.
5. News of the demonstrations spread quickly embarrassing government officials.
6. As things stand now the government has no way to block the visit.
7. At first ten of the jurors thought that he was probably guilty.
8. With the stakes so high lawyers are in no rush to judgment.

9. As familiar as the monsoon cycle may be the winds remain in-
   scrutable.
10. Often as not the women work in the fields.
11. Call us for full details. Better yet call your Travel Agent.
12. Still though most union leaders are publicly backing the AFL-
    CIO leadership, they will make what seem the best deals for their
    members.
13. To obtain the same amount of energy through wind power as-
    suming a windy enough location would require a large capital
    investment.
14. To be honest workers don't stay very long.

7.13 GENITIVES OF NOUNS

In writing we indicate that nouns are genitive (cf. 5.7) by using an apostrophe.
The general rules for forming the genitive are:

1. If the noun is singular, add 's:

the student	the student's expectations
the woman	the woman's options
David	David's brothers

2. If the noun is plural and ends in -s, add just an apostrophe:

the students	the students' expectations
my sisters	my sisters' friends
his parents	his parents' address

3. If the noun is plural and does not end in -s, add 's:

the women	the women's suggestions
the people	the people's decision
the police	the police's reactions

There is some variation among writers regarding singular nouns that end
in -s. On the whole, it is safer to follow the general rule and add 's:

The boss's daughter	Charles's video
Burns's poetry	Dickens's novels

The traditional exceptions, which take just the apostrophe, are:

a. the genitives of <u>Jesus</u> and <u>Moses</u>

Jesus' teaching   Moses' blessing

b. names of more than one syllable that end in <u>-s</u> and have an "eez" sound:

Socrates' death   Xerxes' defeat

In the fixed expressions <u>for</u> . . . <u>sake</u> where the noun in the middle ends in an "s" sound, the noun traditionally takes just the apostrophe:

for goodness' sake   for appearance' sake

============================ **EXERCISE 7.14** ============================

Change the <u>of</u>-phrase into a genitive construction.

EXAMPLE
The father of Susan
Susan's father

1.   the eldest son of my brother
2.   the leaders of our country
3.   the best team of the men
4.   the conviction of the prisoners
5.   the influence of the President
6.   the first papers of the students
7.   the torn coat of somebody
8.   the last play of Shakespeare
9.   the many novels of Dickens
10.   the strike of the air pilots
11.   the catch of the fishermen
12.   the friends of my sister
13.   the accusation of the attorney
14.   the toys of our children
15.   the security of our nation
16.   the flight of the American astronauts
17.   the advice of his father-in-law
18.   the support of the alumni
19.   the desperate plight of the poor
20.   the rights of women

7.14 GENITIVES OF PRONOUNS

Certain indefinite pronouns (cf. 5.23) have a genitive ending in 's. These are one, compounds ending in -one (e.g., someone), and compounds ending in -body (e.g., somebody).

> one's friend   anybody's idea
> nobody's fault   someone's move

In the combinations with else, 's is added to else:

> someone else's coat   no one else's mistake

The indefinite pronoun other follows the general rule for nouns: the genitive singular is other's and the genitive plural is others':

> each other's letters   the others' problems (the problems
>   of the others)
> one another's children

Except for mine and thine, the possessive pronouns (cf. 5.17) end in -s. They should not have an apostrophe:

> hers   its   yours
> his   ours   theirs

Similarly, the genitive of who is whose and should not have an apostrophe. On the possible confusion of such homophones, see A.7 in the Appendix.

=== EXERCISE 7.15 ===

Insert apostrophes where necessary. Some sentences may not require an apostrophe.

1. Eds friends will arrive later.
2. The womans coat was destroyed at the cleaners.
3. The childrens toys were lost in the fire.
4. Everybodys tickets arrived in the mail yesterday.
5. The dog tangled its leash while it was tied outside.
6. The Burns house was put up for sale last week.
7. For heavens sake please don't park your car on the grass.
8. The computer is ours, not theirs.
9. Somebodys bike was stolen last night.
10. We should proofread each others papers before we turn them in.

═══════════════ EXERCISE 7.16: Review ═══════════════

You may often choose to write a pair of sentences as one sentence. Write each pair of sentences as one sentence with two main clauses. Change the punctuation accordingly, using commas between the clauses wherever they are permitted. Do not change words or insert words.

EXAMPLES

We have a problem that affects your generation. And you ought to solve it.
We have a problem that affects your generation, and you ought to solve it.
She had never liked him. However, he had spoken very reasonably that day.
She had never liked him; however, he had spoken very reasonably that day.

1. The videotape camera is a weapon for truth. And yet anyone can use it.
2. You may hear conversation as children help one another. But you won't find long periods of silence.
3. He has cut two record albums of his own songs. Furthermore, he has made three full-length films.
4. They cannot face the shameful facts. And consequently they try to shift the responsibility onto others.
5. A number of technical reforms have been suggested. However, there is no consensus on any of them.
6. We are in danger of losing Yellowstone. Indeed, we will lose it unless we make a determined effort to preserve it.
7. The government profits from the use of alcohol and drugs. And a majority of parents indulge.
8. Their reality was harsh. Yet they faced it steadfastly.
9. You must have been out of the country at the time. Or else I would have asked for your advice.
10. They have recently bought a new car. You can therefore ask them for a lift.
11. Hardly anyone gave New York's canine litter law a chance of succeeding. Nevertheless the cynics were wrong.
12. The windmills resemble oil rigs. But still their overall effect is somehow comforting.
13. Some people spend their surplus money on luxuries. Tom Carley uses his to pay for vacations for poor youngsters.
14. Her back has not been troubling her for the last couple of years. So she has stopped doing the exercises that the physician prescribed.
15. We fought like tigers over the box. Unfortunately, however, Turner was a stronger tiger than I was.
16. I can't help him. Nor can you.

========================= **EXERCISE 7.17: Review** =========================

Each item has one punctuation error. The error may be a wrong punctuation mark or the absence of a punctuation mark. Correct the error in each item.

1. Amnesty estimates that there are half a million political prisoners in the world it is investigating about one percent of these cases.
2. Researchers on the Amnesty staff are generally graduates and can speak several languages, each of them keeps watch on hundreds of political prisoners in a particular country.
3. Torture techniques have become so refined that they rarely leave marks doctors often collaborate in the deception.
4. Amnesty researchers do not feel that human beings are inherently cruel, they should know.
5. One South American officer sent a letter to Amnesty describing the tortures that he had witnessed, he included photographic proof.
6. No one was safe from torture, some cases were more brutal than others, but all prisoners were beaten and tortured.
7. The letters to political prisoners never bear the Amnesty letterhead; and often chat about innocuous matters.
8. A study of torture in one European country showed that the torturers were not sadists who had applied for the job they were youths who had been randomly conscripted.
9. Amnesty won the Nobel Prize for Peace in 1977 complaints from dictatorships all around the world showed that Amnesty's work is effective.
10. To insure impartiality, Amnesty's groups must adopt prisoners from at least two ideological blocs; and cannot work on cases in their own countries.
11. Publicity is Amnesty's only real weapon it is a powerful one.
12. Politicians have begun paying lip service to human rights, Amnesty deserves some credit for this development.

========================= **EXERCISE 7.18: Review** =========================

Each item has one punctuation error. The error may be a wrong punctuation mark or the absence of a punctuation mark. Correct the error in each item.

1. How long will it take before we have peace throughout the world.
2. The answer to this question is quite complex and will require much thought on the part of the people, who attempt to answer it.

3. Many people have asked themselves if "peace is possible or feasible."

4. These people think that worldwide peace is impossible, they advocate that we not try to achieve it.

5. Other people, on the other hand, are idealists they think that we ought to be constantly striving for world peace.

6. Asked about the possibility of world peace, one peace activist replied: Even though world peace is a dream, we must nevertheless keep striving for it.

7. One senator a well known republican who asked not to be identified was less idealistic than the peace activist.

8. He balked at the idea, that we ought to be constantly striving for world peace.

9. Such a goal, he replied; "Only makes us look weaker in the eyes of our enemies."

10. This senator was of the school, who felt that force was a sign of strength.

11. Although many Americans feel as the senator does others think that his ideas are dangerous.

12. They believe that too much force leads to war, consequently, they believe that our foreign policy ought to be directed towards peace instead.

13. While both sides feel that the others position is wrong, such a dialogue is important.

14. It leads to a greater understanding of the issues at hand issues that will shape the form of foreign policy in the future.

CHAPTER EIGHT

Usage Problems

SUBJECT–VERB AGREEMENT

8.1 THE GENERAL RULES

The verb agrees with its subject in number and person. The agreement applies whenever the verb displays distinctions in number and person. For all verbs other than be, the distinctions are found only in the present tense, where the third person singular has the -s form and the third person plural—like the first and second persons—has the base form (cf. 4.13):

[1]   The noise distracts them.
[2]   The noises distract them.

The verb be makes further distinctions in the present and introduces distinctions in the past (cf. 4.12f). For the convenience of the present discussion, I display the set of present and past forms for be:

present tense

	singular	plural
first person	am	
second person	are	are
third person	is	

past tense

	singular	plural
first person	was	
second person	were	were
third person	was	

The distinctions for third person agreement with be are illustrated in [3] and [4] for the present and in [5] and [6] for the past:

[3] The noise is distracting them.
[4] The noises are distracting them.
[5] The noise was distracting them.
[6] The noises were distracting them.

The agreement affects the first verb in the verb phrase, whether it is a main verb as in [1]–[2] or an auxiliary as in [3]–[6]. Modal auxiliaries (cf. 5.29), however, do not make distinctions in number or person:

The noise
The noises } may distract them.

If the subject is a noun phrase, the main noun determines the number of the phrase:

The noise of the { demonstration / demonstrators } is distracting them.

The noises of the { demonstration / demonstrators } are distracting them.

It is a mistake to allow the verb to be influenced by an adjacent noun that is not the main noun.

Noun phrases coordinated with and are generally plural, even though the individual noun phrases are singular:

The President and the Vice-President were at the ceremony.

Clauses are generally singular:

That he needs a shave is obvious.
Playing handball relaxes me.
To make mistakes is only human.

The rule of number agreement between subject (S) and verb applies to all finite clauses, whether they are main clauses or subordinate clauses:

Inflation (S) is decreasing, and productivity (S) is rising.
Nature (S) has arranged that no two flowers (S) are the same,
    even though they (S) appear very similar.

EXERCISE 8.1

Select the appropriate verb form given in parentheses at the end of each sentence, and write it down in the blank space.

EXAMPLES

The slight chest pain *worries* him. (worry, worries)
His wife *has* been urging him to exercise. (have, has)

1. He _____ his neighbor jogging. (see, sees)
2. He _____ know what kind of exercise to do. (don't, doesn't)
3. Exercise for the middle-aged_____ considered a prescription. (am, is, are)
4. Too many people _____ up with heart attacks. (end, ends)
5. To undertake an exercise test _____ prudent. (am, is, are)
6. The test _____ your level of fitness. (determine, determines)
7. Usually the test _____ after a physical examination. (come, comes)
8. Finding out what your heart can do _____ the goal of the test. (am, is, are)
9. Most tests _____ a treadmill. (use, uses)
10. Some clinics also _____ a bicycle. (use, uses)
11. Walking on an elevated fast-moving treadmill_____ hard work. (am, is, are)
12. The doctors constantly _____ your heart rate. (monitor, monitors)
13. On the basis of the tests, the doctor_____ likely to recommend an exercise program. (is, are)
14. To take up a regular program _____ discipline. (require, requires)
15. Static exercise _____ improve the heart. (don't, doesn't)
16. That you shouldn't overexert yourself_____ without saying. (go, goes)
17. On the other hand, we _____ too little exercise. (do, does)
18. I _____ most of the time. (sit, sits)
19. No wonder I _____ overweight. (am, is, are)
20. I_____ to take up a regular exercise program. (have, has)
21. You _____ to do the same. (have, has)
22. We _____ want heart trouble at our age. (don't, doesn't)

8.2 <u>AND</u>

The subject is plural if it consists of two or more phrases that are linked by <u>and</u>, even if each is singular:

> Your kitchen, your living room, and your dining room <u>are</u> too small.

It is also plural if <u>and</u> is implied though not actually present:

> Your kitchen, your living room, your dining room, <u>are</u> too small.

It is plural when one of the main nouns is implied though not actually present:

> British and American English <u>are</u> dialects of one language. (British English and American English are . . .)

> Both the first and the second prize <u>were</u> won by students at our school. (Both the first prize and the second prize were . . .)

On the other hand, if the linked units refer to the same thing, the subject is singular:

> The first serious poem I read in grade school and one I later studied in high school <u>was</u> "Ozymandias" by Shelley. [*The first serious poem was identical with the one later studied.*]

> A conscientious and honest politician <u>has</u> nothing to fear. (A politician who is both conscientious and honest has . . .)

Two linked units may be viewed as either a combination (and therefore singular) or as separate units (and therefore plural):

> Bread and butter <u>is</u> good for you. (Bread with butter on it is . . .)
> Bread and butter <u>have</u> recently gone up in price. (Both bread and butter have . . .)

If the noun phrases are introduced by <u>each</u> or <u>every</u>, the subject is singular:

> Every student and every instructor <u>has</u> to show an I.D. card to borrow books from the library.
> Each adult and each child <u>was</u> given a sandwich.
> Every bank and store <u>was</u> closed that day.

See 8.4 for <u>with</u> and other linking expressions.

8.3 OR, NOR

If the noun phrases are linked by or, either . . . or, or neither . . . nor, the verb may be singular or plural. When both phrases are singular, the verb is singular:

> No food or drink was provided.
> Either the President or Congress has to take drastic measures
>   to combat inflation.
> Neither the time nor the place was appropriate.

When both phrases are plural, the verb is plural:

> Either the miners or the mineowners have to make conces-
>   sions.

When one phrase is singular and the other is plural, the style manuals prefer the verb to agree in number with the phrase closer to it:

> Three short essays or one long essay is required.
> Neither your brother nor your sisters are responsible.

The plural is often used in conversation regardless of which phrase precedes the verb.

When the linked units are pronouns that require different verb forms, it is better to avoid having to make a choice. Instead, rephrase the sentence:

> Neither you are responsible for the arrangements, nor am I.
> Neither of us is responsible for the arrangements.

8.4 WITH

When a singular noun phrase is linked to a following noun phrase by a preposition such as with, the subject is singular even though the preposition is similar in meaning to and:

> The President, together with the Cabinet, is considering how
>   to react to the attacks in the media on the Administration.

The subject is singular because the main noun is singular. Other prepositions used in a similar way include as well as and in addition to:

> The teacher, as well as the students, was enjoying the picnic.

In the following sentence, the preposition is after:

> One Congressman after another has objected to the proposed
>   reform.

8.5 COLLECTIVE NOUNS

A collective noun refers to a group. Some common examples are:

administration	enemy	herd
army	faculty	jury
audience	family	mob
class	fleet	nation
committee	gang	public
crew	government	swarm
crowd	group	team

When members of the group are viewed as a unit, singular verbs and singular pronouns are usual:

> The audience was very noisy.
> The public has a right to know.
> The jury has retired for the night, but it will resume its deliberations early tomorrow.

Plural verbs and plural pronouns are used when the members of the group are viewed as individuals:

> All the team are in their places. (All the members of the team are . . .)
> The faculty have not been able to agree among themselves whether to approve the proposed changes.

8.6 INDEFINITE PRONOUNS

Most indefinite pronouns (cf. 5.23) take singular verbs:

> Everybody is now here.
> Someone has borrowed my comb.

In formal writing, use singular verbs even when a plural phrase follows the pronoun:

> Either of them is prepared to help you.
> Each of our friends has taken the course.

Several indefinite pronouns (none, all, some, any) and the fractions may be either singular or plural. If they refer to one thing, they take a singular verb:

> Some (of the material) is not suitable for children.
> Half (the county) is under water.
> All (the fruit) has been eaten.
> None (of the crop) was in danger.

If they refer to more than one person or thing, they take a plural verb:

> Some (of the pages) <u>are</u> missing.
> Half (of the states) <u>have</u> voted in favor of the amendment.
> All (my friends) <u>were</u> abroad.
> None (of us) <u>have</u> heard about the new regulation.

<u>None</u> is also used with a singular verb:

> None (of us) <u>has</u> heard about the new regulation.

Problems sometimes arise in the choice of pronouns for which singular indefinite pronouns are the antecedent. The traditional choice for formal writing is <u>he</u>, <u>him</u>, <u>his</u>, according to what is required in the context:

[1]   Everybody must declare <u>his</u> major before the end of <u>his</u> sophomore year.

[2]   Does anyone think <u>he</u> can solve this problem?

It is also the traditional choice when noun phrases are introduced by indefinite determiners (cf. 5.24f) or when the phrases refer to a class of people:

[3]   Every lobbyist is required to register <u>his</u> name with Congress.

[4]   An English major may find <u>he</u> has more assignments than <u>he</u> expected.

Changes in attitude have led many to avoid using the masculine pronoun to refer to both male and female. It is generally possible to rephrase the sentence to avoid suggesting a sexist bias. One way is to avoid using any pronoun, as in [1a]; another way is to make the subject plural, as in [2a]–[4a]:

[1a]   Everybody must declare <u>a</u> major before the end of <u>the</u> sophomore year.

[2a]   Do <u>any of you</u> think <u>you</u> can solve the problem?

[3a]   <u>All lobbyists</u> are required to register <u>their</u> names with Congress.

[4a]   <u>English majors</u> may find <u>they</u> have more assignments than <u>they</u> expected.

EXERCISE 8.2

Rewrite each sentence to avoid sexist bias.

1.   Each student must fill out an application form if he wishes to be considered for admission to the university.

2. Everybody worked his hardest to ensure that the telethon was a success.
3. An astronaut runs the risk of serious injury, even death, if his spacecraft malfunctions while he is in orbit.
4. Each worker should show up promptly for work or run the risk of having an hour's pay deducted from his paycheck.
5. The politician of today must raise considerable amounts of money if he wishes to be elected to office.
6. Every individual is responsible for his own welfare.
7. A graduating engineering major will find that his skills are in much demand and that he has many career options.
8. The union worker has found that he has less of an influence in the workplace than he did twenty years ago.
9. The actual mileage one gets will vary according to the type of driving he does, his driving habits, and his car's condition.
10. What somebody serves is often a reflection of himself.

8.7 QUANTITY PHRASES

Plural phrases of quantity or extent take singular verbs when the quantity or extent is viewed as a unit:

> Ten dollars is enough.
> Two years seems too long to wait.
> Five miles was as far as they would walk.

Otherwise, a plural is used:

> Two years have passed since I was last here.
> Twenty-five dollars were stolen from his wallet.

8.8 SINGULAR NOUNS IN -S

Nouns ending in -ics are singular when they refer to a field of study; for example, civics, economics, linguistics, mathematics, physics, statistics:

> Physics is a prerequisite for this course.
> Economics was my favorite subject in high school.

Some of these nouns are used in a different sense and may then be plural:

> Your statistics are inaccurate.
> The acoustics in this hall have been improved.

Names of diseases that end in -s are generally treated as singular; for example, measles, mumps, rickets:

> Measles is a highly infectious disease.

Names of games that end in -s are singular; for example, billiards, checkers, darts, dominoes:

> Dominoes is the only game I play at home.

Individual pieces have singular and plural forms:

> You've dropped a domino on the floor.
> The dominoes are on the floor.

8.9 WHO, WHICH, THAT

The relative pronouns who, which, and that have the same number as the nouns they refer to. The singular is correct in the following sentences:

> I have written a letter for the student who is applying for a job in our department. (The student is applying . . .)

> You need special permission to borrow a book which is kept in the reference section. (The book is kept . . .)

> They noted the tension that has begun to mount in the city. (The tension has begun to mount . . .)

The plural is correct in the following sentences:

> People who live in glass houses shouldn't throw stones. (The people live in glass houses.)

> The weapons which were found during the search were produced as evidence in court. (The weapons were found . . .)

> She reported on the motions that were passed at the meeting. (The motions were passed . . .)

8.10 WHAT

You may use either a singular verb or a plural verb with the pronoun what. The choice depends on the meaning:

What <u>worries</u> them is that he has not yet made up his mind.
(The thing that <u>worries</u> them . . .)

They live in what <u>are</u> called ranch houses. (in houses that <u>are</u>
called . . .)

Similarly, use either the singular or the plural with <u>what</u>-clauses, according to
the meaning:

What they need <u>is</u> a good rest. (The thing that they need
<u>is</u> . . .)

What were once painful ordeals <u>are</u> now routine examina-
tions. (Those things . . . <u>are</u> now . . .)

8.11   <u>THERE IS, THERE ARE</u>

In speech it is common to use a singular verb after introductory <u>there</u> (cf. 6.11)
even when the subject (which follows the verb) is plural:

There<u>'s</u> two men waiting for you.

In formal writing, follow the general rule:

There <u>is</u> somebody waiting for you.
There <u>are</u> two men waiting for you.

8.12   CITATIONS AND TITLES

Citations and titles always take a singular verb, even if they consist of plural
phrases:

"Children" <u>is</u> an irregular plural.
The Power and the Glory <u>is</u> a novel set in Mexico.
The Four Feathers <u>was</u> one of the first novels I read as a child.

=============== **EXERCISE 8.3: Review** ===============

Select the appropriate verb form given in parentheses at the end of each sentence, and write it down in the blank space.

1. Surgeons in the U.S. successfully _____ clouded vision or outright blindness by transplanting about 10,000 corneas a year. (alleviate, alleviates)

2. The congregation _____ mainly of factory workers. (consist, consists)

3. Traditional jobs like cashier and nurse's aide _____ good for women with one or two children. (is, are)

4. Analysis done with the aid of computers _____ those accounts that appear to be conduits for drug money. (select, selects)

5. What makes the situation serious _____ that no new antibiotics have been discovered in the past 15 years. (is, are)

6. Shipping bicycles by air _____ possible, but not easy. (is, are)

7. That athletes are no longer immune from politics _____ made clear by the U.S. decision in 1980 to boycott the Olympic Summer Games in Moscow. (was, were)

8. To drive bicycles in a big city _____ agility, aggressiveness, and guile. (demands, demand)

9. The United States _____ been attracting foreign investments in recent years. (has, have)

10. The most catastrophic example of farming mismanagement in the U.S. _____ the creation of the dust bowls of the Great Plains in the 1920's and the 1930's. (was, were)

11. Each _____ capable of the first 90 minutes of sustained high-altitude running. (is, are)

12. He was fascinated by the stories in the Old Testament that _____ history to be determined by chance meetings and by small, personal incidents. (show, shows)

13. The job of establishing sufficient controls and measurements so that you can tell what is actually going on with athletes _____ tediously complex. (is, are)

14. Both science and medicine _____ to the preparation of athletes for competition. (contribute, contributes)

15. The only equipment they work with _____ a blackboard and some chalk. (is, are)

16. Another area of current research that shows great promise _____ diabetes. (is, are)

17. Either California or Florida _____ the best climate in the U.S. (has, have)

18. The blind _____ not want pity. (does, do)

19. Henry Kissinger's *White House Years* _____ fascinating. (is, are)

20. None of the food _____ fit to eat. (is, are)

========================= **EXERCISE 8.4: Review** =========================

These sentences form a connected passage. The base form of a verb is given in parentheses at the end of each sentence. Write down the appropriate form of the verb in the blank space.

1. The young woman now sitting in the dermatologist's waiting room _____ an itchy rash. (have)
2. The rash on her elbows and legs _____ due to an allergic reaction. (be)
3. There are many allergies that _____ rashes. (cause)
4. The existence of allergies _____ known long before scientists had any understanding of their nature. (be)
5. The nature of allergy _____ still not fully understood. (be)
6. The victims of allergy seldom die and seldom _____. (recover)
7. There _____ nothing like an itchy rash for wearing a person down. (be)
8. Some allergies, such as asthma, _____ no external cause. (have)
9. Others _____ caused by contact with a foreign substance. (be)
10. The young woman's allergy _____ brought about by contact with copper. (be)

_____ **CASE** _____

8.13 SUBJECT COMPLEMENT

When the subject complement is a pronoun, it is usually in the objective case: It's me, That's him. Such sentences tend to occur in speech or written dialogue. In formal style, use the subjective case: It is I, This is he.

8.14 COORDINATED PHRASES

In 5.16 I stated the rules for the selection of subjective and objective cases in pronouns: We use the subjective case for the subject and (in formal style) for the subject complement; otherwise we use the objective case. Errors of case may arise when a pronoun is coordinated with a noun or another pronoun:

[1]   <u>You and her</u> will take charge. [*Correct to* <u>You and she</u>.]

[2]   I think <u>Bob and me</u> have the right approach. [*Correct to* <u>Bob and I</u>.]

[3]   Everybody knows <u>Nancy and I</u>. [*Correct to* <u>Nancy and me</u>.]

[4]   The tickets are for <u>you and I</u>. [*Correct to* <u>you and me</u>.]

The errors do not occur when there is only one pronoun. You can therefore test which form is correct by using just the second pronoun:

[1a]   <u>She</u> will take charge. [<u>She</u> *is subject.*]

[2a]   I think <u>I</u> have the right approach. [<u>I</u> *is subject of the subordinate clause.*]

[3a]   Everybody knows <u>me</u>. [<u>Me</u> *is direct object.*]

[4a]   The tickets are for <u>me</u>. [<u>Me</u> *is complement of the preposition* <u>for</u>.]

There is a similar possibility of error when <u>we</u> or <u>us</u> is accompanied by a noun:

They complained about the way <u>us</u> students were behaving. [*Correct to* <u>we students</u>. *Cf.:* <u>the way we were behaving</u>.]
They will <u>not</u> succeed in pushing <u>we Americans</u> around. [*Correct to* <u>us Americans</u>. *Cf.:* <u>pushing us around</u>.]

========================= **EXERCISE 8.5** =========================

Select the pronoun form given in parentheses that would be appropriate in formal writing, and write it in the blank.

1.   Edward and _____ went for a walk after the talk. (I, me)
2.   Our boss thinks that Mary and _____ talk too much when we work together. (I, me)
3.   The police officer gave the driver and _____ a stern lecture after he pulled us over. (I, me)
4.   _____ Americans should be careful when we travel abroad. (We, Us)
5.   Between you and _____, this class is much harder than I thought it would be. (I, me)
6.   The mayor knows that _____ and the council president do not get along very well. (he, him)
7.   The woman knows Fred and _____ quite well. (I, me)
8.   You should be willing to work with both Mary and _____ on the project. (she, her)

9. Either the president or _____ will be in contact with you about the campaign. (I, me)
10. Everyone except John and _____ was present at the rally. (I, me)

8.15 AFTER AS AND THAN

In formal writing, as and than are always conjunctions in comparisons. The case of the pronoun depends on its function in the comparative clause, though the verb may be absent:

[1] They felt the same way as he. [He is subject.]
[2] She works faster than we. [We is subject.]
[3] They paid him more than me. [Me is indirect object.]
[4] He likes me more than her. [Her is direct object.]

You can test which form is correct by expanding the comparative clause:

[1a] They felt the same way as he did.
[2a] She works faster than we do.
[3a] They paid him more than they paid me.
[4a] He likes me more than he likes her.

8.16 AFTER BUT

But meaning "except" is a preposition. In formal writing, the pronoun following it is always in the objective case:

I know everybody here but her.
Nobody but me can tell the difference.

8.17 AFTER LET

Use the objective case after let:

Let us examine the problem carefully.
Let them make their own decisions.

Take care that a coordinated pronoun is objective:

Let you and me take the matter in hand.
Let Bob and her say what they think.

8.18   WHO, WHOM

Whom is not often used in everyday speech. In formal writing, however, retain the distinction between subjective who and objective whom:

> She is somebody who knows her own mind. [Cf.: She knows her own mind.]
> She is somebody on whom I can rely. [Cf.: I can rely on her.]

Parenthetic clauses like I believe and I think should not affect the choice of case:

[1]   I recently spoke to somebody who I believe knows you well.
      [Cf.: She knows you well, I believe.]

[2]   I recently spoke to somebody whom I believe you know well.
      [Cf.: You know her well, I believe.]

The following example is different:

[3]   She is somebody whom I consider to be a good candidate for promotion. [Cf.: I consider her to be a good candidate for promotion.]

I consider in [3] is not parenthetic. It cannot be omitted like I believe in [1] and [2]. Whom in [3] is the direct object of consider.

Similarly, retain the distinction between subjective whoever and whomever in formal writing:

> Whoever wants to see me should make an appointment with my secretary. [Cf.: She wants to see me.]

> You can show the report to whoever wants to see it. [Cf.: She wants to see it.]

> I will offer advice to whomever I wish. [Cf.: I wish to offer advice to her.]

EXERCISE 8.6

Select the pronoun form given in parentheses that would be appropriate in formal writing, and write it in the blank.

1.   He is the only individual _____ I trust completely. (who, whom)

2. Go to the office and speak to _____ is working the reception desk. (whoever, whomever)

3. He is the only person _____ I think is capable of filling the vacant position. (who, whom)

4. People should vote for the candidate _____ they feel will do the best job. (who, whom)

5. The manager knows _____ is best able to play in cold, rainy weather. (who, whom)

6. _____ is selected to chair the committee has a lot of work ahead of him or her. (Whoever, Whomever)

7. The woman is the person _____ the company transferred to Houston. (who, whom)

8. I will do the work for _____ is made my new boss. (whoever, whomever)

8.19 WITH -ING CLAUSES

When an -ing participle clause has a nominal function (i.e., a function similar to one possible for a noun phrase), if the subject is a pronoun, a name, or other short personal noun phrase, it is preferable, in formal writing, to put it in the genitive case:

> They were surprised at $\begin{cases} \text{Gerald's} \\ \text{his} \end{cases}$ refusing to join the strike.
> He was afraid of my protesting against the new rule.
> I dislike Robert's seeing X-rated movies.
> Do you know the reason for your sister's breaking off the engagement?

Use the common case for long noun phrases:

> I remember a car with a broken rear window being parked alongside our house.

> They were annoyed at the students and faculty demonstrating against cuts in student loans.

Use the common case for nonpersonal nouns:

> I am interested in the car being sold as soon as possible.

Except in formal writing, the subject is often in the common case (for nouns) or objective case (for pronouns):

They were surprised at $\left\{\begin{array}{l}\underline{\text{Gerald}}\\ \underline{\text{him}}\end{array}\right\}$ refusing to join the strike.

In all styles, use the genitive when the clause is the subject:

My forgetting her name amused everybody.

In all styles, use the common case (for nouns) or objective case (for pronouns) after verbs of perception, such as see, or certain other verbs, the most frequent of which are find, keep, and leave:

I kept them waiting.

EXERCISE 8.7: Review

Select the appropriate word given in parentheses at the end of each sentence, and write it down in the blank space. If more than one seems appropriate, give the more formal word.

1. We should help those _____ we know are helping themselves. (who, whom)
2. We don't know _____ to ask. (who, whom)
3. I'll sell the tickets to _____ is there. (whoever, whomever)
4. We have Americans sitting on the bench _____ could play on most clubs. (who, whom)
5. Did you see _____ did it? (who, whom)
6. Pay for the tickets when you next see Bob and _____. (I, me)
7. Speak to the woman _____ is in charge. (who, whom)
8. Joan and _____ are about to leave. (I, me)
9. _____ do you want to see? (Who, Whom)
10. I'm playing the record for _____ is interested. (whoever, whomever)
11. They called while you and _____ were at the party. (I, me)
12. Did you see _____ was there? (who, whom)
13. This is for you and _____. (I, me)
14. Let you and _____ take the initiative. (I, me)
15. He speaks English better than _____. (she, her)
16. It was _____ who seconded the motion. (I, me)
17. They recommended that I consult the lawyer _____ they employed. (who, whom)

EXERCISE 8.8: Review

Select the appropriate word given in parentheses at the end of each sentence, and write it down in the blank space. If more than one seems possible, give the more formal word.

1. I watched _____ playing baseball. (them, their)
2. They were angry at _____ refusing to join the strike. (him, his)
3. Congressmen have found _____ objecting to tax cuts that might increase inflation. (voters, voters')
4. Are you surprised at _____ wanting the job? (me, my)
5. They heard _____ opening the door. (Rhoda, Rhoda's)
6. I saw my _____ boarding a train to Seattle. (brother, brother's)
7. We do not object to _____ paying for the tickets. (them, their)
8. _____ writing a recommendation for me persuaded the manager to give me the position. (You, Your)
9. They were annoyed at their _____ telephoning after eleven. (neighbor, neighbor's)
10. He kept the _____ playing the drums for a long time. (children, children's)

EXERCISE 8.9: Review

Select the appropriate word given in parentheses at the end of each sentence, and write it down in the blank space. If more than one seems possible, give the more formal word.

1. _____ does she resemble most? (Who, Whom)
2. We were pleased to hear of _____ acquiring a new house. (they, them, their)
3. I will introduce you to someone _____ I think can help you. (who, whom)
4. Let Joan and _____ invite your children for the weekend. (I, me)
5. It was _____ who wrote the letter. (he, him)
6. The noise disturbed my parents and _____. (I, me)
7. They will object to _____ you propose for the position. (whoever, whomever)
8. That type of show does not interest either you or _____. (we, us)

9. I heard _____ sing in the shower. (he, him, his)
10. We want to know _____ you expect to visit. (who, whom)
11. They appreciated _____ explaining the differences between the two policies. (I, me, my)
12. People were speculating about _____ was in charge. (who, whom)
13. Everybody except _____ was satisfied with the hotel. (I, me)
14. They accepted weapons from _____ was willing to sell weapons. (whoever, whomever)
15. Peter and _____ share many interests. (I, me)
16. I am sending Susan and _____ an anniversary gift. (he, him)
17. We should help those _____ we know are helping themselves. (who, whom)
18. I saw _____ using the machine. (they, them, their)
19. Their advice is intended for Bruce and _____. (I, me)
20. They will pay the reward to _____ the judges nominate. (whoever, whomever)

===== **EXERCISE 8.10: Review** =====

Select the appropriate word given in parentheses at the end of each sentence, and write it down in the blank space. If more than one seems possible, give the more formal word.

1. Women _____ never truly separate from their mothers are likely to re-create the mother-daughter antagonism in adult relationships. (who, whom)
2. I wondered whether someone would help _____ dig out when the storm was over. (him, his)
3. Grandmother had been one of six sisters, each of _____ had at least five daughters. (who, whom)
4. They can at least prevent _____ infecting others. (him, his)
5. The bank will fire the man _____ was convicted of shoplifting. (who, whom)
6. She handed the baggage to my brother and _____. (I, me)
7. The question was _____ would shoot first. (who, whom)
8. They are preparing supper for _____ wants to eat. (whoever, whomever)
9. My family is paying the rent for Bob and _____. (she, her)
10. We spoke to the official _____ we thought was in charge of the case. (who, whom)

11. They have not yet decided _____ they want as Governor. (who, whom)
12. The Congressmen _____ are now debating the President's tax passage want a smaller tax cut. (who, whom)
13. David and _____ are unhappy about our salary raises. (I, me, my)
14. Nobody knows the way but _____. (she, her)
15. Some students _____ live in the dormitory have complained about the noise. (who, whom)
16. I cannot explain _____ not answering your letter. (they, them, their)
17. They want Bob and _____ to speak. (I, me)
18. We will work for _____ treats us well. (whoever, whomever)
19. We have supervisors _____ are themselves supervised. (who, whom)
20. I heard _____ playing the drums in the attic. (Tom, Tom's)

_____ AUXILIARIES AND VERBS _____

.20 PROBLEMS WITH AUXILIARIES

When it follows a modal (cf. 5.29), the auxiliary <u>have</u> is often pronounced like <u>of</u> and is therefore sometimes misspelled <u>of</u>. The correct spelling is <u>have</u> after the modals in these sentences:

I <u>should have</u> said something about it long ago.
Somebody else <u>would have</u> paid.
You <u>might have</u> helped me.
She <u>could have</u> become the mayor.

<u>Had better</u> is often rendered as <u>'d better</u> or <u>better</u> in speech: He <u>better not</u> be there. Use the full expression in formal writing.

<u>Ought to</u> should be the first verb in the verb phrase. Combinations such as <u>didn't ought to</u> and <u>hadn't ought to</u> are not standard.

.21 LIE, LAY

The intransitive verb <u>lie</u> ("be in a reclining position") and the transitive verb <u>lay</u> ("place") are often confused, because the past tense of <u>lie</u> is <u>lay</u> and the present tense of <u>lay</u> is <u>lay</u> or <u>lays</u>. Here are the forms of the two verbs:

present tense	lie, lies	lay, lays
-ing participle	lying	laying
past tense	lay	laid
-ed participle	lain	laid

Here are examples of sentences with these verbs:

lie

Is she lying on the sofa?
The children lay asleep on the floor.
I have lain in bed all morning.

lay

Are you laying a bet on the next race?
He laid his head on his arms.
The hens have laid a dozen eggs this morning.

8.22   SIT, SET

The verb sit, which is usually intransitive, is sometimes confused with the transitive verb set ("place"). Here are the forms of the two verbs:

base form	sit	set
-s form	sits	sets
-ing participle	sitting	setting
past tense	sat	set
-ed participle	sat	set

Here are examples of sentences with these verbs:

sit

Sit down right here.
They are sitting outside.
We sat talking for a couple of hours.
I had not sat on a committee before.

set

Set your thoughts down in writing.
She is setting her papers in order.
He set his books on the desk.
I have not set eyes on them before.

========================= **EXERCISE 8.11: Review** =========================

Select the verb form given in parentheses that would be appropriate in formal
writing, and write it in the blank.

1. You _____ completed the assignment prior to leaving the
    office. (should have, should of)
2. I wanted to _____ down before preparing dinner. (lie, lay)
3. I _____ played in the game but I had injured my ankle
    the previous day. (could have, could of)
4. I needed to _____ down for a few minutes. (sit, set)
5. John had already _____ the book down on the table be-
    fore realizing that it was freshly painted. (laid, lain)
6. You _____ loiter in the public garden or the police will
    give you a ticket. (ought not to, hadn't ought to)
7. Joan _____ down for a few hours because she wasn't feel-
    ing well. (laid, lay)
8. The worker _____ her tools down while she took her
    lunch break. (sat, set)
9. George has been _____ down during the entire football
    game. (lying, laying)
10. Sue _____ down while the principal informed her of her
    suspension. (sat, set)
11. The children _____ play quietly or they will upset their
    mothers. (had better, better)
12. The former president _____ his notes down in book
    form. (sat, set)
13. The man has _____ down for quite some time. (lain, laid)
14. I _____ written sooner but I have a terrible time compos-
    ing letters. (would have, would of)

8.23 PRESENT TENSE

Standard written English requires the -s inflection for third person singular and
no inflection elsewhere (cf. 8.1 for the verb be):

Johns says.	I say.
She knows.	We know.
The dog bites.	They bite.
It does.	You do.

Forms such as I says, you knows, and it do are heard in casual conversation, but
they are not standard forms and should therefore be avoided in formal writing.

Negative contractions sometimes cause difficulties. The standard contraction of <u>does not</u> is <u>doesn't</u> (<u>she doesn't</u>), not <u>don't</u>. Negative <u>ain't</u> is commonly heard in casual conversation, as a contraction of various combinations, including <u>am not</u>, <u>is not</u>, <u>have not</u>, and <u>has not</u>. However, it should not be used in formal writing.

================= **EXERCISE 8.12** =================

For each verb listed in its base form, give the ·s form (3rd person singular present).

1. think	9. push	17. camouflage
2. taste	10. die	18. do
3. say	11. refuse	19. go
4. imply	12. fly	20. have
5. type	13. be	21. bury
6. cry	14. shout	22. crush
7. make	15. undertake	23. disagree
8. wrong	16. recognize	24. crouch

8.24 PAST AND -ED PARTICIPLE

Regular verbs have the same form for the past and the -ed participle:

> He <u>laughed</u> loudly.
> He hasn't <u>laughed</u> so much for a long time.

Some irregular verbs have different forms:

> She <u>spoke</u> to me about it.
> She has <u>spoken</u> to me about it.

In formal writing avoid nonstandard forms for the past and -ed participle:

> I <u>done</u> my assignment. [*Correct to* <u>did</u>.]
> We <u>seen</u> the movie last week. [*Correct to* <u>saw</u>.]
> He was <u>shook</u> up by the news. [*Correct to* <u>shaken</u>.]
> I must have <u>knew</u> her. [*Correct to* <u>known</u>.]

Some verbs have variant forms that are acceptable for both past and -ed participle: <u>dreamed</u>, <u>dreamt</u>; <u>kneeled</u>, <u>knelt</u>; <u>lighted</u>, <u>lit</u>; <u>shined</u>, <u>shone</u>. <u>Dove</u> is a past variant of <u>dived</u> in some regions. The past and -ed participle of <u>hang</u> is generally <u>hanged</u> in the sense "suspend by neck until dead" and is <u>hung</u> when it refers to pictures on a wall. The -ed participle of <u>get</u> is generally <u>gotten</u> in the sense "obtain possession of" (<u>I've gotten a new car</u>) and is generally <u>got</u> otherwise.

EXERCISE 8.13

For each irregular verb listed in its base form, give the past. For example, <u>live</u> has the past <u>lived</u> as in <u>I lived in New York last year</u>.

1. choose	9. lead	17. shake
2. have	10. hide	18. make
3. bring	11. write	19. see
4. cost	12. put	20. set
5. teach	13. lose	21. keep
6. hold	14. catch	22. throw
7. go	15. do	23. begin
8. draw	16. take	24. tear

EXERCISE 8.14

For each irregular verb listed in its base form, give the -ed participle. For example, <u>lived</u> as in <u>I have lived here for a long time</u>.

1. hear	9. grow	17. drive
2. win	10. tell	18. think
3. fall	11. give	19. see
4. make	12. have	20. find
5. spend	13. forget	21. show
6. go	14. do	22. stand
7. know	15. take	23. come
8. meet	16. read	24. eat

══════════════════ **EXERCISE 8.15: Review** ══════════════════

Select the form given in parentheses that would be appropriate in formal writing, and write it in the blank.

1. We _____ an accident on our way to work this morning. (saw, seen)
2. Mark _____ like staying after school to study in the library. (doesn't, don't)
3. And so I _____ to him, "You'll just have to finish the report without me. I'm going home." (says, said)
4. The young husband _____ home late after a night out with his friends. (came, come)
5. The other workers and I _____ the job without even being asked to do so. (did, done)
6. My mother _____ like it when I show up late for dinner. (doesn't, don't)
7. Our new puppy is lost and hasn't _____ home yet. (come, came)
8. My English teacher _____ that I'm ill, but she continues to mark me absent. (knows, know)
9. You _____ have to talk so loud; I can hear you just fine. (doesn't, don't)
10. The criminal was _____ for the murder that he committed. (hung, hanged)
11. I _____ out the wash so that it would dry. (hung, hanged)
12. I've _____ very good grades this semester in chemistry. (got, gotten)
13. I've _____ some very good advice for you: stay out of trouble. (got, gotten)
14. You should have _____ to me before you decided to come over to visit. (spoke, spoken)

8.25 PAST SUBJUNCTIVE AND PAST

The past subjunctive is used to refer to situations that are very unlikely or that are contrary to the facts (cf. 4.19):

> I wish she <u>were</u> here.
> He behaves as though he <u>were</u> your friend.
> Suppose she <u>were</u> here now.
> If I <u>were</u> you, I wouldn't tell him.

The only past subjunctive is <u>were</u>, which is used for the first and third person singular of the verb <u>be</u> in formal English. In less formal style the simple past <u>was</u> is generally used in the same contexts:

> I wish she <u>was</u> here.
> If I <u>was</u> you, I wouldn't tell him.

For plural and the second person singular of <u>be</u> and for all other verbs, the simple past is used to refer to situations in the present or future that are very unlikely or that are contrary to fact. One very common context is in conditional clauses, clauses expressing a condition on which something else is dependent:

> If they <u>were</u> graduating next year, they would need to borrow less money. [*But they probably will not be graduating next year.*]

> If she <u>lived</u> at home, she would be happier. [*But she does not live at home.*]

> If I <u>came</u> to your party, I would need a new dress. [*But I probably won't come to your party.*]

The verb in the main clause is always a past modal, usually <u>would</u>.

If the situations are set in the past, the past perfect is used in the conditional clause and a past perfect modal, usually <u>would have</u>, in the main clause:

> If we <u>had been</u> there yesterday, we <u>would have seen</u> them. [*But we were not there yesterday.*]
> If he <u>had been given</u> a good grade, he <u>would have told me</u>. [*But it seems that he was not given a good grade.*]

If the auxiliary in the conditional clause is <u>were</u>, <u>had</u>, or <u>should</u>, we can omit <u>if</u> and front the auxiliary:

> <u>Were</u> she here now, there would be no problem.
> <u>Had</u> we stayed at home, we would have met them.
> <u>Should</u> you see him, give him my best wishes.

EXERCISE 8.16

Select the verb form that would be appropriate in formal writing, and write it in the blank.

1. If I _____ you, I'd make an effort to show up at work on time more often. (was, were)

2. If the governor _____ in the state house more frequently, the state government would be running more smoothly. (was, were)

3. If the United States were to become involved in a war in Central America, many U.S. troops _____ have to be sent there. (will, would)

4. _____ we taken the time to do the work correctly, we wouldn't still be here doing it. (Had, Have)

5. The commander acts as though he _____ ready for combat at any time. (was, were)

6. If the child _____ a little more intelligent, he'd have no trouble getting into a very good prep school. (was, were)

7. Had the train arrived a few minutes earlier, we _____ have made the first act of the play. (will, would)

8. I believe strongly that if the committee _____ to pass the amendment our problems would be solved. (was, were)

9. _____ pass the exam, we'll go out to dinner to celebrate. (Should you, Were you to)

10. If I _____ given a second interview, I'd be assured of being offered the position. (was, were)

8.26 MULTIPLE NEGATION

Standard English generally allows only one negative in the same clause. Nonstandard English allows two or more negatives in the same clause:

double negation	They didn't say nothing.
corrected	They said nothing.
	They didn't say anything.
triple negation	Nobody never believes nothing I say.
corrected	Nobody ever believes anything I say.
double negation	I didn't like it, neither.
corrected	I didn't like it, either.

Negative adverbs include not only the obvious negative never, but also barely, hardly, scarcely:

double negation	I can't hardly tell the difference.
corrected	I can hardly tell the difference.

Standard English allows double negation when the two negatives combine to make a positive. When <u>not</u> modifies an adjective or adverb with a negative prefix (<u>unhappy</u>, <u>indecisively</u>), it reduces the negative force of the word, perhaps to express an understatement:

> It was a <u>not unhappy</u> occasion. (a fairly happy occasion)
> She spoke <u>not indecisively</u>. (fairly decisively)

Occasionally both the auxiliary and the main verb are negated:

> You ca<u>n't</u> <u>not</u> obey her instructions. (It's not possible for you not to obey her instructions.)

Other negative combinations also occasionally occur:

> <u>Nobody</u> has <u>no</u> complaints. (There is nobody that has no complaints. Everybody has some complaints.)

<hr>

EXERCISE 8.17

<hr>

Rewrite the sentences containing nonstandard double negatives. Some sentences may not need any revision.

EXAMPLE
> I didn't do nothing all last week.
> *I didn't do anything all last week.*

1. I can't hardly hear with the radio turned up so loud.
2. We didn't do nothing wrong, so why have you pulled us over, officer?
3. We are not displeased with the jury's verdict.
4. Nobody has no alternative ideas.
5. You can't not become involved in such an emotional issue as saving baby seals from being murdered by hunters.
6. I am not unhappy!
7. Those two suspects didn't do nothing to nobody.
8. It is not unusual for there to be cold weather in the northeast, even in April or May.
9. It is not police policy to say nothing about police corruption.
10. I didn't do nothing to deserve the treatment that I've received.

_____ ADJECTIVES AND ADVERBS _____

8.27 CONFUSION BETWEEN ADJECTIVES AND ADVERBS

It is occasionally not obvious whether to use an adjective or a related adverb. One rule is to use an adjective if the word is the subject complement after a linking verb (cf. 3.8). The adjective characterizes the subject:

> She looked <u>angry</u>.
> She feels <u>bad</u>.
> I don't feel <u>well</u>.
> He sounded <u>nervous</u>.
> The flowers smell <u>sweet</u>.
> The food tastes <u>good</u>.

The adverb <u>badly</u> is often used with the linking verb <u>feel</u>, but in formal writing use <u>feel bad</u>. <u>Well</u> in <u>I don't feel well</u> is an adjective meaning "in good health." It is an adverb in <u>He didn't play well</u>.

 If the word characterizes the manner of the action denoted by the verb, use an adverb in formal writing:

> She writes <u>well</u>. [*not* <u>good</u>]
> He hurt his neck <u>badly</u>. [*not* <u>bad</u>]
> Your dog is barking <u>loudly</u>. [*not* <u>loud</u>]
> If the job is done <u>satisfactorily</u>, I will give him other jobs. [*not* <u>satisfactory</u>]

 If the word in question is an intensifier of a verb, adjective, or adverb, use the -<u>ly</u> form in formal writing:

> I <u>sure</u> need a vacation. [*Correct to* <u>certainly</u>.]
> It was a <u>real</u> good story. [*Correct to* <u>really</u>.]

 Some words can have the same form for both the adjective and the adverb: <u>early</u>, <u>deep</u>, <u>fast</u>, <u>hard</u>, <u>late</u>, <u>slow</u>, <u>quick</u>, <u>long</u>, and words in -<u>ly</u> that are formed from nouns denoting time (<u>hourly</u>, <u>daily</u>). The adverbs <u>slow</u>, <u>quick</u>, and <u>deep</u> also have parallel adverb forms in -<u>ly</u>: <u>slowly</u>, <u>quickly</u>, and <u>deeply</u>. These two adverbs formed without the -<u>ly</u> suffix are used mainly with imperatives.

> <u>Drive slow</u>.
> <u>Come quick</u>.
> <u>Dig deep</u> into your pocket for a donation.

═══════════════════════ **EXERCISE 8.18** ═══════════════════════

Correct these sentences where necessary by substituting adjectives for adverbs or
adverbs for adjectives. Some of the sentences do not need to be corrected.

EXAMPLE
  WRONG   He scooped up the coins sudden.
  CORRECTED   He scooped up the coins suddenly.

1.   When she is in the mood, she writes real good.
2.   The child is eating too fast.
3.   When I last saw him, he spoke cheerful.
4.   Do your pants feel tightly?
5.   I sure appreciate your help.
6.   They fought hard against the change.
7.   The sunglasses feel fine.
8.   They seemed right pleased with themselves.
9.   I didn't sleep too good last night.
10.   I thought the policeman was growing rudely.
11.   We left early because I was not feeling well.
12.   The milk tasted sourly this morning.
13.   I felt good about the way they treated you.
14.   Your dog is barking loud.
15.   Many Americans are extreme overweight.
16.   They should think more positive about themselves.
17.   If the job is done satisfactory, I will give him other jobs.
18.   He hurt his neck bad.

.28   COMPARISON

Most adjectives and adverbs are <u>gradable</u> (cf. 5.12): we can view them as being
on a scale of less or more. Gradable words allow comparision (<u>less foolish</u>, <u>more
quickly</u>) and modification by intensifiers that show how far they are along the
scale (<u>somewhat foolish</u>, <u>very quickly</u>). Some adjectives and adverbs are not
gradable. For example, we cannot say <u>more medical</u> or <u>very previously</u>.

Writers vary on whether certain adjectives or adverbs are gradable. Those
who treat them as nongradable think that they express the highest degree (<u>excel-
lent</u>) or that they cannot be measured on a scale (<u>uniquely</u>). The most common
of these disputed words are <u>complete(ly)</u>, <u>perfect(ly)</u>, and <u>unique(ly)</u>. Yet even
in formal writing we find expressions such as <u>a more perfect union</u> or <u>the most
extreme poverty</u>. If you are in doubt, it is better not to treat these words as
gradable in formal writing.

In formal writing use the comparative for two only (the older of the two girls) and the superlative for more than two (the oldest of the three girls).

The comparative of the adjective bad and the adverb badly is worse (not worser); the superlative is worst (not worsest).

Fewer goes with count nouns and less with noncount nouns:

$$
\text{fewer}
\begin{cases}
\text{demonstrators} \\
\text{mistakes} \\
\text{votes}
\end{cases}
\qquad
\text{less}
\begin{cases}
\text{help} \\
\text{sunlight} \\
\text{time}
\end{cases}
$$

Less is often used with count nouns, but doing this is a mistake in formal writing.

EXERCISE 8.19

Give the inflected comparative and superlative of each adjective or adverb.

1. wise	6. strong	11. friendly
2. hard	7. heavy	12. risky
3. sad	8. large	13. fierce
4. angry	9. deep	14. tall
5. rare	10. happy	15. red

8.29 ONLY

Where you put only in a sentence may affect how the reader understands the sentence. In speech you can make your intention clear through your intonation, but when you write, it is best to put only next to the word or phrase it refers to:

> Only children can swim in the lake before noon. [*not adults*]
> Children can only swim in the lake before noon. [*not fish*]
> Children can swim only in the lake before noon. [*not in the pool*]
> Children can swim in the lake only before noon. [*not in the afternoon*]

There are other words that you need to position with care: also, even, just, and merely.

========================= **EXERCISE 8.20** =========================

At the end of each sentence a focusing adverb is given in parentheses. Rewrite the sentence by adding the focusing adverb. Circle the adverb and underline the focused part.

EXAMPLE

Fanatical runners often continue to perform after an injury. (even)
Fanatical runners often continue to perform (even) after an injury.

1. Home plate was a few feet away. (only)
2. She was running two miles. (merely)
3. He stretched a little more on his forehand shot. (just)
4. A heart attack can happen in the middle of a game. (even)
5. Middle-aged athletes remember their youth. (also)
6. Most sport-related injuries do not kill; they do not cripple. (either)
7. Most sport-related injuries incapacitate. (merely)
8. Squash and tennis players suffer knee and ankle injuries. (mainly)
9. They suffer eye injuries. (too)
10. Tennis elbow affects tennis players. (particularly)

.30 DANGLING MODIFIERS

Absolute clauses are nonfinite or verbless adverbial clauses that have their own subjects:

> All their money having been spent on repairs, they applied to the bank for a loan.
> He nervously began his speech, his voice trembling and his face flushed.
> They strolled by the river, their heads bare.

If adverbial clauses have no subject of their own, their implied subject is generally the same as the subject of the sentence:

> Having spent all his money on a vacation to Hawaii, Norman applied to the bank for a loan. [*Norman has spent all his money on a vacation to Hawaii.*]

A **dangling modifier** has no subject of its own, and its implied subject cannot be identified with the subject of the sentence though it can usually be identified with some other phrase in the sentence:

dangling	Being blind, a dog guided her across the street.
corrected	Being blind, she was guided across the street by a dog.
dangling	Although large enough, they did not like the apartment.
corrected	Although the apartment was large enough, they did not like it.
dangling	After turning the radio off, the interior of the truck became silent.
corrected	After she (or I, etc.) turned the radio off, the interior of the truck became silent.
dangling	When sick, the state makes social security payments.
corrected	When you are sick, the state makes social security payments.
dangling	Being an excellent student, her teacher gave her extra assignments.
corrected	Since she was an excellent student, her teacher gave her extra assignments.

EXERCISE 8.21

Rewrite each sentence, avoiding dangling modifiers.

EXAMPLE
   While intoxicated, my car was involved in a serious accident.
   While intoxicated, I was involved in a serious accident.

1. Having successfully completed the project, dinner was in order.
2. Claiming that a new carrier was unnecessary, the bill was vetoed by the president.
3. Having completed the balloon crossing, hundreds of French villagers welcomed the three balloonists.
4. Unwilling to lay down his gun, the police shot dead the escaped convict.
5. When delivered, they found the merchandise spoiled.
6. When attending college, there's always a chance of overworking yourself.
7. When approaching the building, no single feature has an impact on the viewer.
8. Heavy with blossoms, I saw the tree swaying in the wind.

9. A weak student, his teacher gave him extra assignments and went over them with him privately.
10. After completing the first four columns, each should be added separately.

===

EXERCISE 8.22: Review

Each sentence contains an adjective or adverb used inappropriately, a faulty comparison, or a dangling modifier. Rewrite each sentence, correcting the error it contains.

1. By purchasing a bond for 7,500 dollars, at the end of a five-year period it would be worth 12,000 dollars.
2. I did very good on the physics test I took last period.
3. The new contract provides for less working hours per week.
4. While hunting in the woods, a wolf killed him.
5. We had a real nice time on our vacation to London last summer.
6. Being in charge, the accusation was particularly annoying to me.
7. The unions expect less negative votes than last election.
8. John didn't play very good in last night's baseball game.
9. Sue played the most perfect tennis match that I have ever seen.
10. Running out of gasoline, we pulled our car into a service station to have the tank filled.
11. I feel very badly about your accident.
12. Because of inflation, they are likely to have less dollars in real terms.
13. I did very poor on my college entrance exams.

CHAPTER NINE

Style

9.1 STYLE IN WRITING

In normal unprepared conversation we have only a very limited time to monitor what we say and the way we say it. We have much more time when we write, and generally we have the opportunity to revise what we write. Sometimes we are happy with our first decision, but often we think of new things as we write and perhaps want to change both what we write and how we write it.

In our revisions we can draw on the resources that are available to us in various aspects of the language. Our writing style reflects the choices we make. In this chapter we will be looking at the choices we make in grammar. In particular, we will be considering how we can ensure that we convey our message effectively.

————————— EMPHASIS —————————

9.2 END-FOCUS

Given – new

It is normal to arrange the information in our message so that the most important information comes at the end. We follow this principle of **end-focus** when we put such information at the end of a sentence or clause. In contrast, the beginning of a sentence or clause typically contains information that is general knowledge, or is obvious from the context, or may be assumed as given because it has been mentioned earlier:

[1]   The second-quarter increase in U.S. efficiency in producing goods and services was <u>slightly below the 1.6 percent improvement in 1986.</u>

The information that there was a second-quarter increase in 1987 is known from a preceding sentence (in the news item from which this sentence is drawn) and therefore appears at the beginning of the sentence. The new information appears at the end.

If we put a subordinate clause at the end, it receives greater emphasis. For example, [2] emphasizes the action of the committee members, whereas [2a] emphasizes their feelings:

    [2]   <u>Although they were not completely happy with it</u>, the committee members adopted her wording of the resolution.
    [2a] The committee members adopted her wording of the resolution, <u>although they were not completely happy with it</u>.

Similarly, the pairs that follow show how we can choose which information comes at the end by the way we phrase the sentence:

    [3]   The American public is not interested in <u>foreign policy</u>.
    [3a] Foreign policy does not interest <u>the American public</u>.

    [4]   History majors tend to have higher grade point averages than <u>English majors</u>.
    [4a] English majors tend to have lower grade point averages than <u>History majors</u>.

    [5]   Juniors and seniors are <u>difficult to teach</u>.
    [5a] It is difficult to teach <u>juniors and seniors</u>.

═══════════════ EXERCISE 9.1 ═══════════════

Rewrite the following sentences so that the underlined part is placed in the emphatic end position.

EXAMPLE
   <u>General Tomlin</u> outlined the surrender terms.
   The surrender terms were outlined by General Tomlin.

    1. <u>Chicago</u> is similar in many ways to Baltimore.
    2. <u>The administration's energy policy</u> benefits the oil companies.
    3. <u>No other nation in the world</u> consumes more oil than the U.S.
    4. <u>Although police officers no longer have to be above a particular height</u>, doctors make sure that height and weight are in the right proportions.
    5. <u>Rats</u> were crawling all over the building.
    6. I doubt if <u>New York</u> would have such violent race riots.
    7. <u>That car</u> belongs to my sister.

8. All of the students were interested in the lecture on the origins of English words.
9. Last winter's foul weather is part of the reason for inflation.
10. Serious malnutrition affects more than a third of the people in the world.

9.3 FRONT-FOCUS

If we place an expression in an abnormal position, the effect is to make the expression more conspicuous. It is abnormal for the verb and any objects or complements to come before the subject. If these are fronted, they acquire greater prominence:

> Attitudes will not change overnight, but change they will.
> Marijuana they used occasionally, but cocaine they never touched.
> Easily recognizable was the leader of the wolf pack.

When a negative adverbial is fronted, it gains stronger emphasis. The operator comes before the subject, as in questions:

> Never have so many youngsters been unemployed.
> Under no circumstances will they permit smoking in public areas.

EXERCISE 9.2

Put the underlined part in front to give it strong emphasis.

1. The police force no longer excludes short persons.
2. They will sign, or they will not be freed.
3. They not only consult doctors more frequently, but they do so about more minor problems.
4. He rejected the treatment only after thorough investigation.
5. Though they may be reluctant, they will accept the assignment.
6. Affirmative action will never receive as much attention as it does now.

7. I liked <u>the movie version of Jaws</u> but I disliked <u>the book version</u>.
8. The greatest difficulty we had was <u>raising sufficient funds to staff the shelter for the homeless</u>.
9. The man was <u>qualified</u>, but he was still not given the job.
10. You must <u>not only</u> take the class, but you must receive a grade of A in it as well.

9.4 <u>THERE</u>-STRUCTURES AND CLEFT SENTENCES

<u>There</u>-structures give greater prominence to the subject (cf. 6.11). They are particularly useful when the only other elements are the subject and the verb <u>be</u>:

> There are no simple solutions.
> There is more than one kind of octane rating.
> There is no reason to believe that the Administration condoned the attempted assassination of foreign leaders.

Cleft sentences (cf. 6.12) provide greater prominence to one part of the sentence by placing it after a semantically empty subject (<u>it</u>) and a semantically empty verb (<u>be</u>):

> It was <u>a human error</u> that caused the explosion.
> It is <u>the ending</u> that is the weakest part of the novel.

9.5 PARENTHETIC EXPRESSIONS

Parenthetic expressions are marked by intonation in speech and by punctuation in writing. The effect of the interruption is to give greater prominence to the previous unit:

> <u>Freud</u>, of course, thought that he had discovered the underlying causes of many mental illnesses.
> The record business is <u>not</u>, in actual fact, an easy business to succeed in.
> <u>In Australia</u>, for example, the kangaroo is a traffic hazard.
> <u>The unions</u>, understandably, wanted the wage increase to be adjusted to rising inflation.

EXERCISE 9.3

An adverbial is given in parentheses at the end of each sentence. Rewrite each sentence, inserting the adverbial in an appropriate place as a parenthetical adverbial. More than one place may be appropriate.

1. The committee was not as docile as the chairman expected. (as it happens)
2. On a Saturday afternoon you will see crowds in the parks. (perhaps)
3. Heart disease was the principal cause of death. (however)
4. The passenger was able to escape without serious injury. (fortunately)
5. The chair of the committee moved that the motion be approved. (therefore)
6. The president is not the person you should try to contact. (in fact)
7. The coach is very much admired by his colleagues. (indeed)
8. You should make every effort to perform your duties to the best of your ability. (nevertheless)
9. The car is beyond repair and should be junked. (probably)
10. This version of the manuscript illustrates the originality of the author's ideas. (for instance)

EXERCISE 9.4

Rewrite the following paragraph, moving constructions to achieve better emphasis.

Publishing books has become an expensive enterprise. Publishing companies can no longer publish books simply because they are good. Publishers must consider the potential market of the books they intend to publish. Publishers run the risk of losing large amounts of money if they publish unpopular books. Such books will eventually put the publisher out of business. If publishers market popular books, on the other hand, they will make profits enabling them to market a few less popular but equally good books. In fact a great many publishers have this philosophy. They survive, because of it, quite well.

_____ CLARITY _____

9.6 END-WEIGHT

Where there is a choice, it is normal for a longer structure to come at the end. This principle of **end-weight** is in large part a consequence of the principle of end-focus (cf. 9.2), since the more important information tends to be given in fuller detail.

A sentence is clumsy and more difficult to understand when the subject is considerably longer than the predicate. We can rephrase the sentence to shift the weight, or part of it, to the end:

clumsy	The rate at which the American people are using up the world's supply of irreplaceable fossil fuels and their refusal to admit that the supply is limited is the real problem.
improved	The real problem is the rate at which the American people are using up the world's supply of irreplaceable fossil fuels and their refusal to admit that the supply is limited.

Similarly, if there is a considerable difference in length among the units that follow the verb, the longest unit should come at the end:

clumsy	The discovery of a baby mammal in Siberia has provided biochemists, anthropologists, immunologists, zoologists, and paleontologists with ample material.
improved	The discovery of a baby mammal in Siberia has provided ample material for biochemists, anthropologists, immunologists, zoologists, and paleontologists.

Other examples follow where a rephrasing is desirable because of the principle of end-weight:

clumsy	Einstein's theories have made many important technological developments which we now take for granted possible.
improved	Eistein's theories have made possible many important technological developments which we now take for granted.

clumsy	The value of trying to identify the problem and to provide the tools necessary to make the education of these children a success is not questioned.
improved	No one questions the value of trying to identify the problem and to provide the tools necessary to make the education of these children a success.
clumsy	That the recession will be longer, deeper, and more painful than was expected only a few weeks ago is very possible.
improved	It is very possible that the recession will be longer, deeper, and more painful than was expected only a few weeks ago.
clumsy	Thousands of medical volunteers, among them many young American doctors who had just finished their medical training, fought in the war against smallpox.
improved	Thousands of medical volunteers fought in the war against smallpox, among them many young American doctors who had just finished their medical training.
clumsy	A pronunciation set of symbols to enable the reader to produce a satisfactory pronunciation is used.
improved	A pronunciation set of symbols is used to enable the reader to produce a satisfactory pronunciation.

EXERCISE 9.5

Rewrite the following sentences to make them clearer by making the predicate longer than the underlined subject.

1. An open letter beseeching the all-male College of Cardinals to incorporate women into the election of the Pope was issued.
2. One way to limit the complexity of speech synthesis systems which arises from the need for linguistic and contextual knowledge is to limit the scope of the task.
3. A statue of the statesman holding a sword in one hand and a shield in the other hand stood at the entrance.
4. The provocative thought that the bureaucracy is a public service for the benefit of citizens is offered.

5. The difficulty of devising strategies for imparting information about the structure of the language and about the context to the computer makes speech recognition by a computer very difficult.
6. Public health officials, social workers, police, civil liberties lawyers, and even divorce lawyers distract teachers from their teaching.
7. Three of the region's major seabird rookeries and a breeding ground for California and stellar sea lions, northern fur seals, harbor seals, and northern elephant seals are in San Miguel Island.
8. To do whatever can be done to motivate students to improve their reading and writing skills is necessary.
9. Many waste products from the catalytic combustion of gasoline are emitted.

9.7 MISPLACED EXPRESSIONS

We show where an expression belongs by where we place it. For example, [1] and [1a] as written sentences are likely to be understood differently because of the different positions of immediately afterwards:

[1] Immediately afterwards I remembered having met her.
[1a] I remembered having met her immediately afterwards.

A sentence is more difficult to understand when an expression is misplaced, even if there is no danger of misinterpretation. The [a] sentences in the pairs that follow give a corrected placement:

[2] He had not realized how slim she had become before he saw her.
[2a] Before he saw her, he had not realized how slim she had become.

[3] They knew what I meant quite well.
[3a] They knew quite well what I meant.

[4] The students prefer a pass/fail grade who are in the senior year.
[4a] The students who are in the senior year prefer a pass/fail grade.

[5] She told him that it was all a joke in a calm voice.
[5a] She told him in a calm voice that it was all a joke.

Sometimes a sentence has more than one interpretation because an expression is positioned where it might belong in either of two directions. In [6] <u>on several occasions</u> may go with <u>He said</u> or with <u>he suffered from headaches</u>:

    [6]   He said <u>on several occasions</u> he suffered from headaches.

One way of showing it belongs with <u>He said</u> is to insert the conjunction <u>that</u> after it, since <u>on several occasions</u> will then be outside the boundaries of the subordinate clause:

    [6a]   He said <u>on several occasions</u> that he suffered from headaches.

For [7], we can ensure the correct interpretation by moving <u>again</u> to unambiguous positions, as in [7a] and [7b]:

    [7]   I told them <u>again</u> the meeting had been postponed.
    [7a]   I <u>again</u> told them the meeting had been postponed.
    [7b]   I told them the meeting had <u>again</u> been postponed.

For [8], it might be best to rephrase the sentence, as in [8a] and [8b]:

    [8]   Writing <u>clearly</u> is important.
    [8a]   It is important to write clearly.
    [8b]   It is clear that writing is important.

Similarly, [9a] and [9b] clarify the intended meaning of the writer of [9]:

    [9]   Looking at the ages of the subjects <u>first</u> proved not to be very useful.
    [9a]   It proved not to be very useful to look <u>first</u> at the ages of the subjects.
    [9b]   <u>At first</u> it proved not to be very useful to look at the ages of the subjects.

═══════════ EXERCISE 9.6 ═══════════

Rewrite each sentence to avoid the misplaced constructions that are underlined.

1. Brian asked how she was <u>quite routinely</u>.
2. He says <u>sometimes</u> he smokes cigars.
3. Her voice expressed slightly injured surprise, <u>which sounded hoarse</u>.
4. Treating children <u>naturally</u> can be pleasant.

5. To spend a vacation <u>in many ways</u> is necessary for mental health.
6. <u>Based on what the quotations reveal about the meaning of the</u> <u>word</u>, he writes the definitions.
7. The doctor advised her <u>on every occasion</u> to take sedatives.
8. They claimed <u>when they were young</u> they had very little money.
9. A woman conducted the seminar <u>who was very intelligent and</u> <u>interesting</u>.
10. Drinking <u>normally</u> made him happy.

9.8   ABSTRACT NOUNS

It is often possible to make a sentence clearer by rephrasing it to replace abstract nouns (or at least some of them) with verbs or adjectives:

clumsy   Since the <u>decriminalization</u> of public <u>drunkenness</u>, people have been avoiding Broadway Park, where drunks have been congregating.

improved   Since it is no longer a crime to be drunk in public, people have been avoiding Broadway Park, where drunks have been congregating.

clumsy   The report evaluates the <u>effectiveness</u> of the federal regulations in terms of the <u>extent</u> to which exposures to carcinogenic substances have been reduced.

improved   The report evaluates how effective the federal regulations have been in reducing exposures to carcinogenic substances.

clumsy   They should lessen their <u>self-centeredness</u> and increase their <u>assistance</u> to others.

improved   They should be less self-centered and more helpful to others.

General abstract nouns are often redundant. You can easily leave them out by rephrasing the sentence:

redundant   If the fox population were not controlled by <u>the</u> <u>fox-hunting method</u>, other techniques would have to be employed.

improved   If the fox population were not controlled by <u>fox-hunting</u>, other techniques would have to be employed.

redundant The charge that the industry is making excessive profits does not stand on a valid foundation.

improved The charge that the industry is making excessive profits is not valid.

redundant The entertainment aspect of reading is a factor in addition to the informative experience of reading.

improved Reading can provide entertainment as well as information.

or Reading can be entertaining as well as informative.

Some longwinded phrases with general words such as fact are better replaced by simpler conjunctions or prepositions:

longwinded I went to the movie in spite of the fact that I dislike war movies.

improved I went to the movie even though I dislike war movies.

Other examples are on account of the fact that and due to the fact that (both of which can be replaced by "because"), apart from the fact that ("except"), as a consequence of ("because of"), during the course of ("during"), in the neighborhood of ("near"), with the exception of ("except").

EXERCISE 9.7

Rewrite each sentence, eliminating the abstract nouns that are underlined.

EXAMPLE

The implementation of the plan was not done by the committee.
The committee did not implement the plan.

1. The decline of the dollar was noticed by us last week.
2. The importance of a strong economy is sometimes overlooked.
3. The foolishness of the candidate was not noticed by the voters.
4. The writing of the report was done by the two co-workers.
5. The correction of the problems was handled by the mayor's office.
6. One must consider the need of most individuals to have shelter and food.
7. The misanalysis of the situation by the company could be disastrous.
8. The bombing of the port by the army was unnecessary.

=========== **EXERCISE 9.8** ===========

For each word, provide three words that are more specific.

EXAMPLE

<u>artisan</u> → electrician, plumber, carpenter

1. vegetable
2. walk (verb)
3. haircut
4. cook (verb)
5. bad (adjective), as in <u>bad weather</u>
6. rub (verb)
7. colorless (adjective), as in <u>colorless face</u>
8. soft (adjective), as in <u>soft material</u>
9. flow (verb), as in <u>The river flows into the sea</u>
10. dog (noun)
11. look (verb), as in <u>She looked at the pictures</u>
12. think
13. blemish (noun)
14. doctor (noun)

9.9 MODIFIERS IN NOUN PHRASES

Readers may find it difficult to work out the meaning of a noun phrase that has two or more modifiers. If we are writing about American history, it may be obvious what we mean by <u>American history teachers</u>. But if the context fails to make the meaning unambiguous, we should use prepositions to show the relationships: <u>teachers of American history</u> or <u>American teachers of history</u>.

Even if there is no ambiguity, a long noun phrase such as <u>annual human rights progress statements</u> is better written with prepositions that indicate the words that belong together: <u>annual statements on the progress of human rights</u>.

=========== **EXERCISE 9.9** ===========

Rewrite each noun phrase to make it read more clearly.

1. arms control impact statements
2. a real estate law specialist
3. applicant data information cards
4. French language specialists
5. rocket engine booster rockets
6. American sociology teachers

9.10 SUBORDINATION

It is sometimes better to split up a complex sentence:

[1]   She rehearsed the speech <u>which</u> she was to give to the committee <u>which distributed</u> federal funds <u>which had been allocated</u> for training the unemployed.

We can replace the last two <u>which</u> clauses by converting them into nonfinite clauses, as in [1a]:

[1a]   She rehearsed the speech <u>which</u> she was to give to the committee <u>distributing</u> federal funds <u>allocated</u> for training the unemployed.

A similar problem appears in [2]:

[2]   If the college has to admit all students who apply for admission, it will admit many who are not capable of doing college work, <u>which</u> will force them to drop out when they find that they cannot cope with the work, <u>which</u> would be a waste of taxpayers' money and classroom space.

The difficulty with [2] lies in particular with the repetition of the <u>which</u> clauses. Both of them refer back to the part of the sentence that immediately precedes them. We can improve the sentence by dividing it into two sentences and in other ways, as in [2a]:

[2a]   If the college has to admit all students who apply for admission, it will admit many who are not capable of doing college work. Those students will be forced to drop out when they find that they cannot cope with the work, and meanwhile they will have wasted taxpayers' money and taken up classroom space.

═══════════════════ **EXERCISE 9.10** ═══════════════════

Rewrite each sentence, making it less complex.

1.   The dark walls were enlivened by plants hanging from the walls, which gave off an array of colors through the dense smoke which flowed through the air from the many people lighting up their cigarettes, which kept their hands company while their mouths were busy with their drinks.

2. Because many minor revisions were still required in the second draft of the document, contact with individual committee members was made by phone or mail, as they had been dissolved as a standing committee by the board and were to be replaced soon by an entirely new committee made up of members from a different department within the university.

3. Although many alternative energy forms are not safe, for example many people are lost in mining accidents, these kinds of incidents could never compare to the catastrophic effects of nuclear accidents, which can cause immediate death from radiation poisoning, long-term death from cancer, and the destruction of land which cannot be inhabited for years because of radiation contamination.

4. Public confidence in airline safety has been shaky recently because of numerous plane crashes in recent years and because inspections of planes have turned up numerous safety violations which Federal Aviation Administration officials think is the result of deregulation in the 1970s and which many other experts in the field think will continue until new laws are passed.

5. Many politicians and economists believe that entitlement programs such as social security must be cut if we are to achieve a balanced federal budget, which for the past few years has been running a deficit approaching a trillion dollars, a deficit which, if not ended, will lead to a fiscal crisis in the future which will be very difficult to control and which will result in the end of the United States as a world economic power.

9.11 PARALLELISM

Parallel structures provide a pleasing balance between the parallel units, and they emphasize meaningful relationships between the units such as equivalence and contrast.

Parallelism often involves coordination. The coordinate units must be similar in type. Here are examples of faulty parallelism, where the units are wrongly coordinated:

faulty	They discontinued the production of the paint because the results of the field tests were unsatisfactory and a lack of interested customers. [*clause and noun phrase*]
corrected	They discontinued the production of the paint because the results of the field tests were unsatisfactory and there was a lack of interested customers.

or	They discontinued the production of the paint because of <u>the unsatisfactory results of the field tests</u> and <u>a lack of interested customers</u>.
faulty	You will find long lines <u>in the bookstore</u> and <u>to pay your tuition</u>. [*prepositional phrase and infinitive clause*]
corrected	You will find long lines <u>in the bookstore</u> and <u>at the cashier</u>.

The relative pronoun <u>that</u> is generally an alternative to <u>which</u> or <u>who</u>. It is a fault to switch from <u>that</u> to <u>which</u> or <u>who</u>, or vice versa. The fault is illustrated in the following sentence; it can be corrected by using either <u>which</u> or <u>that</u> in both instances:

> Scientists are still trying to explain the UFO <u>which</u> was seen over Siberia in 1908 by thousands of witnesses and <u>that</u> caused an explosion like that of an H-bomb.

In a series of three or more coordinated units, we can often choose whether to repeat words from the first unit or to leave them out. We should be consistent, however:

faulty	The color of her hair, look of self-assurance, and <u>the</u> aristocratic bearing match those in the painting of the beautiful woman staring from the wall of the living room. [*determiner in the third unit, but not in the second*]
corrected	The color of her hair, <u>the</u> look of self-assurance, and <u>the</u> aristocratic bearing . . .
or	The color of her hair, look of self-assurance, and aristocratic bearing . . .

Correlatives (cf. 5.31) <u>both</u> . . . <u>and</u> and <u>either</u> . . . <u>or</u> are pairs of words that must introduce parallel units:

faulty	His collages derive from <u>both</u> art <u>and</u> from popular culture.
corrected	His collages derive from <u>both</u> art <u>and</u> popular culture.
or	His collages derive <u>both</u> from art <u>and</u> from popular culture.
faulty	They <u>neither</u> will help <u>nor</u> hinder her attempts to persuade the workers to join the trade union.
corrected	They will <u>neither</u> help <u>nor</u> hinder . . .

faulty   We realized that we had to make a decision, <u>either</u> marry <u>or</u> we go our separate ways.

corrected   We realized that we had to make a decision, <u>either</u> marry <u>or</u> go our separate ways.

Similarly, expressions that compare or contrast must also introduce parallel units:

faulty   The lung capacity of nonsmokers exposed to tobacco smoke in offices is <u>measurably less than</u> nonsmokers in smoke-free offices.

corrected   . . . is <u>measurably less than</u> that of nonsmokers in smoke-free offices.

faulty   I <u>prefer</u> the novels of Hemingway <u>to</u> Faulkner.

corrected   I <u>prefer</u> the novels of Hemingway <u>to</u> those of Faulkner.

or   I <u>prefer</u> Hemingway <u>to</u> Faulkner.

Both correlatives must be present in comparative structures of the type <u>The more, the merrier</u>:

faulty   If the cost of raw materials keeps rising, <u>the more</u> manufacturers will raise their prices.

corrected   <u>The more</u> the cost of raw materials rises, <u>the more</u> manufacturers will raise their prices.

or   If the cost of raw materials keeps rising, manufacturers will raise their prices.

EXERCISE 9.11

Correct the faulty parallelism in the sentences below.

1. It is a word for people in a hurry and don't have time to speak good English.
2. She strolled down the aisle, her hair in curlers and a faded blouse.
3. She searched for documents, interviewed officials in charge of development programs, and she visited villages near Saigon.
4. At present we know enough neither about animals nor ourselves to make categorical statements on the nature of human communication.

5. Not only would students be involved in college-bound programs,
    but could participate in industry projects.
6. You will find considerable difference between the paragraphs of
    deaf children compared to hearing children.
7. They objected to his complaint and that he refused the assign-
    ment.
8. His shoulder bag contained a pipe, a tobacco pouch, address
    book, and a calculator.
9. He either smokes cigars or cigarettes, but I cannot remember
    which.
10. The optical effects in recent space films are more spectacular
    than past films.
11. I prefer that I grind my own coffee beans and drinking coffee
    without sugar and cream.
12. For his next vacation he thought of visiting his friends in Florida,
    going abroad to Europe, or of learning to drive.
13. They neither will help nor hinder her attempts to persuade the
    workers to join the trade union.
14. College students do not seem as anxious to make friends when
    compared to high school days.

9.12   REPEATED SOUNDS

Avoid putting words near each other if they sound the same or almost the same
but have different meanings. The lack of harmony between sound and sense
may be distracting and sometimes even confusing. I suggest some alternatives
in parentheses:

> Industries and the professions are finding it increasingly dif-
> ficult to find people qualified in basic writing skills. [Re-
> place find by recruit or hire.]
> The subject of my paper is the agreement between subject
> and verb in English. [Replace the first subject by topic.]
> At this point I should point out that I left of my own free will.
> [Replace point out by mention.]
> The television show showed how coal was mined in the
> United States. [Replace showed by demonstrated.]

====== **EXERCISE 9.12** ======

Rewrite the sentences to avoid unnecessary repetition of sounds or of words with different meanings.

1. The audience was noisy at first, but later it became quite quiet.
2. The television show showed how coal was mined in the United States.
3. The public was informed that a formal enquiry would soon be held.
4. My intention is to give more attention in the future to my children.
5. I found that finding a class can be frustrating.
6. He was active in extracurricular activities.
7. You will avoid criticism by stopping pampering yourself.
8. The elderly may decide to own their own homes.
9. You should make reservations at the hotels of your choice before you leave; that way you will not have to look for a hotel on the way.
10. I think that that book of readings recommended for the course is now out of print.
11. Congress rejected the President's plan to establish a gas-rationing plan.

---

13 PRONOUN REFERENCE

A pronoun may refer to something in the situation (this in Give this to your mother), but generally it refers back to another word or phrase—its antecedent (cf. 5.15). The reference to an antecedent should be clear:

unclear	The students worked during the vacation for individuals who were fussy about their work.
clarified	The students worked during the vacation for individuals who were fussy about the students' work.
or	The students worked during the vacation for individuals who were fussy about their own work.

You need to be particularly careful when you intend the pronoun to refer to more than a phrase:

unclear   Some people believe that <u>a person is successful only when he acquires enormous wealth</u> and they cannot be persuaded otherwise. But <u>that</u> is not always true.

clarified   Some people believe that <u>a person is successful only when he acquires enormous wealth</u> and they cannot be persuaded otherwise. But wealth is not always a true measure of success.

Do not use a pronoun to refer vaguely to an antecedent that is implied but is not actually present. Replace the pronoun with a suitable noun phrase:

vague   The airlines and the airports are unable to cope with the flood of passengers. Delays and frustration affect travelers daily. No one saw <u>it</u> coming.

clarified   The airlines and the airports are unable to cope with the flood of passengers. Delays and frustration affect travelers daily. No one anticipated <u>the problem</u>.

You can sometimes improve a sentence by rephrasing it to omit a pronoun:

unnecessary pronoun   In some of the states that have passed the death penalty, <u>they</u> rarely impose it.

improved   Some of the states that have passed the death penalty rarely impose it.

══════════════ EXERCISE 9.13 ══════════════

Rewrite each sentence so that the reference to an antecedent is clear.

1. Ground controllers have twice tried to stabilize Skylab, the American space ship which is showing a dangerous loss of altitude. <u>They</u> didn't work.
2. Panin and Righi are exchanged and <u>he</u> goes to his execution in a Moscow prison.
3. Experience shows that when abortion laws are liberalized, <u>they</u> skyrocket.
4. He spoke about appreciating the beer you are drinking, <u>which</u> starts with the serving.
5. I think you are making a mistake, but <u>that</u> is your decision.
6. The old man told his son that <u>he</u> could not smoke.

7. The teachers made the students put <u>their</u> names on the top of each sheet.
8. In France <u>they</u> do not have political prisoners.
9. In the textbook <u>it</u> says we should make sure that the reference of pronouns is clear.
10. People buy cars to separate <u>them</u> into different social classes.
11. The sermon is to be devoted to peace, <u>which</u> I really appreciate.

CONSISTENCY

9.14 PRONOUN AGREEMENT

Pronouns should agree with their antecedents in number (cf. 5.15):

faulty	Get <u>a university map</u> because <u>they</u> really help.
corrected	Get <u>a university map</u> because <u>it</u> really helps.
faulty	<u>A manager</u> should consider several factors when determining how <u>they</u> will deal with inefficient employees.
corrected	<u>Managers</u> should consider several factors when determining how <u>they</u> will deal with inefficient employees.
faulty	When <u>one partner</u> in a marriage says <u>they</u> will not compromise, the marriage is in danger.
corrected	When <u>one partner</u> in a marriage says <u>he or she</u> will not compromise, the marriage is in danger.

Be consistent in the use of pronouns. Use the same pronouns to refer to the same persons:

inconsistent	Every day <u>you</u> are bombarded with advertisements. It is up to <u>us</u> to decide what is worth buying.
corrected	Every day <u>you</u> are bombarded with advertisements. It is up to <u>you</u> to decide what is worth buying.
or	Every day <u>we</u> are bombarded with advertisements. It is up to <u>us</u> to decide what is worth buying.

<u>One</u> is followed by <u>one</u> or the <u>he</u>-set of pronouns:

inconsistent	One always thinks that the grass is greener on the other side, until <u>you</u> step over and find that it is not.
corrected	One always thinks that the grass is greener on the other side, until <u>one</u> steps over and finds that it is not.
or	One always thinks that the grass is greener on the other side, until <u>he</u> steps over and finds that it is not.
or	<u>We</u> always think that the grass is greener on the other side, until <u>we</u> step over and find that it is not.

The inconsistency in the next example follows from the inconsistent switch from passive to active:

inconsistent	A coordinating conjunction should be used to join two main clauses when <u>you</u> want to give them equal emphasis.
corrected	<u>You</u> should use a coordinating conjunction to join two main clauses when <u>you</u> want to give them equal emphasis.
or	A coordinating conjunction should be used to join two main clauses when equal emphasis is required.

═══ EXERCISE 9.14 ═══

Rewrite each sentence to eliminate inconsistencies in pronouns.

1. If an individual is conscientious, they will do well in their jobs.
2. One does not look at new words and phrases as changes in the language. We look upon them as fads.
3. If one can speak the language fluently, you can negotiate a better price.
4. I recommend that you buy a Milwaukee beer. They're quite good.
5. A person should strive to get the best education possible. That way you can be sure that you will receive a well-paying and satisfying job.
6. Trying one's hardest to get in good shape can ruin your health if you're not careful.

9.15 TENSE CONSISTENCY

Be consistent in your use of tenses:

> A day later you <u>start</u> thinking about the assignment and then you <u>realized</u> that you <u>had</u> been neglecting it. [*Replace* <u>realized</u> *with* <u>realize</u> *and* <u>had</u> *with* <u>have</u>.]
>
> Mr. William Sanders <u>is</u> a loyal and efficient man. He rarely <u>left</u> the house until all his work <u>was</u> done. [*Replace* <u>left</u> *with* <u>leaves</u> *and* <u>was</u> *with* <u>is</u>.]
>
> Sexist society <u>condoned</u> freedom and permissiveness in the male, but <u>forbid</u> it in the female. [*Replace* <u>forbid</u> *with* <u>forbade</u> *or* <u>forbad</u>.]
>
> For the most part they well <u>understood</u> the problems, once <u>being</u> freshmen themselves. [*Replace* <u>once being</u> *with* <u>having once been</u>.]
>
> Although I <u>worked</u> until midnight, I <u>can't</u> finish all my assignments. [*Replace* <u>can't</u> *with* <u>couldn't</u>.]
>
> If you <u>had</u> gone to the bookstore before the semester <u>started</u>, you <u>would be</u> able to buy all your course books. [*Replace* <u>would be</u> *with* <u>would have been</u>.]

==================== **EXERCISE 9.15** ====================

Rewrite each sentence to remove inconsistencies in tenses.

1. He seldom kept the public informed about his policies or take their advice.
2. The spheres rotate and sent out streams of light in every direction.
3. They wanted to show how our culture has changed and affect their life styles.
4. Once she knows a better way to study, she would feel much better.
5. After I spoke to the contractor, but before I sign any contract, I would check with the Better Business Bureau.
6. Before I had begun preparing my survey, I wondered whether the topic was too technical for the average student.
7. The grass was kept very short and the bushes are trimmed.
8. Even though I had done all of the work, I still do poorly on in-class exams.

9.16 SEQUENCE CONSISTENCY

If you mention two or more items and then discuss them or give examples of them, it is clearer to do so in the original order:

> The committee had to decide whether to raise interest rates or to maintain them at their present levels. They faced a difficult choice. Raising the rates might cause a recession, whereas maintaining them at the same levels might worsen inflation.

> Both types of energy production—solar heating and coal-fired electricity plants—require persons to go down the mines: solar heating needs copper for tubing, while coal-fired plants need coal for fuel and iron for turbines.

═══ EXERCISE 9.16: Summary ═══

Rewrite each sentence to achieve the type of emphasis on the underlined items that is indicated in parentheses.

EXAMPLE
  That the work had been done well was noted by my boss. (end-focus)
  My boss noted that the work had been done well.

1. The Soviets will never again interfere with the policies of Hungary. (front-focus)
2. In actuality Darwin's theory of evolution remains controversial. (parenthetic expression)
3. Even though the field of medicine has made great progress in recent years, many poor people live very unhealthy lives. (end-focus)
4. The president's misguided foreign policy caused the flare-up of violence in the region. (cleft sentence)
5. Only three people attended the lecture. (there-structure)
6. The speaker's political views were easily proven simplistic. (front-focus)
7. Moving cross country can be very stressful. (end-focus)
8. In fact inflationary trends cannot be slowed by attempts at manipulating the stock market. (parenthetic expression)
9. Congress, not the White House staff, was responsible for the press leak. (cleft sentence)
10. Einstein's theory of relativity has not as yet been disproven by physicists. (end-focus)

11. <u>Many attempts</u> have been made to communicate with animals such as whales and dolphins. (<u>there</u>-structure)
12. The experiment was conducted by <u>doctors at Massachusetts General Hospital</u>. (cleft sentence)

EXERCISE 9.17: Summary

Rewrite each sentence to make it read more clearly.

EXAMPLE

The scientists were quite excited who made the discovery.
The scientists who made the discovery were quite excited.

1. That world peace will be achieved in the near future is unlikely.
2. Because of the decline in the value of the dollar, American tourists may not travel abroad this summer but will instead vacation in the United States, where they will be able to relax and unwind without having to pay the high prices they would encounter in places such as West Germany and Japan and where they will be able to enjoy the beauty and splendor that only the United States has to offer.
3. If you don't visit your dentist regularly, your teeth will fall out and you'll ultimately end up spending a lot of money on dentures. This is a fact.
4. The man was late for the meeting because the man was held up in traffic for more than an hour.
5. The environmental waste impact report was reviewed by the committee at its last meeting.
6. During the first four to six months, a widower's death rate increases by more than 140 percent, compared with other men of the same age and social class.
7. There is a need for restatement of national policy to encourage the private enterprise development of our national resources in balance with environmental benefits in a total sense.
8. Modifications in housing will help the elderly in overcoming their handicaps.
9. Exercising frequently prolongs one's life.
10. The discussion group discussed the possibility of meeting at a different time.

EXERCISE 9.18: Summary

Rewrite each sentence to avoid pronoun disagreements, tense inconsistencies, and sequence inconsistencies.

EXAMPLE

I was extremely upset with my insurance company. They just wouldn't pay my claim.

I was extremely upset with my insurance company. It just wouldn't pay my claim.

1. My job as a computer analyst has taught me to be responsible and encourages me to work to the best of my ability.
2. As new recruits, one learned that you have to obey your commanding officer or you will be disciplined severely.
3. I used to smoke and drink incessantly, but now I do not drink or smoke at all.
4. If the governor had signed the bill earlier, his reelection campaign would be going more smoothly.
5. Your self-worth is compromised if one doesn't get a job that is challenging and interesting.
6. The two main concerns of Americans are inflation and the energy shortage. They have come to recognize that the nation's energy problems are genuine and they are worried about the apparent inability of the government to cope with inflation.
7. If an individual does not have a college degree, they can still find an interesting career.
8. While many people in the seminar found the material quite difficult, others think it is too superficial.

CHAPTER TEN

Literary Analysis

0.1 THE LANGUAGE OF LITERATURE

Most of what we find in the language of literature, particularly in prose fiction and drama, we also find in other uses of language. Writers select from what is available in the language as a whole. Poetry, however, often departs from the norms of language use in two respects: (1) in deviations from the rules and conventions of ordinary language, and (2) in excessive regularities. For that reason, I will be drawing my examples from poetry. At the same time, it must be said that some poets are more inclined than others to keep close to everyday uses of language, perhaps even to simulate the style of natural conversations.

The deviations that we encounter in poetry are found in various aspects of the language. Poetry is distinctive visually: It is set out in lines that do not go right across the page. Spaces may be left between sets of lines to indicate the beginnings of new sections, and lines within sections may be indented in various ways to indicate connections of some kind, perhaps in rhyme or metrical pattern. The traditional verse convention is for each line to begin with a capital letter, but some modern poets defy this convention. Some modern poets also defy the ordinary language conventions of spelling and punctuation. E. E. Cummings is particularly idiosyncratic in this respect: for example, he regularly writes the first person singular pronoun as "i" and he sometimes inserts a punctuation mark in the middle of a word.

Poets often create new words. These tend to follow the normal rules for word formation rather than being deviant. Some eventually enter the general language. But new words are surprising at their first appearance and they may never be admitted to the general vocabulary, particularly when they are based on word-formation rules that are little used. Gerard Manley Hopkins seems to have invented unfathering ("depriving of a father"). He describes how the snow "Spins to the widow-making unchilding unfathering deeps." The new word and its sense are prepared for by the more transparent widow-making and the parallel <u>unchilding</u> (an existing word, though uncommon). Hopkins has combined the prefix <u>un-</u> with a noun to form a verb <u>unfather</u> in a deprivative sense. This is a rule of word formation that is little used. Even more rare is the formation of a negative noun by prefixing <u>un-</u> to an existing noun. Thomas Hardy introduces the noun <u>unhope</u> as the final word in the last stanza of "In Tenebris":

> Black is night's cope;
> But death will not appal
> One who, past doubtings all,
> Waits in <u>unhope</u>.

We find very few nouns with the prefix <u>-un</u>; two examples are <u>untruth</u> and <u>unrest</u>. Hopkins's <u>unfathering</u> and Hardy's <u>unhope</u> remain **nonce words** (words coined for a single occasion); they have not entered the vocabulary stock of the language.

Conversion is a common process for the formation of new words. We <u>butter</u> bread, take a <u>look</u>, <u>calm</u> somebody. In these everyday examples, words have changed from their original word class to a new word class without any change in their form: <u>butter</u> is a verb derived from a noun ("put butter on"), <u>look</u> is a noun derived from a verb, and <u>calm</u> is a verb derived from an adjective. Poets sometimes introduce nonce formations through conversion. Hopkins converts the adjective <u>comfortless</u> into a noun in "groping round my <u>comfortless</u>" and the abstract noncount noun <u>comfort</u> into a concrete count noun in "Here! creep, /Wretch, under a <u>comfort</u>." Cummings takes conversion to an extreme by converting the past form <u>did</u> and its negative <u>didn't</u> into nouns in "he sang his <u>didn't</u> he danced his <u>did</u>."

Sometimes the poet's lexical innovations are **compounds,** the combination of two words into one: Hopkins's <u>selfyeast</u> in "<u>selfyeast</u> of spirit a dull dough sours"; T. S. Eliot's <u>sea-girls</u>; <u>thought-fox</u> in the title of a poem by Ted Hughes; and <u>gift-strong</u> in John Berryman's "when he was young and <u>gift-strong</u>."

Poets often introduce unusual collocations of words, which may require figurative interpretations. Examples abound. Here are just a few:

> The child's <u>cry</u> / <u>Melts</u> in the wall. [Sylvia Plath]
> Bitter <u>memory</u> like <u>vomit</u> / <u>Choked</u> my throat. [Gary Snyder]
> Your <u>lips</u> are <u>animals</u> [Anne Sexton]
> This <u>grandson</u> of <u>fishes</u> [Robert Bly]
> across the <u>castrate lawn</u> [Richard Wilbur]
> <u>hopeless cathedrals</u> [Allen Ginsberg]

Some deviations are grammatical. Departures from normal word order are common in poetry. In the following line from Walt Whitman the direct object <u>Vigil strange</u> is fronted, an occasional unusual order in nonpoetic language (cf. 9.3):

> <u>Vigil strange</u> I kept on the field one night

What is abnormal is the order <u>vigil strange</u> rather than <u>strange vigil</u>, since adjectives generally come before the nouns they modify. In the next example, by W. H. Auden, the direct object <u>A white perfection</u> is abnormally placed between the subject <u>Swans in the winter</u> and the verb <u>have</u>:

> Swans in the winter air
> <u>A white perfection</u> have

In another example, from Wallace Stevens, the phrase <u>upon a hill</u> is extracted from the first of a pair of coordinated clauses (<u>I placed a jar in Tennessee upon a hill</u>) and placed after the second clause:

> I placed a jar in Tennessee
> And round it was, <u>upon a hill</u>.

In addition, the subject complement <u>round</u> is fronted from its normal position (<u>it was round</u>).

Finally, in these lines from a sonnet by Gerard Manley Hopkins, the verb <u>find</u> is abnormally omitted in the first of two coordinated clauses:

> . . . than blind
> Eyes in their dark can day or thirst can find
> Thirst's all-in-all in all a world of wet.

The sense is "than blind eyes can <u>find</u> day in their dark."

Excessive regularities are expressed in the systematic organization of features that otherwise occur unsystematically in the language. Poetry is often marked by patterns of sound—for example, meter, rhyme, and alliteration. The alliteration of <u>l</u> in this stanza from Philip Larkin's poem "Toads" is so abundant that it could not occur by chance in the ordinary use of language:

> Lots of folk live on their wits:
>   Lecturers, lispers,
> Losels, loblolly-men, louts—
>   They don't end as paupers.

The alternative lines end with identical sounds: <u>ts</u> in <u>wits</u> and <u>louts</u>, and <u>pers</u> in <u>lispers</u> and <u>paupers</u>.

Another type of patterning is **parallelism.** Parallel structures exhibit grammatical, lexical, and semantic similarities or contrasts. Here is an example of close parallelism from "Little Gidding" in T. S. Eliot's "Four Quartets":

> We die with the dying:
> See, they depart, and we go with them.
> We are born with the dead:
> See, they return, and bring us with them.

In the next example, from the end of one of John Donne's sonnets, the final two lines are parallel. This parallelism takes the form of **chiasmus,** a reversal of the order of the two parts of the parallel structures: the <u>except</u>-clause comes first in one line and second in the other:

> Take me to you, imprison me, for I,
> Except you enthrall me, never shall be free,
> Nor ever chaste, except you ravish me.

The two clauses in the first line are also parallel. Grammatically, both clauses are imperative, starting with an imperative verb followed by a direct object. Lexically, both clauses have the same pronoun, <u>me</u>, as direct object, and the verbs <u>take</u> (in this structure) and <u>imprison</u> are partial synonyms. Semantically, both clauses express the poet's request to God (the subject that is understood from the previous context) to take control of him.

One useful approach to literary analysis is to start by looking for the language features that deviate from what we know to be normal in language. This approach is explored in the following section.

EXERCISE 10.1

Identify and explain the examples of deviation given below.

1. Though wise men at their end know dark is right,
   Because their words had forked no lightning they
   Do not go gentle into that good night.
   Dylan Thomas, "Do Not Go Gentle into That Good Night"
2. We build excitement
   General Motors slogan
3. someones married their everyones
   laughed their cryings and did their dance.
   e.e. cummings "Anyone Lived in a Pretty How Town"
4. The houses are haunted
   By white night-gowns.
   Wallace Stevens, "Disillusionment of Ten O'Clock"
5. Personal Faxability
   ad for personal facsimile phone
6. The wrinkled sea beneath him crawls.
   Alfred, Lord Tennyson, "The Eagle"
7. Recently Revealed Rigid Rectangular Receptacle!
   ad for "New Merit Ultra Lights Box"
8. The hour-glass whispers to the lion's roar.
   W.H. Auden "Our Bias"

0.2 FOREGROUNDING

Literary language, especially poetic language, is distinguished by the consistency with which it uses **foregrounding.** The term <u>foregrounding</u> is a visual metaphor; it refers to the language features that stand out from the background of normal use. One of the objectives that literary analysts of the language of literature may set for themselves is to find interpretations of foregrounding. As in all literary criticism, there is scope for more than one interpretation, but some interpretations are more plausible than others.

I take as my first example a poem by Thomas Hardy, entitled "In Tenebris" ("In Darkness"). It has a Latin epigraph from Psalm 102, which is rendered in the King James version "My heart is smitten, and withered like grass." The complete poem follows:

Wintertime nighs;
But my bereavement-pain
It cannot bring again:
Twice no one dies.

(5)   Flower-petals flee;
But, since it once hath been,
No more that severing scene
Can harrow me.

Birds faint in dread:
(10) I shall not lose old strength
In the lone frost's black length:
Strength long since fled!

Leaves freeze to dun;
But friends can not turn cold
(15) This season as of old
For him with none.

Tempests may scath;
But love can not make smart
Again this year his heart
(20)   Who no heart hath.

Black is night's cope;
But death will not appal
One who, past doubtings all,
Waits in unhope.

The poem is divided into six stanzas. The stanza division is made more conspicuous than usual by the indentation of the first and last lines, which are shorter than the middle lines. Sound patterning reinforces the feeling that each stanza is a unit: the two shorter lines rhyme and the two longer lines rhyme, and no rhymes are repeated across stanzas. The metrical scheme is iambic (unstressed syllable followed by stressed syllable), but every stanza begins with a stressed syllable.

The parallelism in appearance and sound has its analogy in a parallelism in sense. The stanzas elaborate the comparison expressed in the epigram from the Psalms: a comparison between desolation in nature and desolation in personal feelings. The first line of each stanza portrays a negative image from nature, an image that conjures up loss or danger. The next three lines relate this image to a negative human experience.

Negation is foregrounded in the poem, which is replete with negative words (no one, no more, none, not, no) and words with negative connotations (such as wintertime, bereavement-pain, flee, lose, black, death). The final word is the nonce formation unhope, which we examined in the previous section. It makes a stronger impact than a possible synonym such as despair might have. As the negative of hope, it intimates the absence of any feeling of hope: a state beyond hope. The contrast with hope is underlined by the collocation Waits in unhope, which brings to mind the normal collocation waits in hope. In its strategic position as the final word of the poem, unhope is the climax to a series of preceding negative expressions.

The negation motif chimes with the imagery and themes of the poem. In each stanza the comments that follow the nature imagery allude to previous experiences of pain and despair. The consequences of past adversities have been permanent, so that a repetition of the adversity can no longer affect the poet. The final stanza refers to the ultimate adversity—death. But even death "will not appal."

In the first half of the poem, the poet treats the experiences as personal to him by using the first person pronouns I, me, my. In the second half, his pain and despair are distanced through the use of the third person pronouns him and his and (in the final stanza) the indefinite pronoun one. Through the change in pronouns, the poet generalizes from his own experiences to the human condition.

My reference to the change in pronouns in the Hardy poem provides a useful transition to a more startling foregrounding of pronouns in the 23rd Psalm, here given in the King James version:

(1)   The LORD is my shepherd; I shall not want.
(2)   He maketh me to lie down in green pastures:
he leadeth me beside the still waters.
(3)   He restoreth my soul: he leadeth me in the
paths of righteousness for his name's sake.
(4)   Yea, though I walk through the valley of the
shadow of death, I will fear no evil: for thou
art with me; thy rod and thy staff they comfort
me.
(5)   Thou preparest a table before me in the
presence of mine enemies: thou anointest my head
with oil; my cup runneth over.
(6)   Surely goodness and mercy shall follow me all
the days of my life: and I will dwell in the house
of the LORD for ever.

In "In Tenebris," the background from which the multiplicity of negative expressions is foregrounded is the language as a whole. In the 23rd Psalm, on the other hand, the norms that form the background lie within the poem: the dominant selection of pronouns to refer to the two main persons in the poem. In Psalm 23 the psalmist and the Lord are predominantly portrayed in an I–he relationship. The psalmist addresses the Lord in the third person: The LORD is my shepherd . . . ; He maketh me to lie down. . . . But in verses 4 and 5 there is a change to an I–thou relationship: for thou art with me . . . ; thou anointest my head. . . . In verse 6 the psalmist reverts to the dominant I–he relationship: I will dwell in the house of the LORD for ever. The changes foreground the person relationship in the psalm, which tallies with the theme of the psalm: the psalmist's trust in God and in his personal relationship with God.

The theme is also expressed in the metaphorical relationships: the psalmist as a sheep and the Lord as his shepherd (verses 1–2); the psalmist as a traveler and the Lord as his guide (3–4); and the psalmist as a guest and the Lord as his host (5–6). The metaphorical progression represents a growing confidence and a deepening personal relationship from complete dependence (of the sheep on his shepherd) to near-equality (of the guest with his host). The change of pronouns to an I–thou relationship coincides with the references to danger: the evil in the valley of the shadow of death and the presence of enemies during the meal. At these times, the psalmist feels the greatest need for the Lord's protection; he expresses his confidence in the Lord's nearness by switching to the thou pronouns. In the final verse the psalmist is most self-confident, assured of staying in the house of the Lord forever, and it is then that he can feel comfortable again with using the third person reference to the Lord.

A final example here of foregrounding involves departures from both external and internal norms. The poem, given in full below, is by Gerard Manley Hopkins. It is titled "Heaven-Haven" and subtitled "A nun takes the veil." The subtitle provides the situational context for the poem. The title not only points to the theme of the poem (heaven as haven) but also introduces the linguistic device that dominates the poem, close parallelism: The two words heaven and haven fall short of complete identity by just one vowel sound as well as one letter:

(1)　　I have desired to go
(2)　　　Where springs not fail,
(3)　To fields where flies no sharp and sided hail
(4)　　And a few lilies blow.

(5)　　And I have asked to be
(6)　　　Where no storms come,
(7)　Where the green swell is in the havens dumb,
(8)　　And out of the swing of the sea.

The close parallelism in grammatical structure between the two stanzas calls attention to itself. The last three lines in each stanza refer to places that are characterized by the negatives not and no and by words that have negative connotations.

   The closeness of the parallelism also foregrounds the differences between
the two stanzas. The first stanza opens with I have desired to go and the second
stanza with I have asked to be. Desire is ambiguous between two meanings: the
stative "wanted" and the dynamic "asked" (cf. 3.14). In the "asked" interpretation, the line is closer in meaning to the opening line of the second stanza. Both
lines then describe a past request. The present perfect have desired and have
asked indicate that the request is relevant to the present time of the poem,
whereas the simple past I desired and I asked might suggest that the person is
no longer interested in having the request granted. On the other hand, in the
"wanted" interpretation, I have desired points to a feeling that has extended
over a period of time to the present but has not necessarily been translated into
the action of making a request. The ambiguity is mimetic of ambivalence. The
ostensible speaker is a woman about to become a nun, and she expresses some
feeling of ambivalence about taking the veil. The change from the ambiguous
desired to the unambiguous asked suggests a progression in the poem.

   Similarly the switch from desired to go to asked to be marks a progression:
the dynamic go points to a striving, whereas the stative be indicates a state
of rest. There are other differences between the stanzas that suggest a similar
advance. There is more deviation from grammatical norms in the first stanza,
perhaps mimetic of the striving: the archaic negation without do in springs not
fail (instead of springs do not fail), the fronting of the verb in flies no sharp and
sided hail, and the separation of the two parts of the compound in sharp and
sided hail (instead of sharp-sided hail).

   There is a difference between where the speaker has desired to go and
where she has asked to be. The first stanza describes a countryside with springs
and fields. It alludes to material needs (springs not fail) and pleasures (a few
lilies blow). The second stanza describes a place of peace and quiet, the haven
of the poem's title. The tension in the first stanza—conveyed in large part by
the grammar—is resolved in the final stanza. The first stanza indicates a desire
for positive things, even though negatives are used: springs that do not fail,
fields without hail, and the presence of a few lilies. The second stanza calls for
the absence of storms and tides: the ideal is the absence of conflict.

   In the next section we will explore the type of foregrounding that derives
from ambiguity.

======================== **EXERCISE 10.2** ========================

Identify instances of foregrounding in the poems below and explain their effects.

   1.   This bread I break was once the oat,
        This wine upon a foreign tree
        Plunged in its fruit;
        Man in the day or wind at night
        Laid the crops low, broke the grape's joy.

Once in this wine the summer blood
Knocked in the flesh that decked the vine,
Once in this bread
The oat was merry in the wind;
Man broke the sun, pulled the wind down.

This flesh you break, this blood you let
Make desolation in the vein,
Were oat and grape
Born of the sensual root and sap;
My wine you drink, my bread you snap.

   Dylan Thomas, "This Bread I Break"

2. After great pain, a formal feeling comes—
The Nerves sit ceremonious, like Tombs—
The stiff Heart questions was it He, that bore,
And Yesterday, or Centuries before?

The Feet, mechanical, go round—
Of Ground, or Air, or Ought—
A Wooden way
Regardless grown,
A Quartz contentment, like a stone—

This is the Hour of Lead—
Remembered, if outlived,
As freezing persons, recollect the Snow—
First–Chill–then Stupor–then letting go—

   Emily Dickinson "After Great Pain"

3. in Just-
spring   when the world is mud-
luscious the little
lame balloonman

whistles   far and   wee

and eddieandbill come
running from marbles and
piracies and it's
spring

when the world is puddle-wonderful

the queer
old balloonman whistles
far   and   wee
and bettyandisbel come dancing

from hop-scotch and jump-rope and

it's
spring
and
     the
        goat-footed
balloonman   whistles
far
and
wee

     e.e. cummings "in Just-"

10.3 AMBIGUITY

In the everyday uses of the spoken language and in most writing, ambiguity is a fault to be avoided because it may cause confusion or misunderstanding. Poets, however, introduce ambiguity intentionally to convey simultaneous meanings.

Puns, which are based on multiple interpretations, are employed playfully in poetry as in jokes and advertisements, though they may also have a serious purpose. This final stanza, from a poem by John Donne, contains two puns, one on <u>Sun</u> and the other on <u>done</u>:

> I have a sin of fear, that when I have spun
>   My last thread, I shall perish on the shore;
> Swear by thyself, that at my death thy <u>Sun</u>
> Shall shine as it shines now, and heretofore;
>   And, having done that, that hast <u>done</u>,
>   I have no more.

Religious poetry traditionally puns <u>Sun</u> with <u>Son</u>, Christ the son of God, blending the associations of natural light with the associations of spiritual light. The second pun is personal, on the name of the poet: <u>thou hast done</u> combines the meaning "you have finished" with "you have Donne." The last two lines of the poem echo a refrain in the previous stanzas:

> When thou hast done, thou hast not done,
>   For I have more.

The poet tells God that when He has forgiven the sins he enumerates He has not finished because he has more sins. At the same time, the pun conveys the added meaning that God has not taken possession of Donne because he has more sins. It is through Christ that at his death the poet will be fully forgiven by God and taken by God.

Poetry may also display grammatical ambiguities. They are generally more difficult to analyze than lexical ambiguities. The first example comes from T. S. Eliot's <u>The Waste Land</u>, in an extract from the section called "The Fire Sermon":

(1)   At the violet hour, when the eyes and back
(2)   Turn upward from the desk, when the human engine waits
(3)   Like a taxi throbbing waiting,
(4)   I Tiresias, though blind, throbbing between two lives,
(5)   Old man with wrinkled female breasts, can see
(6)   At the violet hour, the evening hour that strives
(7)   Homeward, and brings the sailor home from sea,
(8)   The typist home at teatime, clears her breakfast, lights
(9)   Her stove, and lays out food in tins.

The subject of this sentence, <u>I Tiresias</u> (line 4), is followed by two adverbials: a verbless clause <u>though blind</u> and a nonfinite clause <u>throbbing between two lives</u>. Then comes an appositive (cf. 4.7): <u>Old man with wrinkled female breasts</u>. This seems at first reading to be appositive to <u>two lives</u>: one life is an old man, the other perhaps a woman <u>with wrinkled female breasts</u>. But the absence of a description of a second life suggests that the reader has been sent on a false trail. The phrase is then reassigned as appositive to the subject of the sentence <u>I Tiresias</u>. We have two grammatical analyses of the function of the appositive; the second supersedes the first, but the effect of the first lingers. Tiresias is the old man with wrinkled female breasts and the throbbing between two lives is the uneasy straddling of male and female in Tiresias. The grammatical straddling between two analyses reinforces the imagery.

A second false trail is set by what follows the verb <u>can see</u> (line 5). Is <u>see</u> here intransitive ("Tiresias has the ability to see"), or is it transitive ("Tiresias can see somebody or something")? If it is transitive, we expect a direct object to follow later in the sentence. The reader is kept in suspense for several lines. The phrase beginning with <u>the evening hour</u> is appositive to <u>the violet hour</u> (line 6). <u>The evening hour</u> is modified by a relative clause whose predicates are coordinated: <u>that strives</u> / <u>Homeward, and brings the sailor home from sea</u>. It looks as if what follows shares the verb <u>brings</u> and is coordinated, though the coordinator <u>and</u> is implied and not absent; <u>brings the sailor home from sea,</u> / <u>The typist home at teatime</u>. The parallelism of <u>the sailor home</u> and <u>The typist home</u> and the commas after <u>sea</u> and <u>teatime</u> encourage that initial reading. Yet as we read on, we see that <u>The typist</u> has its own set of coordinated predicates: <u>clears her breakfast, lights</u> / <u>Her stove, and lays out food in tins</u> (lines 8–9). <u>The typist</u> could therefore be the subject of a new sentence. Alternatively, <u>The typist home at teatime</u> might indeed be coordinated with <u>the sailor home from sea</u>, and the predicates that follow might be a relative clause (cf. 4.5) with the relative pronoun <u>who</u> omitted, though the omission would be very odd in the ordinary use of language: <u>brings . . . / The typist home at teatime, [who] clears her breakfast, lights</u> / <u>Her stove, and lays out food in tins</u>.

Let us now turn back to the question whether see in line 5 is intransitive or transitive. The question is in fact not resolved, since the grammatical status of see depends on the interpretation of The typist home at teatime (line 8). If this phrase begins a new sentence, see is intransitive. If it is coordinated with the sailor home from sea (line 7), see is still intransitive. But there is yet a third possibility. The phrase may be the subject of a that-clause (whose conjunction that is omitted) which functions as direct object of a transitive see: I Tiresias . . . can see At the violet hour . . . [that] The typist home at teatime, clears her breakfast, lights her stove, and lays out food in tins. This interpretation, which is discouraged by the comma after teatime, is given some support by a parallel sentence five lines later:

> I Tiresias, old man with wrinkled dugs
> Perceived the scene, and foretold the rest—
> I too awaited the expected guest.

Yet the analysis of these lines is also not straightforward. The sentence is parallel if Perceived the scene, and foretold the rest is the predicate of the sentence (I Tiresias . . . / Perceived . . .). But the absence of a comma after dugs allows the possibility that the line is a relative clause with omitted who (I Tiresias . . . [who] / Perceived . . .).

We have seen that the phrase The typist home at teatime faces both ways and that as a result there are three possible interpretations of lines 8–9 that depend on three grammatical analyses. The grammatical ambiguities mimic the paradox of Tiresias, a man who has wrinkled female breasts and a blind man who can see.

The next example of ambiguity comes from the first four lines of a sonnet by Gerard Manley Hopkins. In these lines, the poet calls on himself to turn away from a cycle of self-accusations with which he is tormenting himself:

> (1)   My own heart let me more have pity on; let
> (2)   Me live to my sad self hereafter kind,
> (3)   Charitable; not live this tormented mind
> (4)   With this tormented mind tormenting yet.

Line 1 starts with the fronted My own heart, the complement of the preposition on (cf. 4.25). Later in the line occurs the unusual positioning of more. The oddity of the position of more foregrounds the word and is the cause of its grammatical ambiguity. More may be an adverb ("more often") or an adjective modifying pity. As an adverb, it should come at the end and be accompanied by some time expression such as now or than before: "Let me have pity on my heart more than before." As an adjective, it should precede pity: "Let me have more pity on my heart." The basis of comparison for the adjective is left vague, but two possibilities suggest themselves: "Let me have more pity on myself than on others" or "Let me have more pity on myself than I have had before." The second possibility is closer to the interpretation indicated if <u>more</u> is an adverb, and it receives support from the word <u>hereafter</u> in the parallel sentence that follows.

<u>Live</u> in line 2 seems to be treated as a linking verb, with the adjectives <u>kind, / Charitable</u> as subject complement (cf. 3.8). In normal use, <u>live</u> is an intransitive or a transitive verb, so we would ordinarily expect it to occur with adverbs rather than adjectives (<u>They lived happily ever after</u>, not <u>They lived happy ever after</u>). The grammatical deviation is highlighted by the postponement of the adjectives to the end instead of the normal order as in "Let me live hereafter kind, charitable to my sad self." The unusual structure with a subject complement contributes to the ambiguities of the parallel contrasting sentence in lines 3–4.

The ambiguities lie in the grammatical function of <u>this tormented mind</u>. According to one interpretation the phrase is a subject complement, parallel to <u>kind, / Charitable</u>, and then <u>let me</u> is implied from the preceding sentence: <u>let / Me live to my sad self hereafter kind, / Charitable; [let me] not live this tormented mind / With this tormented mind tormenting yet</u>. If we use <u>be</u> as the linking verb, a simple example of this structure might be <u>Let me be kind to myself, not be a tormentor</u>. As in the preceding sentence, it is odd to have <u>live</u> as a linking verb.

In a second interpretation, <u>this tormented mind</u> is the subject of the intransitive verb <u>live</u> and is parallel to <u>me</u> in the preceding sentence; only <u>let</u> is carried over. The grammatical oddity in this interpretation is that the subject is placed after the verb. If we repositioned the subject in the normal order, we would have <u>[let] this tormented mind not live with this tormented mind tormenting yet</u>.

In the third interpretation, <u>this tormented mind</u> is the direct object of the transitive verb <u>live</u>, and <u>let me</u> is implied from the preceding context. The first part of the sentence might be rephrased "Let me not live this tormented mind." But as a transitive verb, <u>live</u> is highly restricted in the direct objects it may take. We would normally expect a noun phrase with <u>life</u> as its main word ("Let me not live this tormented life"), as in the expresssions <u>live a hard life</u>, <u>live a good life</u>.

The verb <u>torment</u> is ordinarily a transitive verb, but no direct object follows it in line 4. One interpretation is that <u>this tormented mind</u> is the object implied from line 3: <u>With this tormented mind tormenting [this tormented mind] yet</u>. The effect is to suggest an endless cycle of tormentor and tormented, with the poet as a self-tormentor. Alternatively, <u>torment</u> is exceptionally here intransitive, and the sense is "This tormented mind is still experiencing torment." Compare <u>My leg is hurting</u>.

All the interpretations that I have offered for these four lines co-exist and, in doing so, enrich the poem. The dislocations in grammar mimic the psychological dislocations that the poet describes.

The final example comes from the first eight lines of a sonnet by John Milton. The context of the sonnet is the onset of blindness in Milton and his reaction to his disability:

(1)   When I consider how my light is spent,
(2)   Ere half my days in this dark world and wide,
(3)   And that one Talent which is death to hide
(4)   Lodged with me useless, though my Soul more bent
(5)   To serve therewith my Maker, and present
(6)   My true account, lest he returning chide,
(7)   Doth God exact day labour, light denied,
(8)   I fondly ask; . . .

There are various places where multiple interpretations are possible, but I
will focus on the last three lines. In lines 4–6 Milton asserts his eagerness to
present God with a "true account" of his life, lest he returning chide ("lest God
when He returns—or when He replies—rebukes me"). On an initial reading the
question in line 7 seems to be asked by God: Doth God exact day labour, light
denied ("Does God require casual labor when light is denied?"). The question
then appears to be a rhetorical question that God asks in rebuking the poet, and
as a rhetorical question it seeks no answer (cf. 6.2). It implies the strong assertion that of course God does not exact day labour when light is denied. However, when the reader reaches line 8, it becomes transparent that the fronting
of the question before the reporting clause has laid a false trail. The question is
not asked by God, but by the poet: I fondly ask ("I foolishly ask"). The question
now emerges as a genuine yes–no question, which the poet immediately evaluates as a foolish question. The folly of the question is underlined by the previous
reading of it as a rhetorical question, which makes the question unnecessary.
Because God's assertion of His justice is replaced by the poet's questioning of
God's justice, the poet's question is seen to be insolent and presumptuous. The
effect is obtained through the succession of two analyses of the grammar of
lines 6–7: the initial misinterpretation is immediately followed by an accurate
second interpretation. The poet's foolish question is answered in the final line
of the sonnet:

They also serve who only stand and wait.

═══════════════════════ **EXERCISE 10.3** ═══════════════════════

Answer the questions below.

1.   What does the poem below mean if in Spring is one unit functioning as an
      adverbial? What does it mean if in is an adverbial and Spring subject of the
      clause that follows it?

in

Spring comes(no
one
asks his name)

a mender
of things
      e.e. cummings, "in"

2. What does the second line below mean if <u>downeright</u> modifies only <u>violence</u>? What does it mean if it modifies both <u>violence</u> and <u>storme</u>?

> That I did love the Moore, to live with him,
> My downeright violence, and storme of Fortunes,
> May trumpet to the world.

> *Othello,* I.iii.249 (cited in William Empson, *Seven Types of Ambiguity.* New York: New Directions Books, 1947)

3. How does the meaning of the passage below change depending on which words <u>laughable</u> is associated with?

> I am just seventeen years and five months old,
> And, if I lived one day more, three full weeks;
> 'T is writ so in the church's register,
> Lorenzo in Lucina, all my names
> At length, so many names for one poor child,
> —Francesca Camilla Vittoria Angela
> Pompilia Comparini, —laughable!

> Robert Browning, *The Ring and the Book* (cited in Peter Matthews, *Syntax.* Cambridge: Cambridge University Press, 1982)

4. What do the lines below mean if <u>Bitter</u> is a direct object? What do they mean if <u>Bitter</u> is a subject complement?

> I am gall, I am heartburn. God's most deep decree
> Bitter would have me taste: my taste was me;

> G.M. Hopkins, "I wake and feel the fell of dark"

5. What effect does the punctuation of the lines below have on the meaning of the passage?

> To dispense, with justice; or, to dispense
> with justice. Thus the catholic god of France,
> with honours all even, honours all, even
> the damned in the brazen Invalides of Heaven.

> Geoffrey Hill, "The Mystery of the Charity of Charles Peguy"

6. What are the ambiguities in the advertisements given below?
   a. There's more than one litter problem in your neighborhood
      ad for the Massachusetts Society for the Prevention of Cruelty to Animals
   b. Road Service Is Just For Starters
      ad for AAA road service
   c. Seoul Man
      United Airlines ad appealing to international business travelers
   d. Fight cavities with a stick.
      ad for Trident sugarless gum
   e. To get the room you want, you have to push the right buttons.
      ad for toll free number to make reservations at Ramada Hotels

Appendix: Spelling

A.1 SPELLING, PRONUNCIATION, AND MEANING

English spelling is difficult because the pronunciation of a word is not always an accurate guide to its spelling. Two reasons account for most of the discrepancy between pronunciation and spelling.

One reason is that our spelling system is essentially a mixture of two systems: the system used in England before the Norman Conquest in 1066 was mixed with a new system introduced by the Norman-French scribes. We therefore find two spellings for the same sound (as in the final sound of mouse and mice) or two sounds for the same spelling (as in the first sound of get and gem). Later borrowings of words from foreign languages—particularly from French, Latin, and Greek—brought additional spellings; you will recognize as unusual such spellings as the ch of chorus, the ph of philosophy, the g of genre, the oi of reservoir, and the oup of coup. Some spellings were changed to bring words nearer to the form they had in other languages, and the changes introduced letters that have never been pronounced in English. One example is the b in debt: the b was present in the Latin word from which the French equivalent came, but English borrowed the word from French when French no longer had a b. Other examples of such changes are the b in doubt and the p in receipt.

The second reason for the discrepancy between pronunciation and spelling is that spellings have generally remained fixed while pronunciations have changed. During the Middle Ages the few who could write might spell the same word in more than one way; they did not think that only one spelling was correct. When the first printers introduced printing into English in the late fifteenth century they began to establish stable spellings. However, during that century important sound changes took place in English vowels. Those changes and later sound changes are generally not reflected in our spellings. In the centuries that followed, printers continued to work toward a uniform and stable system of spelling, and then the major dictionaries of the eighteenth century established a standard spelling that is close to our present system. On the whole, printers and dictionaries have been a conservative force, preserving old spellings when sounds have changed. We therefore find spellings like the <u>gh</u> of <u>night</u> and the <u>k</u> of <u>know</u>, which retain letters for sounds that we no longer make. Or we find different spellings for the same sound, such as <u>ea</u> in <u>meat</u> and <u>ee</u> in <u>need</u>, because at one time those combinations represented different sounds. Or the sound changed differently in different words, so that the same spelling represents for us two different sounds, such as <u>oo</u> in <u>book</u> and <u>flood</u>.

To some extent our spellings take account of meaning. Sometimes we lose in the spelling–sound relationship but gain in the spelling–meaning relationship.

In the first place, we often distinguish **homophones** (different words pronounced in the same way) by spelling them differently. Here are a few common homophones that we distinguish through spelling:

son – sun   peace – piece
sent – cent – scent   right – write

You will find a list of homophones in A.7.

Second, we often use a similar spelling for parts of words that are related in meaning even though we pronounce them differently. For example, we spell the first two syllables of <u>nation</u> and <u>national</u> identically but the first vowel is pronounced differently in the two words. Similarly, the first three vowels of <u>photography</u> are different from the vowels of <u>photograph</u>, but our spelling connects the two words. We pronounce the words in these sets differently because we shorten vowels that are stressed weakly or not at all. Usually the unstressed or weakly stressed vowel is pronounced like the second vowel of <u>nation</u>. Some common one-syllable words we pronounce in more than one way; in the rapid pace of normal conversation we do not stress them and therefore we shorten their vowels. For that reason we have at least two pronunciations of words like <u>can</u>, <u>does</u>, and <u>your</u>. Sometimes we go further and drop the vowel completely; when we are not writing formally, we can then show the omission in some common words, such as '<u>m</u> for <u>am</u>, '<u>s</u> for <u>is</u> or <u>has</u>, and '<u>ll</u> for <u>will</u>.

A final advantage of the relationship between spelling and meaning is the fact that one spelling of a word may represent different pronunciations, but the spelling shows that it is the same word. English is an international language that is spoken differently in different countries. Even within the United States we do not have a uniform pronunciation; the pronunciation of a word may vary from one area to another or between groups within the same area. For example, some say <u>roof</u> with a long <u>u</u> sound, others with a short <u>u</u> sound; some pronounce the final <u>r</u> in words like <u>car</u>, others do not; some say <u>new</u> with a <u>y</u> sound after the initial <u>n</u>, other do not. Those spellings give some indication of pronunciation, but if we spelled words exactly as we pronounced them, people with different pronunciations of a word would spell the word in different ways. Our spelling usually indicates a shared meaning; it does not necessarily represent an identical pronunciation.

EXERCISE 1.A

The first word in each set has an underlined letter. In each of the other words, underline the spelling that represents the same sound. You may need to underline two letters.

1. zoo, fizz, has, dessert
2. sure, ship, ocean, passion, nation, machine
3. sun, scientific, pass, psychiatry, deceive
4. full, off, rough, telephone
5. no, boat, show, sew, toe
6. away, common, dozen, column, dungeon

EXERCISE 2.A

The spelling ough has a number of different pronunciations. Some common words with ough are listed below in alphabetical order. Rearrange the words in groups so that all the words with the same pronunciation of ough are in the same group.

bough	drought	thorough
bought	enough	though
brought	fought	thought
cough	ought	through
dough	rough	tough

EXERCISE 3.A

Underline the silent letters (letters that have no corresponding pronunciation) in the following words.

climb, weigh, honest, write, knee, condemn, pneumonia, island, listen, guest, two

A.2 LEARNING TO SPELL

English spelling, like English punctuation, is a convention that is helpful to the reader. Spelling mistakes distract and irritate readers. Good spelling is usually considered a sign that the writer is educated.

The spelling of the vast majority of words is now fixed. However, you will encounter some variant spellings in your reading or in dictionaries. For example, you may find <u>catalog</u> and <u>catalogue</u>, <u>archaeology</u> and <u>archeology</u>, <u>judgment</u> and <u>judgement</u>, <u>ax</u> and <u>axe</u>. Do not use more than one spelling in a piece of writing, since inconsistencies are distracting. If you are used to a recognized and acceptable variant, keep to it. If not, select a dictionary and follow its spellings consistently. When a dictionary has variant spellings for a word, it generally puts the preferred spelling first. Consult the introduction to your dictionary to find out how it signals the preferred spelling.

Some spelling variants are exclusively British or are more common in British writing. For example, British spelling uses the -ise and -isation endings (<u>civilise</u>, <u>civilisation</u>) as well as the -ize and -ization endings that are normal for American spelling (<u>civilize</u>, <u>civilization</u>). Be aware of the variants so that you can recognize the words and not be puzzled by them. Here are some common American spellings and the usual British spellings for the same word:

American	British
behavior	behaviour
center	centre
check	cheque
color	colour
draft	draught
harbor	harbour
jewelry	jewellery
labor	labour
meter	metre
neighbor	neighbour
pajamas	pyjamas
rumor	rumour

Because of the constant movement of publications between America and Britain, the national spelling distinctions are becoming acceptable variants in the two countries and also in other English-speaking countries. But as American writers, you should use the common American spellings.

Some students can spell better than others, partly because they have had more experience in reading and writing and have therefore encountered more words and have seen or used them more often. Good spellers may also have a better visual memory than weak spellers. However, everybody can improve his or her spelling. If you are weak in spelling, here is some advice for you to follow:

1. Keep a spelling list of your own. Set aside a few minutes every day to learn spellings. Cross out words when you are sure that you can spell them.

2. Own a college dictionary. If you are not sure how to spell a word, look it up. If the dictionary gives more than one spelling, select the one it indicates as preferred, usually the first. Record the word in your spelling list.

3. Think of ways to remember spellings that are troublesome for you. For example, if you find it difficult to distinguish the homophones stationery and stationary, think of associated words that could help you remember which vowel goes with which meaning: you might associate stationery with letter and stationary with car.

4. In normal conversation we often leave out parts of words or slur them. It will sometimes help you to spell a word if you think of the slow pronunciation. For example, contrast your rapid and slow pronunciations of different and practically. Sometimes the last sound of a word is pronounced identically with the first sound of the next word, as in liked to or likes someone; you might then be tempted to drop a letter and spell like to or like someone. On the other hand, you might add syllables in your pronunciation of certain words that do not correspond to anything in your spelling. For example, some people add the last syllable of disaster when they say disastrous. Check that you do not leave out or add syllables in your spelling.

5. Put into your spelling list the corrected spelling of words that you have spelled wrongly in your writing. Check the spellings carefully in your dictionary before you write them down.

6. Sections A.3–6 contain common spelling rules. Read each rule to see whether it is relevant to the type of spelling mistakes that you make. If it is, memorize the rule and try to apply it when you write.

7. Section A.7 lists sets of words that are spelled differently but are pronounced either identically or similarly. Examine the list. Where you do not know the difference between the spellings, record the set of spellings in your own list and indicate the meaning for each spelling.

8. Section A.8 contains an alphabetical list of words that are frequently misspelled. Since English spelling is not covered by rules completely, you will have to memorize many individual spellings. Go through the list and put into your own list any words that look strange to you. If you do not know the meaning of some of the words, look them up in your dictionary and then write the definitions next to the spellings.

9. Always proofread your writing carefully. Many spelling mistakes are due to inadequate proofreading. You may know the correct spelling, but you can easily miss errors if you proofread too casually.

========================= **EXERCISE 4.A** =========================

Look up the following words in two or more college dictionaries. Do the dictionaries give spelling variants for each word? Do they put the same spelling first?

1. buses	7. fiord	13. mileage
2. collectible	8. guaranty	14. millionaire
3. dependent	9. innuendoes	15. nosy
4. dialogue	10. judgment	16. phantom
5. disc jockey	11. kidnapped	17. phony
6. employee	12. likable	18. vendor

========================= **EXERCISE 5.A** =========================

Say the following words (a) as you normally say them, and (b) very slowly. Have you kept a syllable in your slow pronunciation that you did not have in your normal pronunciation?

1. average	4. incidentally	7. medicine
2. dangerous	5. interest	8. ordinary
3. definite	6. library	9. temporary

A.3 SPELLING RULES FOR SHORT AND LONG VOWEL SOUNDS

1. Doubling of Consonant After Short Vowel

The vowels a, e, i, o, u have both long and short pronunciations; for example, the vowel a has a long pronunciation in rate and a short pronunciation in rat. The following general rule applies if the vowel is stressed.

Generally, a LONG vowel is followed by a single consonant plus a vowel:

V + C + V: LONG vowel + consonant + vowel

and a SHORT vowel is followed by a double consonant; at the end of the word, a SHORT vowel can be followed by just a single consonant:

V + C + C: SHORT vowel + consonant + consonant
V + C: SHORT vowel + consonant (end of word).

Examples:

Long vowel	Short vowel			
	middle		end	
V + C + V	V + C + C		V + C	V + C + C
tape, taping	matter, tapping		tap	camp
scene, scenic	message, begging		beg	sell
ripe, ripen	blizzard, shipping		ship	miss
hope, hopeful	bottom, hopping		hop	fond
amuse, amusement	suffer, cutting		cut	much

This rule is particularly useful when you add a suffix or inflectional ending to a word (cf. A.4[1]).

2.   Addition of Final e to Indicate Long Vowel

A final silent -e indicates that the preceding vowel is long:

Long vowel	Short vowel
mate, debate	mat
theme, extreme	them
fine, polite	fin
robe, explode	rob
cute, amuse	cut

Here are some common exceptions, where the preceding vowel does not have the regular pronunciation:

have
there, where
were
come, done, love, none, some
lose, move, prove, whose
gone
give

A.4   SUFFIXES AND INFLECTIONS

A suffix is a word element that is added to the end of a word to produce another word; for example, the suffix ful is added to help to produce helpful. An inflection is a type of suffix that is added to the end of a word to produce another form of the same word; for example, we add -s to the noun book to produce the plural <u>books</u>, and we add <u>-ed</u> to the verb <u>walk</u> to produce the past <u>walked</u>. The general rules for suffixes in (1)–(3) below apply also to inflections, and the examples include words with inflections added to them.

1. Doubling of Consonant Before Suffix

We often double a final consonant when we add a suffix beginning with a vowel.

Double the final consonant before a suffix beginning with a vowel:

    (a) if the word ends in a single consonant, and
    (b) if a single vowel comes before the consonant, and
    (c) if the syllable before the suffix is stressed.

Condition (c) always applies if the suffix is added to a monosyllabic word:

Suffix added to monosyllabic word	Polysyllabic word: suffix follows stressed syllable
stop + ed → stopped	permit + ed → permitted
swim + ing → swimming	prefer + ed → preferred
big + er → bigger	forget + ing → forgetting
old + est → oldest	begin + ing → beginning
red + ish → reddish	occur + ence → occurrence
drug + ist → druggist	
win + er → winner	

The vowel before the final consonant is a short vowel (cf. A.3).

In the following sets of related words, the final consonant is doubled when the suffix follows a stressed syllable, but not when it follows an unstressed syllable:

Suffix follows stressed syllable	Suffix follows unstressed syllable
deferred, deferring	deference
inferred, inferring	inference
preferred, preferring	preference
referred, referring	reference

Exceptions for words of one syllable:

    <u>buses</u>, <u>bused</u>, <u>busing</u>, and <u>gases</u> are more common with
      single <u>s</u>; but spell <u>gassing</u>, <u>gassed</u>.

Do not double the final consonant:

   (a) if the word ends in two consonants:
       <u>finding</u>, <u>lifted</u>, <u>recorded</u>, <u>resistance</u>
   (b) if there are two vowels:
       <u>meeting</u>, <u>rained</u>, <u>beaten</u>, <u>trainer</u>, <u>repeated</u>, <u>appearance</u>
   (c) if the stress is not on the last syllable of the word to which
       the suffix is added:
       <u>limit</u>, <u>limiting</u>; <u>deliver</u>, <u>delivered</u>; <u>differ</u>, <u>difference</u>

Exceptions for words of two or more syllables:

   (a) Some words, most of them ending in <u>l</u>, have variants in a
       double consonant; for example, <u>traveler</u>, <u>traveller</u>; <u>quarreled</u>,
       <u>quarrelled</u>; <u>diagramed</u>, <u>diagrammed</u>. If you do not already
       have a preference, follow the regular rule and use a single
       consonant.
   (b) Final <u>c</u> is usually spelled <u>ck</u> when a suffix is added, to indi-
       cate the <u>k</u> sound:
       <u>mimic</u>, <u>mimicking</u>; <u>panic</u>, <u>panicky</u>; <u>picnic</u>, <u>picnicked</u>; <u>traffic</u>,
       <u>trafficked</u>.
   (c) spell <u>handicapped</u> with double <u>p</u>.

=============================== **EXERCISE 6.A** ===============================

Form words by joining the parts.

1. panel + ing	6. snob + ish	11. short + er
2. loyal + ist	7. sin + er	12. similar + ity
3. green + ish	8. dark + en	13. paint + er
4. sad + en	9. rag + ed	14. confer + ence
5. commit + ed	10. differ + ence	15. big + est

2.   Dropping of Final -e Before Suffix

Drop the final silent -<u>e</u> before a suffix beginning with a vowel:

        have + ing → having   explore + ation → exploration
        debate + ed → debated   cure + able → curable
        fame + ous → famous   refuse + al → refusal

Exceptions where the e is kept before a vowel:

    (a)   Keep the e in dyeing (from dye) and singeing (from singe) to distinguish the words from dying (from die) and singing (from sing).

    (b)   Keep the e in ce and ge before a suffix beginning with a or o to preserve the s and j sounds: enforceable, noticeable, peaceable, traceable, advantageous, courageous, knowledgeable.

Do not drop the e before a suffix beginning with a consonant:

    movement, forceful, hopeless, strangely

Exceptions where the e is dropped before a consonant:

    (a)   argument, awful, duly, truly, wholly

    (b)   abridgment, acknowledgment, and judgment; these words have less common variants with the e.

EXERCISE 7.A

Form words by joining the parts.

1. segregate + ion	6. advantage + ous	11. type + ing
2. care + ful	7. argue + ment	12. rare + ly
3. waste + age	8. deplore + able	13. true + ly
4. revive + al	9. delete + ion	14. courage + ous
5. style + ize	10. base + less	15. rare + ity

3.   Change of -y to -i Before Suffix

When a word ends in a consonant plus y, change the y to i before any suffix except -ing or 's:

    happy + ly → happily   study + es → studies
    amplify + er → amplifier   mystery + ous → mysterious
    beauty + ful → beautiful   ratify + cation → ratification
    apply + ed → applied   empty + ness → emptiness

Exceptions where the y after a consonant is kept:

(a) A few words of one syllable keep the y before a suffix:
     dryness, shyness, slyness.
(b) The y is kept in busyness to distinguish it from business.

Keep the y before -ing: studying, applying.
Keep the y before 's: the spy's name, July's weather.
Keep the y in most words that end in a vowel + y:

employ + er → employer   play + ful → playful
annoy + ance → annoyance   destroy + s → destroys
spray + ed → sprayed   pay + ment → payment

Exceptions where the y after a vowel is changed to i:

daily, laid, paid, said, slain

EXERCISE 8.A

Form words by joining the parts.

1. dry + ing   6. simplify + cation   11. biography + cal
2. necessary + ly   7. lazy + ness   12. shy + ness
3. pity + ful   8. day + ly   13. luxury + ous
4. momentary + ly   9. symmetry + cal   14. funny + ly
5. play + ful   10. identify + able   15. happy + ness

4. Plurals of Nouns and -s Forms of Verbs

Similar rules apply for making the plurals of regular nouns and the -s forms of
regular verbs. Indeed, many words can be either nouns or verbs.
    (a) General rule: add -s:

Noun plurals   **Verb -s forms**

street → streets   speak → speaks
eye → eyes   bring → brings
winter → winters   write → writes

(b) If the ending is pronounced as a separate syllable (like the sound in is), add -es:

Noun plurals	**Verb -s forms**
church → churches	touch → touches
box → boxes	buzz → buzzes
bush → bushes	wash → washes

When the word already ends in an -e, add just -s:

Noun plurals	**verb -s forms**
base → bases	curse → curses
judge → judges	trace → traces

(c) If the word ends in a consonant plus y, change y to i and then add -es:

Noun plurals	**Verb -s forms**
worry → worries	carry → carries
spy → spies	dry → dries

(d) For some words ending in -o, add -es. Some of them have a less common variant in -s:

Noun plurals	**Noun plurals and Verb -s forms**
archipelago → archipelagoes	echo → echoes
buffalo → buffaloes	embargo → embargoes
cargo → cargoes	go → goes
hero → heroes	torpedo → torpedoes
motto → mottoes	veto → vetoes
potato → potatoes	
tomato → tomatoes	
tornado → tornadoes	
volcano → volcanoes	

(e) For some nouns ending in -f or -fe, form the plural by changing the -f or -fe to -ves:

calf → calves	life → lives	thief → thieves
elf → elves	loaf → loaves	wife → wives
half → halves	self → selves	wolf → wolves
knife → knives	sheaf → sheaves	
leaf → leaves	shelf → shelves	

═══════════════════════ **EXERCISE 9.A** ═══════════════════════

Give the plurals of these nouns.

1. day	6. century	11. thief
2. beach	7. race	12. journey
3. wife	8. loaf	13. hero
4. historian	9. stove	14. coach
5. potato	10. speech	15. belief

═══════════════════════ **EXERCISE 10.A** ═══════════════════════

Give the -s forms of these verbs.

1. imply	6. fly	11. marry
2. think	7. die	12. type
3. refuse	8. push	13. bury
4. agree	9. taste	14. try
5. camouflage	10. crouch	15. reach

5. Verb Forms: -ing Participles

The rules for making the -ing participle apply to both regular and irregular verbs.

(a) General rule: add -ing:

play → playing   carry → carrying
go → going   wash → washing

(b) If the word ends in -e, drop the e before the -ing:

lose → losing   write → writing
save → saving   judge → judging

But if the word ends in -ee, -ye, or -oe, keep the e:

see → seeing   dye → dyeing
agree → agreeing hoe → hoeing

Also, <u>singe</u> keeps the <u>e</u> in <u>singeing</u>, in contrast with <u>sing–singing</u>.

(c) If the word ends in -<u>ie</u>, change <u>i</u> to <u>y</u> and drop the <u>e</u> before the -<u>ing</u>:

  die → dying tie → tying
  lie → lying

Contrast <u>die–dying</u> with <u>dye–dyeing</u>.

(d) The rules for doubling a single consonant before -<u>ing</u> are given in A.4(1):

  beg → begging boat → boating
  prefer → preferring enter → entering

EXERCISE 11.A

Give the ·ing participles of these verbs.

1. apply	4. occur	7. make	10. win	13. bring
2. see	5. lie	8. get	11. support	14. create
3. continue	6. begin	9. die	12. brag	15. spot

6. Verb Forms: Simple Past and -<u>ed</u> Participles

The simple past and -<u>ed</u> participle are the same in regular verbs. The spelling rules given above apply to regular verbs.

(a) General rule: add -<u>ed</u>:

  play → played load → loaded
  mail → mailed echo → echoed

(b) If the word ends in -<u>e</u>, add just -<u>d</u>:

  save → saved note → noted
  agree → agreed tie → tied

(c) If the word ends in a consonant plus <u>y</u>, change the <u>y</u> to <u>i</u> before the -<u>ed</u>:

  dry → dried apply → applied
  cry → cried imply → implied

There are three exceptions, where the <u>y</u> is changed to <u>i</u> after a vowel and just <u>d</u> is added:

lay → laid   pay → paid   say → said

(d) The rules for doubling a single consonant before -<u>ed</u> are given in A.4(1):

beg → begged   boat → boated
prefer → preferred enter → entered

═══════════════ **EXERCISE 12.A** ═══════════════

Give the –<u>ed</u> form (simple past and –<u>ed</u> participle) of these verbs.

1. study	6. delay	11. deliver
2. persuade	7. point	12. surprise
3. trick	8. parallel	13. pay
4. dot	9. occupy	14. taste
5. comfort	10. distinguish	15. reply

7. <u>-ize</u> or -ise; -ization

The usual spelling is -<u>ize</u> and -<u>ization</u>:

memorize   criticize
colonize   memorization
apologize   colonization

The following words, and words formed from them, are usually spelled with -<u>ise</u>:

advertise	compromise	enterprise	revise
advise	despise	exercise	supervise
arise	devise	franchise	surprise
comprise	disguise	merchandise	televise

8. Addition of <u>-ally</u> to Adjectives Ending in <u>-ic</u> to Form Adverbs

Add -<u>ally</u> to adjectives ending in -<u>ic</u> to form the corresponding adverbs. In normal conversation, the -<u>al</u> of -<u>ally</u> is not sounded:

basic → basically   realistic → realistically
emphatic → emphatically specific → specifically

Exception: <u>publicly</u>.

9. <u>-ful</u>

The suffix is -<u>ful</u>:

> beautiful successful useful
> hopeful teaspoonful wonderful

Notice also the usual spellings of <u>fulfill</u> and <u>fulfillment</u>.

A.5 PREFIXES

Do not add or subtract letters when you add a prefix:

un + easy → uneasy
un + necessary → unnecessary
dis + obey → disobey
dis + satisfied → dissatisfied
mis + inform → misinform
mis + spell → misspell

over + eat → overeat
over + rule → overrule
under + take → undertake
under + rate → underrate
in + expensive → inexpensive
in + numerable → innumerable

The prefix <u>in</u>- is regularly changed to <u>il</u>-, <u>im</u>-, or <u>ir</u>- according to the first letter of the word that it is added to. The prefix often means "not," as in the examples that follow:

<u>il</u>- before <u>l</u>	<u>ir</u>- before <u>r</u>	<u>im</u>- before <u>m</u> or <u>p</u>
illegal	irrational	immoral
illegible	irregular	immortal
illegitimate	irrefutable	impartial
illiterate	irrelevant	impossible
illogical	irresponsible	impure

=========== **EXERCISE 13.A** ===========

Form words by joining the parts.

1. dis + similar
2. mis + apprehend
3. ir + reverent
4. un + informed
5. im + mobile
6. un + natural
7. dis + associate
8. il + licit
9. under + expose
10. out + talk
11. mis + shapen
12. over + rated
13. out + argue
14. dis + solve
15. hyper + active

A.6 OTHER AIDS TO SPELLING

1. Words Run Together

A common type of spelling error is to run words together by writing two words as one. Always write these phrases as separate words:

a lot	even if	in fact	no one
all right	even though	just as	of course

In some cases the spelling depends on the meaning. For example, write <u>nobody</u> as one word when it is a synonym of <u>no person</u>, but write <u>no body</u> as two words in other meanings (for example, "no corpse"). Write <u>anyway</u> when it is a synonym of <u>anyhow</u>, but <u>any way</u> when it means "any direction" or "any manner"; <u>awhile</u> is an adverb meaning "for a brief period" (e.g. <u>You can stay awhile</u>), but <u>a while</u> is a noun phrase meaning "a period of time" (e.g. <u>We'll be there in a (little) while</u> and <u>We haven't seen them for a (long) while</u>).

Here are some pairs that you write either as one or as two words, depending on the meaning you intend:

One word	Two words
already	all ready
altogether	all together
always	all ways
anybody	any body
anyone	any one
anyway	any way
awhile	a while
everybody	every body
everyone	every one
however	how ever
into	in to
maybe	may be
nobody	no body
somebody	some body
someone	some one
whatever	what ever
whoever	who ever

If you are not sure of the differences between the pairs, consult your dictionary.

2. ie or ei

When the sound of the vowel is as in brief, spell it ie; but after c, spell it ei:

ie		ei after c	
brief	thief	ceiling	deceit
belief	achieve	conceive	perceive
believe	field	conceit	receive
diesel	niece	deceive	receipt
relief	priest		
relieve	siege		

Exceptions for spelling ei:

either, neither, leisure, seize, weird

Exceptions for spelling ie:

(a) financier, species
(b) Words in which y has changed to i (cf. A.4[3]) end in ies even after c: prophecies, democracies.

In most words that do not have the pronunciation as in brief, the usual order is e before i: neighbor, weigh, reign. The most common exception is friend.

3. could, should, would

Notice the silent l in these three auxiliaries.

4. -cede, -ceed, -sede

The most common spelling is -cede:

antecede, concede, precede, recede, secede

We find -ceed in three words:

exceed, proceed, succeed

We find -sede in one word:

supersede

A.7 WORDS PRONOUNCED SIMILARLY

You will find here a list of common **homophones** (words that are pronounced in the same way but have different meanings) that are spelled differently. The list includes some words that are pronounced not identically but similarly. If you are not sure of the differences in meaning, look up the words in a dictionary.

We begin with a group of very common homophones. The other homophones or near-homophones are listed alphabetically; they include several sets of three homophones. The list has been broken up into groups so that you can review them conveniently.

1. he's/his, it's/its, you're/your, they're/their/there, who's/whose

Some contractions of <u>is</u>, <u>has</u>, and <u>are</u> result in words that can be confused with homophones:

(a) <u>he's</u> = <u>he is</u> or <u>he has</u>

He'll tell you when <u>he's</u> back home. (= <u>he is</u>)
I know that <u>he's</u> sent the check. (= <u>he has</u>)

Distinguish between <u>he's</u> and possessive <u>his</u>:

Do you know <u>his</u> name?

(b) <u>it's</u> = <u>it is</u> or <u>it has</u>

It's in the kitchen. (= <u>It is</u>)
I believe <u>it's</u> stopped raining. (= <u>it has</u>)

Distinguish between <u>it's</u> and possessive <u>its</u>:

The dog is wagging <u>its</u> tail.

(c) <u>you're</u> = <u>you are</u>

Did you say that <u>you're</u> willing to volunteer? (= <u>you are</u>)

Distinguish between <u>you're</u> and possessive <u>your</u>:

They enjoyed <u>your</u> jokes.

(d) <u>they're</u> = <u>they are</u>

I wonder where <u>they're</u> staying. (= <u>they are</u>)

Distinguish <u>they're</u> from possessive <u>their</u> and the adverb <u>there</u>:

> We met <u>their</u> parents.
> - All my friends were <u>there</u>.

For the adverb <u>there</u>, compare the spellings of the related words <u>here</u> and <u>where</u>.

(e) <u>who's</u> = <u>who is</u> or <u>who has</u>

> Can you see <u>who's</u> ringing the bell? (= <u>who is</u>)
> <u>Who's</u> found the reference? (= <u>Who has</u>)

Distinguish between <u>who's</u> and possessive <u>whose</u>:

> <u>Whose</u> book is that?
> There is no charge for patients <u>whose</u> income is below a specified level.

2. List of Words Pronounced Similarly

(a)
accept	except
access	excess
advice	advise
affect	effect
aid	aide
aisle	isle
altar	alter
assistance	assistants
ate	eight

(b)
bare	bear
beach	beech
beer	bier
berry	bury
berth	birth
board	bored
born	borne
brake	break
bread	bred
breadth	breath
business	busyness
buy	by

(c)
canvas	canvass
capital	capitol

	cell	sell	
	censor	censure	
	cereal	serial	
	climactic	climatic	
	coarse	course	
	complement	compliment	
	conscience	conscious	
	council	counsel	

(d)	dairy	diary	
	decent	descent	dissent
	desert	dessert	
	device	devise	
	dew	due	do
	discreet	discrete	
	dual	duel	
	dyeing	dying	

(e)	elicit	illicit
	emigrate	immigrate
	eminent	imminent
	envelop	envelope
	fair	fare
	father	farther
	flour	flower
	for	four
	formally	formerly
	forth	fourth

(f)	gorilla	guerrilla
	grate	great
	hair	hare
	hear	here
	heard	herd
	higher	hire
	hostel	hostile

(g)	idle	idol
	in	inn
	ingenious	ingenuous
	instance	instants
	irrelevant	irreverent
	knew	new
	know	no

(h) lead   led
      lessen   lesson
      loan   lone
      loose   lose

      made   maid
      main   mane
      maize   maze
      meat   meet
      medal   meddle
      miner   minor

      oar   ore   or
      of   off
      one   won

(i)   pain   pane
      passed   past
      patience   patients
      peace   piece
      peak   peek   pique
      pear   pair   pare
      personal   personnel
      pier   peer
      plane   plain
      poor   pour   pore
      precede   proceed
      presence   presents
      principal   principle
      profit   prophet
      prophecy   prophesy

(j) quiet   quite
      rain   reign   rein
      raise   rays
      read   red
      right   write
      role   roll

      sail   sale
      scent   sent   cent
      seed   cede
      seem   seam

(k) shone   shown
      sight   site   cite

sole	soul	
son	sun	
stake	steak	
stationary	stationery	
steal	steel	
straight	strait	

(l)
taught	taut	
team	teem	
than	then	
threw	through	
tide	tied	
to	too	two
vain	vein	vane

(m)
wander	wonder	
waste	waist	
wave	waive	
way	weigh	
weak	week	
weather	whether	
were	where	wear
which	witch	
wood	would	
wrote	rote	

A.8   WORDS OFTEN MISSPELLED

You will find here an alphabetical list of words that might cause spelling difficulties. Memorize those that look strange to you. If you are not sure of the meanings of some of the words, look them up in a dictionary. The list has been broken up into groups of ten so that you can review them conveniently:

(1) accident	(2) allege	(3) approach
accommodate	amateur	appropriate
accurate	analysis	argument
achieve	anniversary	assign
acknowledge	annual	athlete
acquaintance	answer	attempt
acquire	anxious	attendance
across	apparent	average
address	appearance	bargain
adventure	appreciate	beauty
(4) because	(5) ceremony	(6) conscientious
beginning	certain	controversy

believe
benefit
budget
build
bureaucracy
business
calendar
cemetery
(7) definite
description
desperate
dictionary
difference
dilemma
disappoint
disastrous
discipline
educate
(10) fiction
foreign
fortunate
forty
friend
genius
government
guarantee
guess
guilty
(13) library
lightning
listen
literature
machine
marriage
mathematics
medicine
message
minute
(16) permanent
personal
persuade
police
politician
possession
possible
practically

climate
college
column
committee
condemn
confusion
conscious
conscience
(8) efficient
embarrass
enough
environment
equation
especially
estimate
every
exaggerate
exceed
(11) handkerchief
height
hierarchy
hygiene
hypocrite
imagine
immediately
incidentally
inconvenient
independent
(14) mission
mortgage
nation
naturally
necessary
neighbor
neither
nervous
nuisance
obstinate
(17) privilege
probable
probably
procedure
proceed
professor
profession
pronunciation

convenient
country
courage
creature
criticism
damage
dangerous
daughter
(9) excellent
exercise
existence
experience
extension
failure
famous
fashion
fatigue
February
(12) initiate
interest
irrelevant
irresistible
jeopardy
journey
knowledge
laboratory
language
leisure
(15) occasion
occurred
omission
opportunity
opposite
ordinary
original
parallel
parliament
people
(18) psychology
purchase
purpose
pursue
question
questionnaire
ratio
receipt

	preferred		propaganda		receive
	prejudice		psychiatry		recommend
(19)	reference	(20)	satellite	(21)	soldier
	referred		schedule		solemn
	relevant		science		speak
	religious		secretary		special
	restaurant		sense		speech
	rhetorical		sentence		subtle
	rhyme		separate		succeed
	rhythm		serious		sufficient
	ridiculous		siege		suggest
	sandwich		similar		surprise
(22)	suspicious	(23)	tragedy	(24)	vague
	technique		translate		valuable
	temperature		tries		variety
	temporary		trouble		various
	tendency		truly		vengeance
	therefore		unanimous		village
	though		unnecessary		villain
	thought		until		Wednesday
	till		usual		width
	tongue		usury		writing

Glossary

ABSOLUTE CLAUSE.   An absolute clause is an adverbial clause that either has a nonfinite verb (as in 1 below) or no verb at all (as in 2 below) but has its own subject:

1. <u>The work having been finished</u>, the gardener came to ask for payment.
2. The prisoners marched past, <u>their hands above their heads</u>.

ACTIVE.   Sentences and verb phrases with transitive verbs are either active or passive. The active is commonly used. The passive involves differences in the structure of the verb phrase: The passive verb phrase has the addition of a form of the verb <u>be</u>, which is followed by an -ed **participle:**

ACTIVE   <u>loves</u>   PASSIVE   <u>is loved</u>
         <u>will proclaim</u>   <u>will be proclaimed</u>
         <u>is investigating</u>   <u>is being investigated</u>

The passive sentence differs from the corresponding active sentence in that the active subject corresponds to the passive object:

ACTIVE   <u>The FBI</u> (S) is investigating <u>the crime</u> (O).
PASSIVE   <u>The crime</u> (S) is being investigated.

If the active subject (here <u>The FBI</u>) is retained in the passive sentence, it is put into a <u>by</u>-phrase:

The crime is being investigated <u>by the FBI</u>.

ADJECTIVE.   An adjective is a word that can modify a noun and usually can itself be modified by <u>very</u>; for example, <u>(very) wise</u>, <u>(very) careful</u>. Adjectives are called "attributive" when they are used as premodifiers in a noun phrase (a conscientious student). They are called "predicative" when they are used as complements (She is conscientious). Adjectives that can be used both attributively and predicatively are called "central" adjectives.

ADJECTIVE PHRASE. The main word in an adjective phrase is an **adjective**. Other constituents that often appear in the phrase are **premodifiers** (which come before the adjective) and **complements** (which come after the adjective):

> quite (prem.) hungry (adj.)
> extremely (prem.) happy (adj.) to see you (comp.)

ADVERB. The class of words that are called adverbs is a miscellany, since not all adverbs can have the same range of functions. An adverb is a word that is used chiefly as a modifier of an adjective (extremely in extremely pale), or a modifier of another adverb (very in very suddenly), or as an **adverbial** (frequently in I visit my family frequently).

ADVERB PHRASE. The main word in an adverb phrase is an **adverb**. Other constituents that often appear in the phrase are premodifiers (which come before the adverb) and complements (which come after the adverb):

> very (prem.) neatly (adv.)
> very (prem.) luckily (adv.) for me (comp.)

ADVERBIAL. An adverbial is an optional sentence element that is chiefly used to convey information about the circumstances of the situation depicted in the basic structure of the sentence (cf. 3.14). There may be more than one adverbial in a sentence.

> Every year (A1) they rented a truck for two weeks (A2) to haul out 100 tons of jade (A3).

In the above sentence, the adverbials convey information on frequency in time (A1), duration of time (A2), and purpose (A3).

We should distinguish the adverbial from the **adverb**. Like a noun, an adverb is a member of a word class.

An adverbial complement is an element that conveys the same information as some adverbials but is required by the verb:

> I am now living in Manhattan.

The verb that most commonly requires an adverbial complement to complete the sentence is the verb be. An adverbial complement is also required by some transitive verbs to follow a direct object. See **Object**.

> I put my car (dO) in the garage (AC).

ADVERBIAL CLAUSE. An adverbial clause is a clause that functions as **adverbial** in sentence structure.

ADVERBIAL COMPLEMENT. An adverbial complement is an obligatory element in sentence structure. See **Adverbial**.

ALTERNATIVE QUESTION. An alternative question is a question that presents two or more choices and asks the hearer to choose one of them:

> Do you want a cookie or a piece of cake?

ANTECEDENT. The antecedent of a pronoun is the unit that the pronoun refers to. The antecedent usually comes before the pronoun:

> The brakes were defective when I examined them.

ANTICIPATORY IT. The pronoun it is called "anticipatory it" when the sentence is so structured that the pronoun takes the position of the subject and the subject is moved to the end:

> It is a pity that Sue is not here. [Cf.: That Sue is not here is a pity.]
> It's good to see you. [Cf.:To see you is good.]

APPOSITION. Apposition is a type of relation between two or more units.

> Peter, your youngest brother, has just arrived.

Typically, the two units are identical in the kind of unit (here two noun phrases), in what they refer to (Peter and your youngest brother refer to the same person), and in having the same potential function (so that either can be here omitted—Peter has just arrived and Your youngest brother has just arrived are both acceptable). See also **Appositive Clause**.

APPOSITIVE CLAUSE. An appositive clause is a type of clause that functions as a postmodifier in a noun phrase:

> the reason that I am here today

The conjunction that does not function in the clause (cf. **Relative Clause**). Since the clause is in apposition to the noun phrase, the two units correspond to a sentence structure in which they are linked by a form of the verb be:

> The reason is that I am here today.

ASPECTS. Aspect is the grammatical category in the verb phrase that refers to the way that the time of the situation is viewed by the speaker. There are two aspects: perfect and progressive. The perfect combines a form of auxiliary have with the -ed **participle**: has shouted, had worked, may have said. The progressive combines a form of auxiliary be with the -ing **participle**: is shouting, was working, may be saying.

AUXILIARY.   Auxiliary ("helping") verbs typically come before the **main verb** (<u>see</u> in the following examples) in a verb phrase: <u>can see</u>, <u>has been seeing</u>, <u>should have been seen</u>. The auxiliaries are:

    (1)   modals: e.g., <u>can</u>, <u>should</u>
    (2)   perfect: auxiliary <u>have</u>
    (3)   progressive: auxiliary <u>be</u>
    (4)   passive: auxiliary <u>be</u>
    (5)   dummy operator: <u>do</u>

BASE FORM.   The base form of the verb is the form without any **inflection**. It is the entry word for a verb in dictionaries.

BASIC SENTENCE STRUCTURE.   The seven basic sentence or clause structures are:

        SV: subject + verb
        SVA: subject + verb + adverbial (complement)
        SVC: subject + verb + (subject) complement
        SVO: subject + verb + (direct) object
        SVOO: subject + verb + (indirect) object + (direct) object
        SVOA: subject + verb + (direct) object + adverbial (complement)
        SVOC: subject + verb + (direct) object + (object) complement

See 3.13. One or more **adverbials** may be added to the basic structures.

CASE.   Case is a distinction in nouns and pronouns that is related to their grammatical functions. Nouns have two cases: the common case (<u>child</u>, <u>children</u>) and the genitive case (<u>child's</u>, <u>children's</u>). The genitive noun phrase is generally equivalent to an <u>of</u>-phrase:

        <u>the child's</u> parents
        the parents <u>of the child</u>

In <u>the child's parents</u>, the genitive phrase is a determinative genitive: it functions like a **determiner**. When the phrase is not dependent on a following noun, it is an independent genitive:

        The party is at <u>Susan's</u>.

Personal pronouns and the pronoun <u>who</u> have three cases: subjective (e.g., <u>I</u>, <u>we</u>, <u>who</u>), objective (e.g., <u>me</u>, <u>us</u>, <u>whom</u>), and genitive (e.g., <u>my</u>, <u>mine</u>; <u>our</u>, <u>ours</u>; <u>whose</u>). The two genitive forms of the personal pronouns have different functions: <u>My</u> is a possessive determiner in <u>my parents</u>, and <u>mine</u> is a possessive pronoun in <u>Those are mine</u>.

The distinctions in case are neutralized in some personal pronouns. For example, <u>you</u> may be either subjective or objective. See **Subjective Case**.

Chiasmus. See **Parallelism.**

Clause. A clause is a sentence or sentence-like construction that is contained within another sentence. Constructions that are sentence-like are **nonfinite clauses** or **verbless clauses**. Nonfinite clauses have a **nonfinite verb phrase** as their verb, whereas verbless clauses do not have a verb at all. They are like sentences because they have sentence elements such as **subject** and **direct object**.

We can parallel the nonfinite clause in [1] with the finite clause in [1a]:

[1]   Being just a country boy, I'd ...
[1a] Since I'm just a country boy, I'd ...

We can show similar parallels between the verbless clause in [2] and the finite clause in [2a]:

[2]   Though fearful of road conditions, they ...
[2a] Though they were fearful of road conditions, they ...

In a wider sense, a clause may coincide with a sentence, since a **simple sentence** consists of just one clause.

Cleft Sentence. A cleft sentence is a sentence divided into three parts: The first has the subject it and a form of the verb be; the emphasized part comes next; and the final part is what would be the rest of the sentence in a regular pattern:

> It was Betty that I wanted. [*Cf.* I wanted Betty.]
> It was after lunch that I phoned John. [*Cf.* I phoned John after lunch.]

Collective Noun. A collective noun refers to a group, e.g., class, family, herd, jury.

Comma Splice. See **Run-on Sentence**.

Comparative Clause. Comparative clauses are clauses that are introduced by than or as and involve a comparison:

> Maurice is happier than he used to be.
> Terence is as good a student as you are.

Complement. The term "complement" is used in two senses:

1. A complement is a sentence element that is required, by the meaning of the verb, to complete the sentence. There are three complements of this kind: adverbial complement, subject complement, and object complement.

2. A complement is the unit that normally follows a preposition to complete the prepositional phrase. This prepositional complement is typically a noun phrase; for example, the noun phrase <u>my best friend</u> is the complement of the preposition in the prepositional phrase <u>for my best friend</u>. Adjectives and adverbs may also have complements.

COMPLEX SENTENCE. A complex sentence is one that contains one or more subordinate clauses. The subordinate clause may function as a sentence element [1], as a postmodifier in a phrase [2], or as a complement in a phrase [3]:

[1] Jean told me <u>that she would be late</u>.
[2] This is <u>the man who was asking for you</u>.
[3] We are <u>glad that you could be here</u>.

COMPOUND. A compound is a word formed from the combination of two words: <u>handmade</u>, <u>user-friendly</u>.

COMPOUND SENTENCE. A compound sentence is one that consists of two or more clauses linked by a coordinator. The coordinators are <u>and</u>, <u>or</u>, and <u>but</u>; <u>but</u> can link only two clauses:

She is a superb administrator, <u>and</u> everybody knows that.

See 6.6.

CONDITIONAL CLAUSE. A conditional clause is a clause that expresses a condition on which something else is dependent:

<u>If they hurry</u>, they can catch the earlier flight.

The sentence conveys the proposition that their ability to catch the earlier flight is dependent on their hurrying.

CONJUNCTION. The two classes of conjunctions are **coordinators** (or coordinating conjunctions) and **subordinators** (or subordinating conjunctions). The coordinators are <u>and</u>, <u>or</u>, and <u>but</u>. They link units of equal status (those having a similar function), e.g., clauses, phrases, premodifiers. Subordinators (e.g., <u>because</u>, <u>if</u>) introduce **subordinate clauses:**

The baby is crying <u>because</u> she is hungry.

CONVERSION. Conversion is the process by which a word is changed from one class to a new class without any change in its form. For example, the verb <u>bottle</u> ("put into a bottle") is derived by conversion from the noun <u>bottle</u>.

COORDINATION.   Coordination is the linking of two or more units with the same function. The coordinators (or coordinating conjunctions) are <u>and</u>, <u>or</u>, and <u>but</u>:

> There is a state tax on <u>cigarettes</u>, <u>cigars</u>, and <u>pipe tobacco</u>.
> They pierced their <u>ears</u> or <u>noses</u>.
> <u>We waited</u>, but <u>nobody came</u>.

COORDINATOR.   See **Conjunction.**

COUNT.   Count nouns refer to things that can be counted, and they therefore have a singular and a plural: <u>college</u>, <u>colleges</u>. Noncount nouns have only the singular form: <u>information</u>.

DANGLING MODIFIER.   A dangling modifier is an adverbial clause that has no subject, but its implied subject is not intended to be identified with the subject of the sentence:

> <u>Being blind</u>, a dog guided her across the street.

The implied subject of <u>being blind</u> is not intended to be <u>a dog</u>.

DECLARATIVE.   A declarative sentence is a type of sentence structure used chiefly for making statements. In declaratives, the **subject** generally comes before the **verb:**

> Sandra is on the radio.
> I'm not joking.
> The sea lashed out harshly, jabbing the shoreline.
> Much more work will be required to analyze the data before
>   we can announce our conclusions.

DECLARATIVE QUESTION.   A declarative question has the form of a declarative sentence but the force of a question:

> She agrees with us?

DEFINITE.   Noun phrases are definite when they are intended to convey enough information, in themselves or through the context, to identify uniquely what they refer to:

> You'll find <u>the can of beer</u> in <u>the refrigerator</u>.

A likely context for using the definite article <u>the</u> here is that this particular can of beer has been mentioned previously and that it is obvious which refrigerator is being referred to. Noun phrases are indefinite when they are not intended to be so identifiable:

> You'll find <u>a can of beer</u> in the refrigerator.

DEFINITE ARTICLE.   The definite article is <u>the</u>. Contrast **Indefinite Article.**

DEMONSTRATIVE.   The demonstrative pronouns are <u>this</u>, <u>these</u>, <u>that</u>, and <u>those</u>. The same forms are demonstrative **determiners.**

DESCRIPTIVE RULES.   See **Grammar**.

DETERMINATIVE GENITIVE.   See **Case**.

DETERMINER.   Determiners introduce noun phrases. They fall into several classes: the **definite** and **indefinite articles, demonstratives, possessives, interrogatives, relatives,** and **indefinites**.

DIRECTIVE.   The major use of **imperative** sentences is to issue directives, that is, requests for action. Directives include a simple request [1], a command [2], a prohibition [3], a warning [4], and an offer [5]:

> [1]   Please send me another copy.
> [2]   Put your hands up!
> [3]   Don't move!
> [4]   Look out!
> [5]   Have another piece of cake.

You can convey a directive through sentence types other than imperatives:

> I want you to send me another copy, please.
> Would you please send me another copy?
> I need another copy.

DIRECT OBJECT.   See **Object.**

DIRECT SPEECH.   Direct speech quotes the actual words that somebody has said. Indirect speech reports what has been said but not in the actual words used by the speaker:

> [1]   Mavis asked me, "Have you any friends?" [*direct speech*]
> [2]   Mavis asked me whether I had any friends. [*indirect speech*]

In both [1] and [2], <u>Mavis asked me</u> is the reporting clause.

DOMAIN.   The domain of language use is the type of activity in which the language is used; for example, scientific English or legal English.

DUMMY OPERATOR.   The dummy operator is the verb <u>do</u>. It is used to perform the functions of an **operator** when an operator is otherwise absent:

> <u>Does</u> (op) Polly know?

The three verb forms are <u>do</u> and <u>does</u> for the present **tense** and <u>did</u> for the past tense.

DYNAMIC. See **Stative**.

ELEMENT. An element is a constituent of sentence or clause structure. Seven elements combine to form the **basic sentence structure**:

subject	S		
verb	V		
object	O:	direct object	dO
		indirect object	iO
complement	C:	subject complement	SC
		object complement	OC
		adverbial complement	AC

In addition, the adverbial (A) is an optional element.

END-FOCUS. The principle of end-focus requires that the most important information come at the end.

END-WEIGHT. The principle of end-weight requires that a longer unit come after a shorter unit whenever there is a choice of relative positions.

EXCLAMATIVE. An exclamative sentence is a type of sentence structure used chiefly to express strong feeling. Exclamatives begin with <u>what</u> or <u>how</u>. <u>What</u> is used with a **noun phrase** and <u>how</u> elsewhere:

> <u>What a good time</u> we had! (We had a very good time.)
> <u>How well</u> she plays! (She plays very well.)

FINITE. Finite is a term used in contrast with nonfinite in the classification of verbs, verb phrases, and clauses. A finite verb allows contrasts in **tense** and **mood**. All verb forms are finite except **infinitives** and **participles**. A verb phrase is finite if the first or only verb is finite; all the other verbs are nonfinite. A finite clause is a clause whose verb is a finite verb phrase:

> [1]   Marian <u>has been working</u> hard.

A finite clause can constitute an independent sentence, as in [1]. Contrast the nonfinite clause <u>to work hard</u> in [2]:

> [2]   Daniel was reluctant <u>to work hard</u>.

FOREGROUNDING. Foregrounding refers to the features that stand out in the language of a literary work.

FORMAL DEFINITION. A formal definition defines a grammatical term, such as adverb, by the form of members of the category. For example, most adverbs end in -ly. In a wider sense, form includes **structure**. The form or structure of a noun phrase may be described as consisting of a noun or pronoun as the main word plus other possible constituents, such as **determiners** and modifiers. See **Structure**. Formal definitions are contrasted with **notional definitions**.

FRAGMENTARY SENTENCE.   Fragmentary sentences are irregular sentences from which some part or parts are missing that are normally present in corresponding regular sentences. We can "regularize" the fragmentary sentence <u>in the kitchen</u> in this exchange:

> A: Where are you?
> B: <u>In the kitchen</u>.

<u>In the kitchen</u> corresponds to the regular sentence <u>I am in the kitchen</u>.

FRONT-FOCUS.   Front-focus is a device for fronting an expression from its normal position so that it will acquire greater prominence:

> <u>Ronald</u> I like, but <u>Doris</u> I respect.

Here the two direct objects have been fronted from their normal position after the verb.

FUNCTION.   The function of a unit refers to its use within another unit. For example, the function of <u>your sister</u> is **subject** in [1] and **object** in [2]:

> [1]   <u>Your sister</u> is over there.
> [2]   I have already met <u>your sister</u>.

GENDER.   Gender is a grammatical distinction among words of the same word class that refers to contrasts such as masculine, feminine, neuter. In English this distinction is found mainly in certain pronouns and in the **possessive determiners**.

GENERIC.   Noun phrases are generic when they refer to a class as a whole:

> <u>Dogs</u> make good pets.

They are nongeneric when they refer to individual members of a class:

> <u>My dogs</u> are good with children.

GENITIVE CASE.   See **Case**.

GRADABLE.   Words are gradable when they can be viewed as being on a scale of degree of intensity. Adjectives and adverbs are typically gradable: They can be modified by intensifiers such as <u>very</u> (<u>extremely hot</u>, <u>very badly</u>), and they can take comparison (<u>happier</u>, <u>more relevant</u>).

GRAMMAR. The grammar is the set of rules for combining words into larger units. For example, the rules for the grammar of standard English allow:

Home computers are now much cheaper.

They disallow:

[1] Home computers now <u>much</u> are cheaper.
[2] Home computers <u>is</u> now much cheaper.

They disallow [1] because <u>much</u> is positioned wrongly. They disallow [2] because the subject and the verb must agree in number, and the subject <u>Home computers</u> is plural whereas the verb <u>is</u> is singular.

Such rules are **descriptive rules**: they describe what speakers of the language use. There are also **prescriptive rules**: they advise people what they should use. These prescriptive rules are found in style manuals, handbooks, and other books that advise people how to use their language, telling people which usages to adopt or avoid. The prescriptive rules refer to usages that are common among speakers of standard English, perhaps mainly when they are speaking informally; for example:

Don't use <u>like</u> as a conjunction, as in <u>Speak like I do</u>.

GRAMMATICAL SENTENCE. A grammatical sentence in English is a sentence that conforms to the rules of the grammar of **Standard English.** In a wider sense, grammatical sentences are sentences that conform to the rules of any variety, so that it is possible to distinguish between grammatical and nongrammatical sentences in different varieties of nonstandard English.

HOMOGRAPH. See **Homonym.**

HOMONYM. Homonyms are two or more words that are identical in sound or spelling but different in meaning: The verb <u>peep</u> refers either to making a kind of sound or to taking a kind of look. **Homophones** share the same sound but not necessarily the same spelling: <u>weigh</u> and <u>way</u>. **Homographs** share the same spelling but not necessarily the same sound: <u>row</u> ("line of objects" when it rhymes with <u>no</u>, or "quarrel" when it rhymes with <u>now</u>).

HOMOPHONE. See **Homonym.**

IMPERATIVE. An imperative sentence is a type of sentence structure used chiefly for issuing a **directive**. The imperative verb has the **base form**. The subject is generally absent, and in that case the missing subject is understood to be <u>you</u>:

Take off your hat.
Make yourself at home.

There are also first and third **person** imperative sentences with <u>let</u> and a subject:

> Let's go now.
> Let no one move.

INDEFINITE ARTICLE. The indefinite article is <u>a</u> or (before a vowel sound) <u>an</u>. Contrast **Definite Article**.

INDEFINITE PRONOUN. Indefinite pronouns are pronouns that refer to the quantity of persons or things. They include sets of words ending in -<u>one</u> and -<u>body</u> (<u>someone</u>, <u>nobody</u>, <u>everybody</u>), <u>many</u>, <u>few</u>, <u>both</u>, <u>either</u>, <u>neither</u>, <u>some</u>, <u>any</u>. Some of these pronouns have the same form as indefinite **determiners**.

INDEPENDENT GENITIVE. See **Case**.

INDICATIVE. See **Mood**.

INDIRECT OBJECT. See **Object**.

INDIRECT SPEECH. See **Direct Speech**.

INFINITIVE. The infinitive is the base form of the verb. It is often preceded by <u>to</u> (<u>to stay</u>, <u>to knock</u>), but the infinitive without <u>to</u> is used after the central **modals** (<u>may stay</u>, <u>will knock</u>) and after **dummy operator** <u>do</u> (<u>did say</u>).

INFLECTION. See **Suffix**.

INTERROGATIVE. An interrogative sentence is a type of sentence structure used chiefly for asking questions. In interrogatives the **operator** comes before the **subject**, or the sentence begins with an interrogative word (e.g., <u>who</u>, <u>how</u>, <u>why</u>) or with an interrogative expression (e.g., <u>on which day</u>, <u>for how long</u>):

> Did you hear that noise?
> Why is Pat so annoyed?
> At which point should I stop?

INTERROGATIVE PRONOUN. The interrogative pronouns are <u>who</u>, <u>whom</u>, <u>which</u> and <u>what</u>.

INTRANSITIVE VERB. An intransitive verb does not require another element to complete the sentence:

> The baby is crying.
> It has been raining.

Intransitive verbs contrast with transitive verbs, which take an object; for example, the transitive verb <u>read</u> is followed by the object <u>the book</u> in this next sentence:

>   Everybody has read the book.

Many verbs may be either intransitive or transitive, for example <u>eat</u>:

>   They have eaten.
>   They have eaten breakfast.

IRREGULAR SENTENCE. See **Regular Sentence**.

LINKING VERB. See **Subject Complement**.

MAIN CLAUSE. A **simple sentence** [1] or a **complex sentence** [2] consists of one main clause:

>   [1] You should be more careful.
>   [2] You should be more careful when you cross the street.

A **compound sentence** [3] consists of two or more main clauses:

>   [3] I know that you are in a hurry, <u>but</u> you should be more careful when you cross the street.

In [3], <u>but</u> joins the two main clauses.

MAIN VERB. A main verb is the main word in a verb phrase. Regular main verbs have four forms: the base, -<u>s</u>, -<u>ing</u>, and -<u>ed</u> forms. The base form (e.g., <u>talk</u>) has no inflection; the other three forms are named after their inflections (<u>talks</u>, <u>talking</u>, <u>talked</u>). Some irregular verbs have five forms, two of them corresponding to the two uses of the regular -<u>ed</u> form: past (<u>spoke</u>) and -<u>ed</u> participle (<u>spoken</u>); others have four forms, but the -<u>ed</u> form is irregular (<u>spent</u>); others still have only three forms, since the base and the -<u>ed</u> forms are identical (<u>put</u>). The highly irregular verb <u>be</u> has eight different forms. See 4.12 and 5.9.

MEDIUM. The medium is the channel in which the language is used. The main distinction is between speech and writing.

MODAL. The central modals (or central modal auxiliaries) are <u>can</u>, <u>could</u>, <u>may</u>, <u>might</u>, <u>will</u>, <u>would</u>, <u>shall</u>, <u>should</u>, <u>must</u>.

MOOD. Mood is the grammatical category that indicates the attitude of the speaker to what is said. Finite verb phrases have three moods: **indicative, imperative,** and **subjunctive.** The indicative is the usual mood in **declarative, interrogative,** and **exclamative** sentences. The imperative mood is used in **imper-**

ative sentences. The subjunctive mood commonly conveys uncertainty or tentativeness. See 4.19.

MORPHOLOGY. Morphology deals with the structure of words. Words may be combinations of smaller units. For example, <u>books</u> consists of the stem <u>book</u> and the **inflection** -<u>s</u>. <u>Sometimes</u> is a compound formed from the two stems <u>some</u> and <u>times</u>. <u>Review</u> consists of the **prefix** <u>re</u>- and the stem <u>view</u>, and <u>national</u> consists of the stem <u>nation</u> and the suffix -<u>al</u>.

MULTIPLE SENTENCE. See **Simple Sentence**.

MULTI-WORD VERB. Multi-word verbs are combinations of a verb and one or more other words. The major types are phrasal verbs (<u>give in</u>), prepositional verbs (<u>look at</u>), and phrasal-prepositional verbs (<u>put up with</u>).

NEUTRALIZATION. Neutralization involves reducing distinctions to one form. For example, <u>you</u> represents both the subjective form (<u>You saw them</u>) and the objective form (<u>They saw you</u>).

NOMINAL CLAUSE. Nominal clauses are subordinate clauses that have a range of functions similar to that of noun phrases. For example, they can function as subject [1] or direct object [2]:

    [1] <u>That it's too difficult for him</u> should be obvious to everyone.
    [2] I think <u>that you should take a rest now</u>.

Nominal relative clauses are introduced by a nominal relative pronoun. The pronoun functions like a combination of **antecedent** and **relative pronoun**:

    You can take <u>whatever you want</u>. (anything that you want)

NOMINAL RELATIVE CLAUSE. See **Nominal Clause**.

NOMINAL RELATIVE PRONOUN. Nominal relative pronouns introduce **nominal relative clauses**. The pronouns are <u>who</u>, <u>whom</u> (formal), <u>which</u>, <u>whoever</u>, <u>whomever</u> (formal), <u>whichever</u>, <u>what</u>, and <u>whatever</u>. Several of these have the same form as nominal relative determiners.

NONCOUNT. See **Count**.

NONFINITE. See **Finite**.

NONGENERIC. See **Generic**.

NONRESTRICTIVE APPOSITION. See **Restrictive Apposition**.

NONRESTRICTIVE RELATIVE CLAUSE. See **Restrictive Relative Clause**.

NONSENTENCES. Nonsentences may be perfectly normal even though they cannot be analyzed as sentences. For example, the greeting Hi! is a nonsentence grammatically, and so is the written sign Exit.

NONSPECIFIC. See **Specific**.

NONSTANDARD ENGLISH. See **Standard English**.

NOTIONAL DEFINITION. A notional definition defines a grammatical term, such as a noun, by the meaning that members of the category are said to convey. For example, a traditional notional definition of a noun is "the name of a person, thing, or place." Notional definitions can help to identify a category such as a noun by indicating typical members of the category, but the definitions are usually not comprehensive. Nouns include words such as happiness, information, and action that are not covered by the traditional notional definition. Notional definitions are contrasted with **formal definitions**.

NOUN. Proper nouns are names of people (Mary), places (Chicago), days of the week (Monday), holidays (Christmas), and the like. The **noun phrases** in which common nouns function refer to people (teachers), places (the city), things (your car), qualities (elegance), states (knowledge), actions (action), and so on. Most common nouns take a plural form: car, cars.

NOUN PHRASE. The main word in a noun phrase is a noun or a pronoun. If the main word is a noun, it is often introduced by a **determiner** and may have modifiers. Premodifiers are modifiers that come before the main word and postmodifiers are modifiers that come after it:

> an (det.) old (prem.) quarrel (noun) that has recently flared up
> again (postm.)

NUMBER. Number is a grammatical category that contrasts singular and plural. It applies to nouns (student, students), pronouns (she, they), and verbs (he works, they work).

OBJECT. Transitive verbs require a direct object to complete the sentences, as in [1]:

> [1] Dennis introduced the speaker (dO).

Some transitive verbs allow or require a second element: indirect object, which comes before the direct object [2]; **object complement** [3]; **adverbial complement** [4]:

> [2] Nancy showed me (iO) her book (dO).
> [3] Pauline made him (dO) her understudy (OC).
> [4] Norma put the cat (dO) in the yard (AC).

The direct object typically refers to the person or thing affected by the action. The indirect object typically refers to the person who receives something or benefits from the action. The object in an **active** structure (whether the object is direct or indirect) usually corresponds to the subject in a passive structure:

> The sentry fired <u>two shots</u> (dO).
> <u>Two shots</u> (S) were fired.
> Ted promised <u>Mary</u> (iO) <u>two tickets</u> (dO).
> <u>Mary</u> (S) was promised two tickets.
> <u>Two tickets</u> (S) were promised to Mary.

OBJECT COMPLEMENT. Some transitive verbs require or allow an object complement to follow the direct object:

> The heat has turned <u>the milk</u> (dO) <u>sour</u> (oC).

The relationship between the direct object and the object complement resembles that between the subject and the **subject complement**:

> <u>The milk</u> (S) turned <u>sour</u> (sC).

See **Object**.

OBJECTIVE CASE. See **Subjective Case**.

OPERATOR. The operator is the part of the predicate that (among other functions) interchanges with the subject when we form questions [1] and comes before <u>not</u> or contracted <u>n't</u> in negative sentences [2] and [3]:

> [1] <u>Have</u> (op) <u>you</u> (S) seen my pen?
> [2] I <u>have</u> (op) <u>not</u> replied to her letter.
> [3] I <u>haven't</u> replied to her letter.

The operator is usually the first auxiliary in the verb phrase, but the main verb <u>be</u> is the operator when it is the only verb in the verb phrase, as in [4]:

> [4] <u>Are</u> you ready?

See also **Dummy Operator**.

ORTHOGRAPHIC SENTENCE. An orthographic sentence is a sentence in the written language, signaled by an initial capital letter and a final period.

ORTHOGRAPHY. Orthography is the writing system in the language: the distinctive written symbols and their possible combinations.

PARALLELISM. Parallelism is an arrangement of similar grammatical structures. In parallel structures at least some of the words have similar or contrasting meanings:

It was too hot to eat; it was too hot to swim; it was too hot
    to sleep.
They tended the wounded and they comforted the dying.
The more you talk, the madder I get.

Chiasmus is a form of parallelism in which the order of parts of the structures is reversed:

I respect Susan, but Joan I admire.

PARTICIPLE.   There are two participles, the -ing participle (playing) and the
-ed participle. The -ing participle always ends in -ing. In all regular verbs and
in some irregular verbs, the -ed participle ends in -ed. In other irregular verbs
the -ed participle may end in -n (speak, spoken), or may have a different vowel
from the base form (fight, fought), or may have both characteristics (wear,
worn), or may be identical with the base form (put, put).

The -ing participle is used to form the progressive (was playing). The -ed
participle is used to form the perfect (has played) and the passive (was played).
Both participles can function as the verb in **nonfinite** clauses:

Knowing Carol, I am sure you can trust her.
When captured, he refused to give his name.

See **Aspect, Active, Finite.**

PARTICLE.   A particle is a word that does not change its form (unlike verbs
that have past forms or nouns that have plural forms) and, because of its specialized functions, does not fit into the traditional classes of words. Particles include not, to as used with the infinitive, and the words like up and out that
combine with verbs to form **multi-word verbs,** for example, blow up and look
out.

PASSIVE.   See **Active**.

PERFECT.   See **Aspect**.

PERSON.   Person is the grammatical category that indicates the relationship
to the speaker of those involved in the situation. There are three persons: the
first person refers to the speaker, the second to those addressed, and the third
to other people or things. Differences are signaled by the **possessive determiners** (my, your, etc.), some pronouns (e.g., I, you), and verb forms (e.g., I know
versus She knows).

PERSONAL PRONOUN.   The personal pronouns are:

(1) subjective case: I, we, you, he, she, it, they
(2) objective case: me, us, you, him, her, it, them

See **Subject Case.**

PHONETICS.   Phonetics deals with the physical characteristics of the sounds in the language, their production, and their perception.

PHONOLOGY.   Phonology is the sound system in the language: the distinctive sound units and the ways in which they may be combined.

PHRASAL AUXILIARY.   Phrasal auxiliaries convey meanings that are similar to the auxiliaries but do not share all their grammatical characteristics. For example, only the first word of the phrasal auxiliary <u>have got to</u> functions as an **operator**:

> <u>Have</u> we <u>got to</u> go now?

Phrasal auxiliaries include <u>have to</u>, <u>had better</u>, <u>be about to</u>, <u>be going to</u>, <u>be able to</u>.

PHRASAL-PREPOSITIONAL VERB.   See **Multi-Word Verb.**

PHRASAL VERB.   See **Multi-Word Verb.**

PHRASE.   A phrase is a unit below the **clause**. There are five types of phrases:

noun phrase	<u>our family</u>
verb phrase	<u>was talking</u>
adjective phrase	<u>quite right</u>
adverb phrase	<u>very loudly</u>
prepositional phrase	<u>for you</u>

   The first four phrases above are named after their main word. The prepositional phrase is named after the word that introduces the phrase.
   In this book, and in many other works on grammar, a phrase may consist of one word, so that both <u>talked</u> and <u>was talking</u> are verb phrases. See 4.1.

POSSESSIVE DETERMINER.   The possessive determiners are <u>my</u>, <u>our</u>, <u>your</u>, <u>his</u>, <u>hers</u>, <u>its</u>, <u>theirs</u>. See **Case**.

POSSESSIVE PRONOUN.   The possessive pronouns are <u>mine</u>, <u>ours</u>, <u>yours</u>, <u>his</u>, <u>hers</u>, <u>its</u>, <u>theirs</u>. See **Case**.

PRAGMATICS.   Pragmatics deals with the use of utterances in particular situations. For example, <u>Will you join our group?</u> is a question that might be intended as either a request for information or a request for action.

PREDICATE.   We can divide most **clauses** into two parts: the **subject** and the predicate. The main parts of the predicate are the verb and any of its objects or complements.

PREFIX. A prefix is added before the stem of a word to form a new word, e.g., <u>un-</u> in <u>untidy</u>.

PREPOSITION. Prepositions introduce **prepositional phrases**. The preposition links the complement in the phrase to some other expression. Here are some common prepositions with complements in parentheses: <u>after</u> (lunch), <u>by</u> (telling me), <u>for</u> (us), <u>in</u> (my room), <u>since</u> (seeing them), <u>to</u> (Ruth), <u>up</u> (the road).

PREPOSITIONAL OBJECT. A prepositional object is a word or phrase that follows the preposition of a prepositional verb:

> Tom is looking after <u>my children</u>.
> Norma is making fun of <u>you</u>.

PREPOSITIONAL PHRASE. The prepositional phrase consists of a preposition and the complement of the preposition:

> for (prep.) your sake (comp.)
> on (prep.) entering the room (comp.)

PREPOSITIONAL VERB. See **Multi-Word Verb.**

PRESCRIPTIVE RULES. See **Grammar**.

PROGRESSIVE. See **Aspect**.

PRONOUN. A pronoun is a closed class of words that are used as substitutes for a noun phrase or (less commonly) for a noun. They fall into a number of classes, such as personal pronouns and demonstrative pronouns. See 5.15.

RECIPROCAL PRONOUN. The reciprocal pronouns are <u>each other</u> and <u>one another</u>.

REFLEXIVE PRONOUN. The reflexive pronouns are <u>myself</u>, <u>ourselves</u>, <u>yourself</u>, <u>yourselves</u>, <u>himself</u>, <u>herself</u>, <u>itself</u>, <u>themselves</u>.

REGULAR SENTENCE. A regular sentence conforms to the major patterns of sentences in the language. Those that do not conform are irregular sentences. See **Basic Sentence Structure.**

RELATIVE CLAUSE. A relative clause functions as a postmodifier in a noun phrase:

> the persons <u>who advised me</u>

The relative word or expression (here <u>who</u>) functions as an element in the clause (here as subject; cf. <u>they advised me</u>).

RELATIVE PRONOUN.   Relative pronouns introduce **relative clauses**. The relative pronouns are <u>who</u>, <u>whom</u> (formal), <u>which</u>, and <u>that</u>. The relative pronoun is omitted in certain circumstances: <u>the apartment (that) I live in</u>; the omitted pronoun is known as a zero relative pronoun. <u>Which</u> and <u>whose</u> are relative determiners.

REPORTING CLAUSE.   See **Direct Speech**.

RESTRICTIVE APPOSITION.   **Apposition** may be restrictive or nonrestrictive. A restrictive appositive identifies:

> the fact <u>that they have two cars</u>
> my sister <u>Clarissa</u>

A nonrestrictive appositive adds further information:

> the latest news, <u>that negotiations are to begin next Monday</u>,
> my eldest sister, <u>Clarissa</u>,

See **Restrictive Relative Clause**.

RESTRICTIVE RELATIVE CLAUSE.   Relative clauses may be either restrictive or nonrestrictive. A restrictive relative clause identifies more closely the noun it modifies:

> the sister <u>who was in your class</u>

A nonrestrictive relative clause does not identify. It adds further information:

> your youngest sister, <u>who was in your class</u>,

RHETORICAL QUESTION.   A rhetorical question has the form of a question but the force of a strong assertion:

> How many times have I told you to wipe your feet? ("I have
> told you very many times to wipe your feet.")

RUN-ON SENTENCE.   A run-on sentence is an error in punctuation arising from the failure to use any punctuation mark between sentences. If a comma is used instead of a major mark, the error is a comma splice. See 7.3.

SEMANTICS.   Semantics is the system of meanings in the language: the meanings of words and the combinatory meanings of larger units.

SENTENCE FRAGMENT.   A sentence fragment is a series of words that is punctuated as a sentence even though it is not grammatically an independent sentence:

> You're late again. <u>As usual</u>.

SIMPLE SENTENCE. A simple sentence is a sentence that consists of just one clause:

> I'm just a country boy.

A multiple sentence consists of more than one clause:

> I'm just a country boy, and I'd never been out of the state before.
>
> Since I'm just a country boy, I'd never been out of the state before.

See **Complex Sentence** and **Compound Sentence**.

SPECIFIC. Noun phrases are specific when they refer to specific persons, places, things, and so on: I hired a horse and a guide for the trip along the mountain trail. They are nonspecific when they do not have such reference:

> I have never met a Russian. [*nonspecific*: any Russian]

STANDARD ENGLISH. Standard English is the variety of English that normally appears in print. Its relative uniformity is confined to grammar, vocabulary, spelling, and punctuation. There is no standard English pronunciation. There are some differences in the standard English used in English-speaking countries, so we can distinguish, for example, between standard English in the United States, in Canada, and in Britain. Varieties other than the standard variety are called **nonstandard**.

STATIVE. Stative verbs introduce a quality attributed to the subject (Tom seems bored) or a state of affairs (We know the way). Dynamic verbs are used in descriptions of events (The kettle is boiling; Cathy listened intently). Dynamic verbs can occur with the -ing form, as in is boiling, has been listening.

STRUCTURE. The structure of a unit refers to the parts that make up the unit. For example, a sentence may have the structure **subject, verb, object,** as in:

> Dinah (S) has written (V) a good paper (O).

Or a noun phrase may have the structure **determiner, premodifier, noun,** as in:

> a (D) good (P) paper (N)

SUBJECT. The subject is an **element** that usually comes before the verb in a **declarative** sentence [1] and after the **operator** in an interrogative sentence [2]:

> [1] We (S) should consider (V) the rights of every class.
>
> [2] Should (op) we (S) consider the rights of every class?

Except in **imperative** sentences, the subject is an obligatory element. In active structures, the subject typically refers to the performer of the action.

SUBJECT COMPLEMENT. Linking verbs require a subject complement to complete the sentence. The most common linking verb is <u>be</u>. Subject complements are usually **noun phrases** [1] or **adjective phrases** [2]:

[1]   Leonard is <u>Mary's brother</u>.

[2]   Robert looks <u>very happy</u>.

The subject complement typically identifies or characterizes the subject.

SUBJECTIVE CASE. The **personal pronouns** and the pronouns <u>who</u> and <u>whoever</u> distinguish between subjective case and objective case. The subjective case is used when a pronoun is the subject (<u>I</u> in <u>I know</u>). The objective case is used when a pronoun is a direct object (<u>me</u> in <u>He pushed me</u>) or indirect object (<u>me</u> in <u>She told me the truth</u>) or complement of a preposition (<u>for me</u>). The subject complement takes the subjective case in formal style (<u>This is she</u>), but otherwise the objective case (<u>This is her</u>) is usual.

SUBJECT–OPERATOR INVERSION. In subject–operator inversion, the usual order is inverted: the **operator** comes before the **subject.**

[1]   <u>Are</u> (op) <u>you</u> (S) staying?

Subject–operator inversion occurs chiefly in questions, as in [1]. It also occurs when a negative element is fronted, as in [2]:

[2]   <u>Not a word</u> did we hear.

Compare [2a] and [2b]:

[2a]   We did <u>not</u> hear <u>a word</u>.

[2b]   We heard <u>not a word</u>.

SUBJECT–VERB AGREEMENT. The general rule is that a verb agrees with its subject in number and person whenever the verb displays distinctions in number and person:

The dog <u>barks</u>.   I <u>am</u> thirsty.

The dogs <u>bark</u>.   She <u>is</u> thirsty.

SUBJUNCTIVE. The present subjunctive is the base form of the verb:

I demanded that Norman <u>leave</u> the meeting.

The past subjunctive is <u>were</u>:

If Tess <u>were</u> here, she would help me.

See 4.19.

SUBORDINATE CLAUSE. See **Complex Sentence**.

SUBORDINATOR. See **Conjunction**.

SUFFIX. A suffix is added after the stem of a word to form a new word, e.g., -ness in goodness. A suffix that expresses a grammatical relationship is an **inflection**, e.g., plural -s in crowds or past -ed in cooked.

SUPERORDINATE CLAUSE. A superordinate clause is a clause that has a subordinate clause as one of its elements:

> I hear (A) that you know (B) where Ken lives.

The (A) clause that you ... lives is superordinate to the (B) clause where Ken lives. The subordinate (B) clause is the direct object in the (A) clause.

SYNTAX. This is another term for **Grammar**, as that term is used in this book.

TAG QUESTION. A tag question is attached to a sentence that is not interrogative. It invites agreement:

> You remember me, don't you?
> Please don't tell them, will you?

TENSE. Tense is the grammatical category that refers to time and is signaled by the form of the verb. There are two tenses: present (laugh, laughs) and past (laughed).

THERE-STRUCTURE. In a there-structure, there is put in the subject position and the subject is moved to a later position.

> There is somebody here to see you. [*Cf.*: Somebody is here to see you.]

TRANSITIVE VERB. See **Object**.

VERB. A verb is either (like a noun) a member of a word class or (like a subject) an element in sentence or clause structure. As a verb, it functions in a **verb phrase**. The verb phrase may be playing is the verb of the sentence in [1]:

> [1] She may be playing tennis this afternoon.

It is the verb of the that-clause in [2]:

> [2] She says that she may be playing tennis this afternoon.

See **Main Verb**.

VERBLESS CLAUSE. A verbless clause is a reduced clause that does not have a verb:

> Send me another one <u>if possible</u>. (if it is possible)
> <u>Though in pain</u>, Joan came with us. (Though she was in pain)

VERB PHRASE. A verb phrase consists of a **main verb** preceded optionally by a maximum of four **auxiliaries**.

VOICE. Voice is a grammatical category that applies to the structure of the sentence and to the structure of the verb phrase. There are two voices: the active voice and the passive voice. See **Active**.

WH-QUESTION. A <u>wh</u>-question is a question beginning with an interrogative word or with a phrase containing an interrogative word. All interrogative words except <u>how</u> begin with <u>wh</u>-: <u>who</u>, <u>whom</u>, <u>whose</u>, <u>what</u>, <u>where</u>, <u>when</u>, <u>why</u>, <u>which</u>.

YES-NO QUESTION. A <u>yes-no</u> question is a question that expects the answer <u>yes</u> or <u>no</u>. <u>Yes-no</u> questions require **subject–operator inversion**:

> <u>Can</u> (op) <u>I</u> (S) have a word with you?

ZERO RELATIVE PRONOUN. See **Relative Pronoun**.

Index